Concise
Chinese–English
Romanized
Dictionary

*Containing nearly 10,000
romanized Chinese words and
expressions, Chinese characters,
and English equivalents.*

James C. Quo

TUTTLE PUBLISHING
Tokyo • Rutland, Vermont • Singapore

Published by Tuttle Publishing, an imprint of Periplus Editions (HK) Ltd., with editorial offices at 364 Innovation Drive, North Clarendon, Vermont 05759 U.S.A. and 130 Joo Seng Road #06-01, Singapore 368357.

LCC Card No. 60-14372
ISBN-13: 978-0-8048-3872-6
ISBN-10: 0-8048-3872-0

Printed in Singapore

First edition, 1960

Distributed by:

North America, Latin America & Europe
Tuttle Publishing,
364 Innovation Drive, North Clarendon, VT 05759-9436 U.S.A.
Tel: 1 (802) 773-8930   Fax: 1 (802) 773-6993
info@tuttlepublishing.com
www.tuttlepublishing.com

Japan
Tuttle Publishing,
Yaekari Building, 3rd Floor
5-4-12 Osaki, Shinagawa-ku, Tokyo 141-0032
Tel: (81) 03 5437-0171   Fax: (81) 03 5437-0755
tuttle-sales@gol.com

Asia Pacific
Berkeley Books Pte. Ltd.,
130 Joo Seng Road #06-01, Singapore 368357
Tel: (65) 6280-1330   Fax: (65) 6280-6290
inquiries@periplus.com.sg
www.periplus.com

09 08 07 06   6 5 4 3 2

CONTENTS

ABBREVIATIONS

a.	adjective
adv.	adverb
art.	article
conj.	conjunction
int.	interjection
n.	noun
prep.	preposition
pron.	pronoun
v.	verb
v. aux.	auxiliary verb
*	indicates a Republic of China term
**	indicates a Chinese Communist term

chem.	chemistry	*med.*	medical
elec.	electrical	*mil.*	military
engin.	engineering	*off.*	official
math.	mathematics	*U.S.*	United States

A

A¹ 啊 [a final particle, an exclamation]

AI² 挨 *v.* suffer. ~¹ *a.* near

AI¹ tz'u⁴ ~次 *a.* orderly
  ~²~e⁴ ~餓 *v.* suffer from hunger
  ~ma⁴ ~罵 *v.* be blamed
  ~ta³ ~打 *v.* be beaten

AI⁴ 愛 *a.* fond; *v.* love, like; *n.* love, affection
  ~ch'ing² ~情 *n.* love
  ~jen² ~人 *n.* sweetheart, lover
  ~kuo² ~國 *n.* patriotism
  ~kuo² che³ ~國者 *n.* patriot
  ~kuo² ssu¹ hsiang³ ~國思想 *n.* patriotism
  ~kuo² tseng¹ ch'an³ yün⁴ tung⁴ ~國增產運動 *n.* patriotic production campaign**
  ~lien⁴ ~戀 *v.* love
  ~shen² ~神 *n.* Venus, Cupid

AI⁴ 礙 *n.* obstacle; *v.* hinder, obstruct

AN¹ 安 *a.* quiet, calm, safe; *v.* tranquilize
  ~chih⁴ ~置 *v.* settle, lay down
  ~ching⁴ ~靜 *a.* quiet, peaceful; *v.* keep quiet
  ~ch'üan² ~全 *n.* safety; *a.* safe
  ~ch'üan² chieh⁴ ~全界 *n.* safety zone
  ~ch'üan² yin¹ su⁴ ~全因素 *n.* factor of safety (*engin.*)
  ~hsi² jih⁴ ~息日 *n.* sabbath
  ~hsien² ~閒 *n.* leisure; *adv.* leisurely
  ~i⁴ ~逸 *n.* comfort, easy
  ~le⁴ ~樂 *a.* comfortable
  ~mien² yao⁴ ~眠藥 *n.* hypnotic (drug)
  ~p'ai² ~排 *v.* arrange
  ~shih⁴ ~適 *a.* comfortable
  ~ting⁴ ~定 *n.* tranquillity
  ~tsang⁴ ~葬 *v.* inter, bury
  ~wei⁴ ~慰 *v.* comfort
  ~wen³ ~穩 *a.* firm, stable, steady, safe
  ~wo⁴ ~臥 *v.* sleep

1

AN⁴ 岸 *n.* bank, shore
AN⁴ 按 *v.* press down, massage, hold, stop; *prep.* according to
  ~chao⁴ ～照 *prep.* according to
  ~shih² ～時 *v.* keep time
AN⁴ 案 *n.* table, record, case
  ~chien⁴ ～件 *n.* law case
  ~cho¹ ～桌 *n.* desk
  ~chüan⁴ ～卷 *n.* record (*off.*)
AN⁴ 暗 *a.* dark, gloomy; *adv.* secretly
  ~ch'i¹ ～漆 *n.* lusterless paint
  ~hao⁴ ～號 *n.* secret sign, secret mark
  ~kou¹ ～溝 *n.* culvert
  ~ma³ ～碼 *n.* cipher
  ~sha¹ ～殺 *n.* murder
  ~shih⁴ ～示 *v.* hint
  ~shih⁴ ～室 *n.* darkroom
  ~ti⁴ ～地 *adv.* secretly
  ~t'an⁴ ～探 *n.* detective

CH

CHA⁴ 炸 *v.* explode. ～² *v.* fry
  ~ch'en² ～沉 *v.* sink (by bombing)
  ~hui³ ～毀 *v.* blow up
  ~kao¹ ～高 *n.* height of burst
  ~lieh⁴ ～裂 *n.* burst (explosion)
  ~tan⁴ ～彈 *n.* bomb
  ~yao⁴ ～藥 *n.* explosive
CHAN¹ 粘 *v.* paste up, stick. **NIEN²** *a.* glutinous
  ~¹ t'ieh¹ ～貼 *v.* paste
  t'u³ ～土 *n.* clay
CHAN³ 展 *v.* unfold, open
  ~ch'i¹ ～期 *v.* postpone
  ~hsien⁴ ～限 *v.* extend
  ~k'ai¹ ～開 *v.* deploy
  ~lan³ hui⁴ ～覽會 *n.* exhibition
  ~wang⁴ k'ung³ ～望孔 *n.* vision slit
CHAN⁴ 佔 *v.* occupy

~**chü⁴** ~據 v. occupy; n. occupation
~**ling³ chen⁴ ti⁴** ~領陣地 v. occupy a position
~**ling³ chün¹** ~領軍 n. occupation forces
~**ling³ ch'ü¹** ~領區 n. occupied area (by our own forces)

CHAN⁴ 站 v. stand; n. station
~**chang³** ~長 n. station master
~**chu⁴** ~住 v. halt
~**kang³** ~崗 v. post
~**li⁴** ~立 v. stand up
~**wen³** ~穩 v. stand firmly

CHAN⁴ 暫 n. a short time; adv. temporarily, briefly
~**shih²** ~時 a. temporary; adv. temporarily
~**t'ing²** ~停 n. suspension

CHAN⁴ 戰 v. fight, fear, tremble; n. fight, battle, war
~**cheng¹** ~爭 n. war
~**chien⁴** ~艦 n. battleship, warship
~**ch'ang³** ~場 n. battlefield, field
~**ch'ü¹** ~區 n. theater of operations
~**fei⁴** ~費 n. military expenditure
~**hao²** ~壕 n. trench
~**hsien⁴** ~線 n. battle front
~**i⁴** ~役 n. campaign
~**kung¹** ~功 n. exploit
~**k'uang³** ~況 n. tactical situation
~**li⁴** ~慄 v. tremble
~**li⁴ p'in³** ~利品 n. trophy
~**lüeh⁴** ~略 n. strategy; a. strategic
~**lüeh⁴ chi⁴ hua⁴ wei³ yüan² hui⁴** ~略計劃委員會 n. Strategy Planning and Research Committee*
~**pai⁴** ~敗 v. defeat
~**sheng⁴** ~勝 v. win (a battle); n. victory
~**shih²** ~時 n. wartime
~**shih³** ~史 n. war history
~**shih⁴** ~士 n. warrior
~**shu⁴** ~術 n. tactics
~**ti⁴ chi⁴ che³** ~地記者 n. war correspondent
~**tou⁴ chi¹** ~鬭機 n. combat airplane

3

~**tou⁴ li⁴** ~鬪力 *n.* battle efficiency

~**tou⁴ ying¹ hsiung²** ~鬪英雄 *n.* combat hero**

CHANG¹ 張 *n.* sheet; *v.* display, open, expand

~**kung¹** ~弓 *v.* draw a bow

~**k'ai¹** ~開 *v.* open

~**lo²** ~羅 *v.* raise money

CHANG¹ 章 *a.* elegant; *n.* essay, rule, chapter; *v.* manifest

~**ch'eng²** ~程 *n.* regulation, rule

~**fa³** ~法 *n.* phraseology

CHANG³ 掌 *n.* palm, sole; *v.* control

~**kuei⁴** ~櫃 *n.* accountant, shop-owner

~**kung¹** ~工 *n.* blacksmith

~**li³** ~理 *v.* manage

~**wo⁴** ~握 *v.* control

CHANG³ 長 *a.* older; *n.* head, chief, commander, length. **CH'ANG²** *a.* long

~**³ chin⁴** ~進 *n.* progress

~**hsiung¹** ~兄 *n.* oldest brother

~**lao³ hui⁴** ~老會 *n.* rectory

~**tzu³** ~子 *n.* oldest son

~**² teng⁴** ~凳 *n.* bench

~**tuan³** ~短 *n.* length

~**t'u² tien⁴ hua⁴** ~途電話 *n.* long-distance telephone

CHANG⁴ 漲 *v.* overflow, expand

~**chia⁴** ~價 *v.* raise the price

~**ch'ao²** ~潮 *n.* flood-tide

~**shui³** ~水 *n.* tide

CHANG⁴ 丈 *n.* Chinese linear measure for 11.75 feet

~**fu¹** ~夫 *n.* husband

~**jen²** ~人 *n.* father of one's wife (father-in-law)

~**mu³** ~母 *n.* mother of one's wife (mother-in-law)

CHANG⁴ 仗 *n.* weapon; *v.* rely on, depend on

CHANG⁴ 帳 *n.* curtain, tent. [Same as 賬] account

~**fang²** ~房 *n.* cashier's department

~**mu⁴** ~目 *n.* account

~**p'eng²** ~蓬 *n.* tent

~**tan¹** ~單 *n.* bill

4

CHAO¹ 招 *v.* beckon, confess, invite
~**chi²** ~集 *v.* muster
~**chih⁴** ~致 *v.* invite attack
~**hu¹** ~呼 *v.* beckon
~**je³** ~惹 *v.* incur
~**ping¹** ~兵 *v.* recruit
~**p'ai²** ~牌 *n.* signboard (store)
~**tai⁴** ~待 *v.* entertain
~**tai⁴ yüan²** ~待員 *n.* usher
~**t'ieh¹** ~貼 *n.* poster
~**tsu¹** ~租 *v.* be let for rent
~**yao²** ~搖 *v.* exaggerate
CHAO¹ 朝 *see* **CH'AO²**
CHAO² 着 *v.* cause, send, put on; [a prep.] **CHE¹** [a suffix]
CHAO³ 找 *v.* seek, look for
~**ch'iao⁴ men²** ~竅門 *v.* find a secret technical contrivance**
~**hsün²** ~尋 *v.* find
~**t'ou²** ~頭 *n.* change (money)
CHAO⁴ 召 *v.* call, summon
~**chi²** ~集 *v.* assemble
CHAO⁴ 照 *v.* enlighten, illuminate
~**ch'ang²** ~常 *adv.* as usual
~**hsiang⁴** ~相 *n.* photograph; *v.* take photograph of
~**hsiang⁴ chi¹** ~相機 *n.* camera
~**hsiang⁴ shu⁴** ~相術 *n.* photography
~**ku⁴** ~顧 *v.* patronize, take care of
~**liao⁴** ~料 *v.* take care of, look after
~**ming⁴ tan⁴** ~明彈 *n.* flare bomb
~**ming² teng¹** ~明燈 *n.* illuminating light
~**yao⁴** ~耀 *v.* shine on
CHE¹ 遮 *v.* screen, intercept, hide
~**hu⁴** ~護 *v.* shelter
~**man²** ~瞞 *v.* conceal
~**pi⁴** ~庇 *v.* protect
~**pi⁴** ~避 *v.* screen, blind, mask
~**pi⁴ ting³** ~避頂 *n.* grazing point
CHE¹ 着 *see* **CHAO²**
CHE² 折 *v.* bend, discount

~k'ou⁴ ~扣 *n.* discount

~shih² chia⁴ ~實價 *n.* net price

~shih² kung¹ chai⁴ ~實公債 *n.* parity bond**

~shih² tan¹ wei⁴ ~實單位 *n.* parity unit**

CHE³ 者 [a final particle, a suffix]

CHE⁴ 這 *a. & pron.* this; *adv.* here. [Also read **CHEI⁴**]

~hsieh¹ ~些 *a. & pron.* these

~ko⁴ ~個 *a. & pron.* this

~li³ ~裏 *adv.* here

~yang⁴ ~樣 *adv.* thus, so

CHEI⁴ 這 *see* **CHE⁴**

CHEN¹ 眞 *a.* real, true, genuine

~cheng⁴ ~正 *a.* real, true

~chu¹ ~珠 *n.* pearl

~hua⁴ ~話 *n.* truth

~k'ung¹ ~空 *n.* vacuum

~k'ung¹ kuan³ ~空管 *n.* vacuum tube

~li³ ~理 *n.* truth

CHEN¹ 針 *n.* needle, pin

~hsien⁴ ~線 *n.* needlework

~hsien⁴ pao¹ ~線包 *n.* sewing kit

~tz'u⁴ fa³ ~刺法 *n.* acupuncture

CHEN⁴ 振 *v.* arouse, stimulate

~chiu⁴ ~救 *v.* save from danger

~hsing¹ ~興 *v.* develop

~tung⁴ ~動 *v.* vibrate; *n.* vibration

~tso⁴ ~作 *v.* stimulate, encourage

CHIH³ 紙 *n.* paper

~pi⁴ ~幣 *n.* paper money

~san³ ~傘 *n.* paper umbrella

~shan⁴ ~扇 *n.* paper fan

~yen⁴ ~煙 *n.* cigarette

~yüan¹ ~鳶 *n.* kite

CHEN⁴ 鎭 *n.* town; *v.* keep, protect

~shou³ ~守 *v.* guard

~ya¹ ~壓 *v.* suppress

CHEN⁴ 陣 *n.* tactics, array, moment

~chung¹ jih⁴ chi⁴ ~中日記 *n.* war diary

~hsien⁴ ~綫 *n.* line of battle

~ti⁴ ~地 *n.* fire position (*mil.*)

6

~wang² ~亡 *v.* be killed in action

~yü³ ~雨 *n.* shower

CHENG¹ 爭 *v.* quarrel, dispute, debate

~lun⁴ ~論 *n.* & *v.* quarrel

~to² ~奪 *v.* contest (for a position)

~tou⁴ ~鬪 *v.* fight

CHENG¹ 征 *v.* invade, attack, levy

~chan⁴ ~戰 *v.* fight a battle

~fa² ~伐 *v.* invade, attack

~fu² ~服 *v.* conquer

~ping¹ ~兵 *v.* conscript

~shou¹ ~收 *v.* levy, collect

~shui⁴ ~稅 *v.* levy taxes

CHENG³ 整 *v.* adjust, arrange; *a.* entire, whole

~ch'i² hsien⁴ ~齊線 *n.* alignment

~ko⁴ ~個 *a.* integral, whole, entire

~li³ ~理 *v.* reorganize

~tun⁴ ~頓 *v.* reorganize

CHENG⁴ 正 *a.* upright, proper; *v.* make right, correct

~¹ yüeh⁴ ~月 *n.* January

~⁴ chih² ~直 *a.* righteous, upright

~fang¹ ~方 *n.* square

~i⁴ ~義 *n.* justice

~mien⁴ ~面 *n.* positive

~shih⁴ ~式 *a.* formal; *adv.* formerly

CHENG⁴ 政 *n.* government, administration, executive, politics

~chieh⁴ ~界 *n.* political circle

~chih⁴ ~治 *n.* politics

~chih⁴ chia¹ ~治家 *n.* statesman

~chih⁴ chü² ~治局 *n.* politburo

~chih⁴ fa³ lü⁴ wei³ yüan² hui⁴ ~治法律委員會 *n.* Committee of Political and Legal Affairs**

~chih⁴ fan⁴ ~治犯 *n.* political prisoner

~chih⁴ hui⁴ i⁴ ~治會議 *n.* political conference

~chih⁴ huo² tung⁴ ~治活動 *n.* political activity

~chih⁴ hsüeh² ~治學 *n.* political science

~chih⁴ kung¹ tso⁴ ~治工作 *n.* political work

~chih⁴ pu⁴ ~治部 *n.* political department

~chih⁴ sheng¹ huo² ~治生活 *n.* political life

~chih⁴ wang² ming⁴ ～治亡命 n. political refugee

~ch'üan² ～權 n. political power

~fa³ ～法 n. politics and law

~fu³ ～府 n. government

~k'o⁴ ～客 n. politician

~pien⁴ ～變 n. revolution, coup d'etat

~tang³ ～黨 n. political party

~t'i³ ～體 n. form of government

~ts'e⁴ ～策 n. policy

~wu⁴ yüan⁴ ～務院 n. Government Administrative Council**

CHENG⁴ 證 n. evidence, legal testimony, proof; v. prove, testify, verify

~chü⁴ ～據 n. evidence

~jen² ～人 n. witness

~ming² ～明 v. prove

~shu¹ ～書 n. certificate

CHI¹ 機 n. machine; a. opportune, motive

~ch'i⁴ chiao³ t'a⁴ ch'e¹ ～器脚踏車 n. motorcycle

~ch'iao³ ～巧 a. skillful

~hui⁴ ～會 n. opportunity, chance

~hsieh⁴ ～械 n. machinery; a. mechanical

~hsieh⁴ hua⁴ ～械化 v. mechanize

~hsieh⁴ kung¹ ch'eng² ～械工程 n. mechanical engineering

~hsieh⁴ shih¹ ～械師 n. mechanist

~hsieh⁴ wei² wu⁴ lun⁴ ～械唯物論 n. mechanistic materialism**

~i² ～宜 n. policy, line of action

~kuan¹ ～關 n. organ, organization

~kuan¹ ch'iang¹ ～關鎗 n. machine gun

~mi⁴ ～密 a. secret, confidential (security classification)

~mou² ～謀 n. stratagem

~tung⁴ ～動 a. mobile

~yao⁴ ～要 a. confidential, classified

~yu² ～油 n. oil

CHI¹ 激 n. rush; v. rouse, excite; a. indignant

~ang² ～昂 a. spirited, passionate

~li⁴ ～勵 *v.* encourage
~lieh⁴ ～烈 *a.* bitter, violent (combat)
~nu⁴ ～怒 *v.* enrage
~tung⁴ ～動 *v.* rouse, excite

CHI¹ 積 *v.* gather, store up, accumulate
~chi² ～極 *a.* positive, constructive
~hsü¹ ～蓄 *n. & v.* deposit

CHI¹ 績 *n.* meritorious service; *v.* spin, twist

CHI¹ 饑 *n.* famine, dearth; *a.* hungry
~chin³ ～饉 *n.* famine
~e⁴ ～餓 *n.* hunger
~min² ～民 *n.* starving person

CHI¹ 鷄 *n.* chicken, hen, cock
~chiao⁴ ～叫 *v.* crow (cock)
~kuan¹ ～冠 *n.* cock's comb
~tan⁴ ～蛋 *n.* hen's egg

CHI¹ 基 *n.* foundation, base, land, property
~ch'u³ ～礎 *n.* foundation, base
~hsien⁴ ～線 *n.* base line
~pen³ chin¹ ～本金 *n.* reserve fund
~pen³ tan¹ wei⁴ ～本單位 *n.* basic unit
~pen³ te¹ ～本的 *a.* fundamental
~ti⁴ ～地 *n.* base (of operations)
~tu¹ chiao⁴ ～督敎 *n.* Christianity

CHI¹ 擊 *v.* strike, beat, attack, whip
~fa¹ ～發 *v.* firing mechanism
~k'uei⁴ ～潰 *v.* rout
~lo⁴ ～落 *v.* bring down (aircraft)
~pai⁴ ～敗 *v.* defeat
~p'o⁴ ～破 *v.* break (by striking)
~t'ui⁴ ～退 *v.* repel, repulse

CHI² 吉 *a.* lucky, fortunate
~chao⁴ ～兆 *a.* lucky
~li⁴ ～利 *n.* good luck
~p'u³ ch'e¹ ～普車 *n.* jeep

CHI² 急 *a.* urgent, hasty; *n.* urgent message
~chin⁴ chu³ i⁴ ～進主義 *n.* radicalism
~chin⁴ p'ai⁴ ～進派 *n.* radical party
~chiu⁴ ～救 *n.* first aid
~hsing² chün¹ ～行軍 *n.* rapid march
~hsing² ch'e¹ ～行車 *n.* express (train, bus)

~**mang²** ~忙 *a.* hasty

~**su²** ~速 *a.* quick, fast, swift

~**tien⁴** ~電 *n.* urgent telegram

~**tsao⁴** ~踩 *a.* passionate

~**ts'u⁴** ~促 *n.* & *v.* hurry

~**yü³** ~雨 *n.* shower

CHI² 及 *v.* reach to; *prep.* & *conj.* till

CHI² 即 *adv.* immediately, now

~**k'o⁴** ~刻 *adv.* immediately, at once

~**shih³** ~使 *adv.* even if, though

CHI² 籍 *n.* record, register, list

~**kuan⁴** ~貫 *n.* birthplace

~**mo⁴** ~沒 *v.* confiscate

CHI² 集 *v.* collect; *n.* market

~**chieh¹** ~結 *n.* troop concentration

~**chung¹** ~中 *v.* focus, concentrate

~**chung¹ ying²** ~中營 *n.* concentration camp

~**ch'üan²** ~權 *n.* centralized control

~**ho²** ~合 *v.* assemble, rally

~**ho² ti⁴** ~合地 *n.* assembly area

~**hui⁴** ~會 *v.* hold a meeting

~**t'i³ nung² ch'ang³** ~體農場 *n.* collective farm**

CHI² 極 *n.* zenith, end; *adv.* very, extremely

~**chia¹** ~佳 *a.* best

~**e⁴** ~惡 *a.* worst

~**hsing²** ~刑 *n.* capital punishment

~**ta⁴** ~大 *a.* greatest, largest

~**tuan¹** ~端 *n.* extremity, extreme

CHI² 級 *n.* class, grade, step

CHI³ 己 *pron.* I, myself

CHI³ 幾 *v.* be near, approximate; *adv.* almost

~**ho²** ~何 *n.* geometry

CHI³ 擠 *v.* crowd, press, milk

~**ju³** ~乳 *v.* milk

CHI³ 給 *see* KEI³

CHI⁴ 計 *v.* count, calculate, compute; *n.* calculation, plot

~**hua⁴** ~劃 *n.* plan, scheme

~**hua⁴ kuan³ li³** ~劃管理 *n.* planned management**

10

~**i⁴** ~議 *v.* discuss
~**mou²** ~謀 *n.* plot, trick
~**suan⁴** ~算 *v.* calculate
~**suan⁴ ch'i⁴** ~算器 *n.* calculating machine
~**suan⁴ ch'ih³** ~算尺 *n.* slide rule
CHI⁴ 季 *n.* season
~**hou⁴ feng¹** ~候風 *n.* monsoon
~**k'an¹** ~刊 *n.* quarterly
~**p'iao⁴** ~票 *n.* season ticket
CHI⁴ 既 *conj.* since, whereas
CHI⁴ 寄 *v.* send, lodge at, deliver to
~**su⁴** ~宿 *v.* lodge at
~**su⁴ she⁴** ~宿舍 *n.* dormitory
~**sheng¹ wu⁴** ~生物 *n.* parasite
~**shou⁴** ~售 *n.* consignment
~**t'o¹** ~託 *v.* entrust
~**ts'un²** ~存 *v.* deposit
~**wang⁴** ~望 *v.* expect
CHI⁴ 記 *v.* record, remember, write down
~**chang⁴ pu⁴** ~帳簿 *n.* cashbook
~**hao⁴** ~號 *n.* sign, mark, symbol
~**hsing⁴** ~性 *n.* memory
~**i⁴** ~憶 *v.* recollect
~**i⁴ li⁴** ~憶力 *n.* memory
~**nien⁴** ~念 *n.* remembrance
~**shih⁴ pu⁴** ~事簿 *n.* notebook
~**shou²** ~熟 *v.* memorize
~**te²** ~得 *v.* remember
CHI⁴ 紀 *n.* century, record
~**lu⁴** ~錄 *n.* record
~**lü⁴** ~律 *n.* discipline
~**nien⁴** ~念 *v.* commemorate
~**nien⁴ hui⁴** ~念會 *n.* memorial meeting
~**nien⁴ jih⁴** ~念日 *n.* anniversary
~**nien⁴ pei¹** ~念碑 *n.* stone monument
~**nien⁴ p'in³** ~念品 *n.* souvenir, memorial
~**shih⁴** ~事 *n.* memorandum
~**yüan²** ~元 *n.* epoch, era
~**yüan² ch'ien²** ~元前 *n.* before Christ (B.C.)
~**yüan² hou⁴** ~元後 *n.* after Christ (A.D.)
CHI⁴ 際 *n.* limit, juncture, occasion, time

CHI⁴ 濟 *v.* aid, relieve

CHI⁴ 繼 *n.* adoption; *v.* continue, succeed
~**ch'eng²** ~承 *v.* inherit; *n.* inheritance
~**fu⁴** ~父 *n.* stepfather
~**hsü⁴** ~續 *v.* continue; *n.* continuation
~**mu³** ~母 *n.* stepmother
~**nü³** ~女 *n.* stepdaughter
~**tzu³** ~子 *n.* stepson

CHI⁴ 技 *n.* art, skill, talent
~**ch'iao³** ~巧 *a.* skillful
~**i⁴** ~藝 *n.* art
~**neng²** ~能 *n.* skill, talent, ability
~**shu⁴** ~術 *n.* technique; *a.* technical
~**shu⁴ ho² tso⁴** ~術合作 *n.* technical cooperation

CHIA¹ 家 *n.* home, family, house
~**chang³** ~長 *n.* head of a family
~**cheng⁴** ~政 *n.* household affairs
~**cheng⁴ fu⁴** ~政婦 *n.* housekeeper
~**chü⁴** ~具 *n.* furniture
~**hsiang¹** ~鄉 *n.* native place
~**t'ing²** ~庭 *n.* home, family
~**yung⁴** ~用 *n.* family expenditure

CHIA¹ 加 *v.* add; *n.* addition; *a.* additional; *prep.* plus
~**pei⁴** ~倍 *v.* double
~**su²** ~速 *v.* speed, accelerate
~**yu²** ~油 *v.* lubricate, oil, fuel

CHIA¹ 夾 *n.* pincers, clip, wallet; *v.* hold tight
~**chiao³** ~角 *n.* offset angle
~**ch'a¹** ~叉 *n.* gunnery bracket
~**kung¹** ~攻 *n.* converging attack
~**pan³** ~板 *n.* splint
~**tsa²** ~雜 *a.* mixed

CHIA³ 甲 *n.* armor; *a.* first
~**chou⁴** ~冑 *n.* armor
~**pan³** ~板 *n.* deck
~**teng³** ~等 *n.* first class

CHIA³ 假 *a.* false. ~⁴ *n.* leave
~³**chuang¹** ~裝 *v.* disguise, pretend
~**fa³** ~髮 *n.* wig
~**hua⁴** ~話 *n.* lie

12

~hsiang³ ti² ~想敵 *n.* imaginary enemy

~hsiao⁴ ~笑 *v.* smirk

~mei⁴ ~寐 *n.* nap

~mien⁴ chü⁴ ~面具 *n.* mask

~shih³ ~使 *conj.* if; *prep.* in case of

~shih⁴ ~釋 *n.* parole

~ting⁴ ~定 *v.* suppose

~wu⁴ ~物 *n.* counterfeit

~⁴ jih⁴ ~日 *n.* holiday

CHIA⁴ 價 *n.* price, cost, value

~ang² ~昂 *a.* expensive

~chih² ~值 *n.* value

~ko² ~格 *n.* price

~lien² ~廉 *a.* cheap

~mu⁴ piao³ ~目表 *n.* price list

CHIA⁴ 架 *n.* shelf, stand, rack, frame; *v.* kidnap

~ch'iao² ~橋 *v.* build a bridge over

~ch'iao² tso⁴ yeh⁴ tui⁴ ~橋作業隊 *n.* bridging party

~hsien⁴ ~線 *n.* wire laying

CHIA⁴ 稼 *n.* crops

CHIA⁴ 嫁 *v.* marry

~chuang¹ ~妝 *n.* dowry, portion

CHIANG¹ 將 *v.aux.* shall, will; *v.* be ready to.

~⁴ *v.* command; *n.* side, general, marshal

~¹ chin⁴ ~近 *adv.* nearly, presently

~lai² ~來 *a. & n.* future

~⁴ chün¹ ~軍 *n.* general

~kuan¹ ~官 *n.* general officer

CHIANG¹ 江 *n.* river

CHIANG³ 講 *v.* explain, talk

~chieh³ ~解 *v.* explain; *n.* explanation

~ho² ~和 *v.* negotiate

~hua⁴ ~話 *v.* talk, speak

~tao⁴ ~道 *v.* preach

~t'ai² ~台 *n.* platform, pulpit

~shih¹ ~師 *n.* lecturer, instructor

~yen³ ~演 *n. & v.* lecture

CHIANG³ 獎 *v.* praise, encourage, reward

~chang¹ ~章 *n.* meritorious medal

~li⁴ ~勵 *v.* encourage

13

~p'in³ ~品 *n.* prize, reward

CHIANG⁴ 醬 *n.* soy sauce, jam

~ts'ai⁴ ~菜 *n.* vegetables (pickled)

~yu² ~油 *n.* sauce

CHIANG⁴ 匠 *n.* workman, craftsman, mechanic

CHIANG⁴ 降 *v.* drop, reduce, descend. **HSIANG²** *v.* surrender

~chi² ~級 *v.* reduce in rank, demote

~hsüeh³ ~雪 *v.* snow

~lao⁴ ~落 *v.* descend, land (from the air)

~lao⁴ san³ ~落傘 *n.* parachute

~yü³ ~雨 *v.* rain

hsiang² fu² ~服 *v.* surrender

CHIANG⁴ 喉 *see* **MA²**

CHIAO¹ 交 *v.* associate, pay, deliver, give

~chan⁴ ~戰 *v.* fight; *n.* hostilities

~chieh² ~結 *v.* associate with

~chieh⁴ ~界 *n.* boundary, border

~ch'ing² ~情 *n.* friendship

~fu⁴ ~付 *v.* pay, deliver

~huan² ~還 *v.* return

~huan⁴ ~換 *v.* exchange

~hsiang³ ch'ü³ ~響曲 *n.* symphony

~i⁴ ~易 *n.* trade, bargain, business deal

~i⁴ so³ ~易所 *n.* stock exchange

~kou⁴ ~媾 *v.* copulate; *n.* coition

~liu² tien⁴ ~流電 *n.* alternative current

~she⁴ ~涉 *v.* negotiate

~tai⁴ ~代 *v.* hand over

~tai⁴ cheng⁴ ts'e⁴ ~代政策 *v.* explain policy to one's immediate subordinate**

~t'i⁴ ~替 *v.* substitute

~t'ung¹ ~通 *v.* communicate; *n.* traffic

~t'ung¹ pu⁴ ~通部 *n.* Ministry of Communications

~yu³ ~友 *v.* make friends with

CHIAO¹ 焦 *a.* burned, anxious; *v.* scorch

~chi² ~急 *a.* anxious

~tien³ ~點 *n.* focus

~t'an⁴ ~炭 *n.* coke (coal)

CHIAO¹ 膠 *n.* glue; *a.* sticky

14

~**chih²** ~質 *n.* glue, gum
~**chu⁴** ~住 *n.* stick fast
~**chüan³** ~卷 *n.* photographic film
~**p'i²** ~皮 *n.* rubber
~**shui³** ~水 *n.* glue, mucilage
~**wan²** ~丸 *n.* capsule
CHIAO³ 角 *n.* horn, corner, angle
~**chu²** ~逐 *v.* compete
~**li⁴** ~力 *n.* wrestling
~**tu⁴** ~度 *n.* angle
~**t'ieh³** ~鐵 *n.* angle iron
CHIAO³ 脚 *n.* foot
~**ch'i⁴ ping⁴** ~氣病 *n.* beriberi
~**t'a⁴ ch'e¹** ~踏車 *n.* bicycle
CHIAO⁴ 叫 *v.* cry, call, shout
~**han³** ~喊 *v.* shout
~**hua⁴ tzu¹** ~化子 *n.* begger
CHIAO⁴ 教 *n.* doctrine, sect, school; *v.* cause, make. ~¹ *v.* teach
~¹ **yang³** ~養 *n.* breeding (manners)
~⁴ **huang²** ~皇 *n.* The Pope, pontiff
~**hui⁴** ~會 *n.* religious mission
~**hsün⁴** ~訓 *n.* instruction
~**i⁴** ~義 *n.* doctrine
~**kuan¹** ~官 *n.* instructor, officer
~**k'o¹ shu¹** ~科書 *n.* textbook
~**lien⁴** ~練 *v.* train
~**shih⁴** ~室 *n.* classroom
~**shou⁴** ~授 *n.* professor
~**t'ang²** ~堂 *n.* church
~**t'iao² chu³ i⁴ che³** ~條主義者 *n.* doctrinaires**
~**t'iao² chu³ i⁴ ssu¹ hsiang³** ~條主義思想 *n.* doctrinaire ways of thought**
~**t'u²** ~徒 *n.* disciple
~**yü⁴** ~育 *v.* educate; *n.* education
~**yü⁴ chi¹ chin¹** ~育基金 *n.* educational fund
~**yü⁴ pu⁴** ~育部 *n.* Ministry of Education
~**yü⁴ ying³ p'ien⁴** ~育影片 *n.* training film
~**yüan²** ~員 *n.* teacher, professor
CHIAO⁴ 較 *v.* compare, examine, compete; *n.* comparison

15

~**ch'a¹** ~差 *a.* worse
~**hao³** ~好 *a.* better
~**hsiao³** ~小 *a.* smaller
~**kao¹** ~高 *a.* higher, taller
~**kuei⁴** ~貴 *a.* dearer
~**lien²** ~廉 *a.* cheaper
~**shao³** ~少 *a.* less
~**ta⁴** ~大 *a.* bigger
~**ti¹** ~低 *a.* lower
~**to¹** ~多 *a.* more
~**tuan³** ~短 *a.* shorter

CHIAO⁴ 校 *v.* revise. **HSIAO⁴** *n.* school
~**kao³** ~稿 *v.* proofread
~**ting⁴** ~訂 *v.* revise
~**tui⁴** ~對 *v.* proofread
~**tui⁴ che³** ~對者 *n.* proofreader
hsiao⁴ **chang³** ~長 *n.* school principal, college
  president

CHIEH¹ 街 *n.* street
~**shih⁴** ~市 *n.* city street
~**tao⁴** ~道 *n.* avenue

CHIEH¹ 接 *v.* receive, connect, follow, succeed to
~**chi⁴** ~濟 *v.* supply
~**chin⁴** ~近 *prep.* near, by; *v.* approach
~**ch'u⁴** ~觸 *v.* contact
~**ho²** ~合 *v.* join, assemble
~**hsien⁴ sheng¹** ~線生 *n.* telephone operator
~**hsü⁴** ~續 *v.* continue
~**shou¹** ~收 *v.* take office
~**tai⁴** ~待 *v.* receive friends
~**tai⁴ shih⁴** ~待室 *n.* drawing room, parlor
~**wen³** ~吻 *v.* kiss

CHIEH¹ 階 *n.* rank, step, degree
~**chi²** ~級 *n.* rank, grade
~**chi² tou⁴ cheng¹** ~級闘爭 *n.* class struggle**
~**t'i¹** ~梯 *n.* step

CHIEH² 節 *n.* joint, knot, verse
~**chih⁴** ~制 *v.* control (restrain)
~**jih⁴** ~日 *n.* holiday, festival
~**ts'ao¹** ~操 *a.* chaste
~**yü⁴** ~育 *n.* birth control

16

~yüeh¹ ~約 *a.* frugal

CHIEH² 結 *v.* tie

~**chang⁴** ~賬 *v.* settle an account

~**chiao¹** ~交 *v.* make friends, associate

~**ching¹** ~晶 *n.* crystal

~**chü²** ~局 *n.* end, conclusion

~**ho²** ~合 *v.* assemble weapons

~**ho²** ~核 *n.* tuberculosis

~**hun¹** ~婚 *n.* wedding

~**kou⁴** ~構 *n.* structure

~**kuo³** ~果 *n.* result, consequence

~**lun⁴** ~論 *n.* conclusion

~**ping¹** ~冰 *v.* freeze

~**shu⁴** ~束 *v.* close, end, finish

CHIEH² 潔 *a.* pure, clean, neat, chaste

CHIEH³ 姐 *n.* older sister

~**fu¹** ~夫 *n.* older sister's husband (brother-in-law)

CHIEH³ 解 *v.* undo, loosen, explain. ~⁴ *v.* convey

~**chüeh²** ~決 *v.* solve

~**ch'u² ching³ pao⁴ hsin⁴ hao⁴** ~除警報信號 *v.* all clear signal

~**ch'u² ch'i⁴ yüeh¹** ~除契約 *n.* termination of contract

~**ch'u² wu³ chuang¹** ~除武裝 *v.* disarm

~**fang⁴ chün¹** ~放軍 *n.* liberation army**

~**fang⁴ ch'ü¹** ~放區 *n.* liberated area**

~**fang⁴ pao⁴** ~放報 *n.* Liberty Daily** (newspaper)

~**hsi¹** ~析 *n.* analysis

~**hsi¹ chi³ ho²** ~析幾何 *n.* analytic geometry

~**k'ai¹** ~開 *v.* untie

~**san⁴** ~散 *v.* disband a unit

~**shih⁴** ~釋 *v.* explain

~**tu² chi⁴** ~毒劑 *n.* antidote

CHIEH⁴ 界 *n.* border, boundary, circle (group)

~**hsien⁴** ~限 *n.* limitation

~**shuo¹**.~說 *n.* definition

CHIEH⁴ 介 *prep.* between

~**hsi⁴ tz'u²** ~系詞 *n.* preposition

~**i⁴** ~意 *v.* care

17

~**shao⁴** ~紹 *v.* introduce

~**yü²** ~於 *prep.* between

CHIEH⁴ 借 *v.* borrow, lend

~**chü⁴** ~據 *n.* promissory note

~**k'uan³** ~款 *v.* make a loan

CHIEH⁴ 戒 *v.* refrain

~**chih³** ~指 *n.* finger ring

~**ch'ih³** ~尺 *n.* ferule

~**yen²** ~嚴 *n.* martial law, curfew

CHIEN¹ 間 *n.* room, space. ~⁴ *v.* separate

~⁴ **chieh¹** ~接 *a.* indirect

~**chieh¹ ching¹ yen⁴** ~接經驗 *n.* indirect experience**

~**huo⁴** ~或 *adv.* occasionally

~**hsi⁴** ~隙 *n.* gap (in line of battle)

~**ko²** ~隔 *n.* interval

~**tieh²** ~諜 *n.* spy

~**tieh² huo² tung⁴** ~諜活動 *n.* espionage

~**tuan⁴** ~斷 *v.* interrupt

CHIEN¹ 漸 *v.* soak. ~⁴ *adv.* gradually

CHIEN¹ 堅 *a.* strong, durable, firm, hard

~**ch'iang²** ~強 *a.* vigorous

~**ch'ih²** ~持 *v.* insist

~**ku⁴** ~固 *a.* hard

~**ting⁴** ~定 *a.* firm

~**ying⁴** ~硬 *n.* rigid

CHIEN¹ 肩 *n.* shoulder

~**chang¹** ~章 *n.* epaulet

CHIEN¹ 監 *v.* oversee; *n.* jail. ~⁴ *n.* college

~**ch'a² yüan⁴** ~察院 *n.* control yuan*

~**fan⁴** ~犯 *n.* criminal

~**shih⁴** ~視 *v.* overlook

~**tu¹** ~督 *v.* supervise; *n.* supervision, supervisor

~**yü⁴** ~獄 *n.* jail, prison

CHIEN¹ 尖 *n.* point; *a.* sharp

~**li⁴** ~利 *a.* sharp

CHIEN¹ 艱 *n.* difficulty, suffering, distress; *a.* malicious

~**hsien³** ~險 *a.* difficult and dangerous

~**k'u³** ~苦 *n.* trouble

18

~nan² ～難 *a.* difficult; *n.* difficulty
CHIEN¹ 奸 *a.* crafty, tricky, villainous
  ~cha⁴ ～詐 *a.* deceitful
  ~hua² ～滑 *a.* tricky, knavish
  ~hsi⁴ ～細 *n.* traitor, spy
CHIEN³ 簡 *n.* letter, document, record; *v.* a-
  bridge; *a.* simple, easy
  ~lüeh⁴ ～略 *a.* abridged
  ~pien⁴ ～便 *a.* convenient
  ~tan¹ ～單 *a.* simple; *n.* simplicity
  ~tuan³ ～短 *a.* short, brief
  ~yao⁴ ～要 *a.* terse
CHIEN³ 檢 *v.* arrange, collate, gather; *n.* label,
  envelope
  ~ch'a² ～查 *v.* examine, check, inspect, censor
  ~ch'a² kuan¹ ～察官 *n.* inspector
  ~ting⁴ ～定 *a.* authorized
  ~yüeh⁴ ～閱 *v.* inspect troops
CHIEN³ 儉 *a.* frugal, economical
  ~p'u² ～僕 *n.* frugality, thrift
  ~sheng³ ～省 *a.* frugal
CHIEN³ 減 *v.* decrease, reduce, subtract; *n.* reduction
  ~ch'ing¹ ～輕 *v.* relieve
  ~fa³ ～法 *n.* subtraction
  ~hao⁴ ～號 *n.* minus, minus sign
  ~hsin¹ ～薪 *n.* reduction in pay
  ~shao³ ～少 *v.* reduce, decrease
CHIEN³ 剪 *v.* cut
  ~fa³ ～髮 *n.* haircut
  ~fa³ chü⁴ ～髮具 *n.* clippers (tool)
  ~tao¹ ～刀 *n.* scissors
  ~tuan³ ～短 *v.* cut short, clip
  ~tuan⁴ ～斷 *v.* cut
CHIEN⁴ 見 *v.* see
  ~cheng⁴ ～證 *n.* witness
  ~hsiao⁴ ～效 *a.* effective
  ~mien⁴ ～面 *n.* interview
  ~shih⁴ ～識 *n.* experience, knowledge
CHIEN⁴ 件 *n.* article, item
CHIEN⁴ 建 *v.* establish, build, construct

~chu⁴ shih¹ ～築師 *n.* architect

~i⁴ ～議 *v.* suggest ; *n.* suggestion

~kuo² fang¹ lüeh⁴ ～國方略 *n.* plans for national reconstruction*

~kuo² ta⁴ kang¹ ～國大綱 *n.* fundamentals of national reconstruction*

~li⁴ ～立 *v.* establish

~she⁴ ～設 *n.* construction

~she⁴ kung¹ tso⁴ ～設工作 *n.* construction work

~tsao⁴ ～造 *v.* build, construct

CHIEN⁴ 賤 *a.* mean, cheap, low, worthless

~chia⁴ ～價 *n.* low price

~jen² ～人 *n.* worthless, good-for-nothing

CHIEN⁴ 健 *a.* strong, vigorous

~chuang⁴ ～壯 *a.* strong

~k'ang¹ ～康 *a.* healthy ; *n.* health

~k'ang¹ cheng⁴ ming² shu¹ ～康證明書 *n.* health certificate

~mei³ ～美 *n.* physical beauty

~wang⁴ ～忘 *a.* absent-minded

CHIH¹ 知 *v.* know, understand

~chiao¹ ～交 *a.* intimacy

~chüeh² ～覺 *n.* sensation

~ch'ih³ ～恥 *v.* feel ashamed

~shih⁴ ～識 *n.* knowledge

~shih⁴ chieh¹ chi² ～識階級 *n.* intelligentsia, intellectual

~shih⁴ li³ shou³ ～識裏手 *n.* wiseacre**

~tao⁴ ～道 *v.* known

~tsu² ～足 *a.* satisfied

CHIH¹ 支 *n.* branch ; *v.* draw

~ch'ih² ～持 *v.* support, hold up

~ch'u¹ ～出 *v.* disburse, pay out

~fu⁴ ～付 *v.* pay, defray

~liu² ～流 *n. & a.* tributary

~pu⁴ ～部 *n.* branch office

~p'ei⁴ ～配 *v.* manage, control, conduct, handle, direct

~p'iao⁴ ～票 *n.* check

~p'iao⁴ pen³ ～票本 *n.* checkbook

~tien⁴ ～店 *n.* branch store

20

CHIH¹ 隻 *a.* one, single
CHIH¹ 織 *v.* weave, spin
  ~**chi¹** ～機 *n.* loom
  ~**kung¹** ～工 *n.* weaver
  ~**pu⁴** ～布 *v.* weave cloth
  ~**wu⁴** ～物 *n.* fabric, textile
CHIH¹ 之 *v.* go to, arrive at; *pron.* he, she, it, this, that; *prep.* of, for; *a.* possessive
CHIH² 職 *n.* duty
  ~**ch'üan²** ～權 *n.* authority
  ~**tse²** ～責 *n.* duty
  ~**wu⁴** ～務 *n.* duty, service, work
  ~**yeh⁴** ～業 *n.* occupation, vocation, profession
  ~**yüan²** ～員 *n.* staff employee
CHIH² 植 *n. & v.* plant
  ~**shu⁴ chieh²** ～樹節 *n.* Arbor Day (U.S.), Tree Planting Day
  ~**wu⁴** ～物 *n.* plant
  ~**wu⁴ hsüeh²** ～物學 *n.* botany
  ~**wu⁴ hsüeh² chia¹** ～物學家 *n.* botanist
CHIH² 直 *a.* straight, direct, frank
  ~**chiao³** ～角 *n.* right angle
  ~**chieh¹** ～接 *a.* direct
  ~**chieh¹ ching¹ yen⁴** ～接經驗 *n.* direct experience**
  ~**ching⁴** ～徑 *n.* diameter
  ~**chüeh²** ～覺 *n.* intuition
  ~**te¹** ～的 *a.* straight
  ~**yen²** ～言 *v.* speak frankly
CHIH² 值 *v.* cost; *n.* worth, price; *a.* worthy
  ~**ch'ien²** ～錢 *a.* valuable
  ~**jih⁴** ～日 *v.* be on duty for the day
  ~**jih⁴ kuan¹** ～日官 *n.* officer of the day
  ~**pan¹** ～班 *v.* be on duty
  ~**te²** ～得 *a.* worthy
CHIH² 質 *n.* substance, matter, material. ～⁴ *n.* pledge; *v.* pawn
  ~**liang⁴** ～量 *n.* quality
  ~**p'u² te¹** ～樸的 *a.* plain, simple
  ~**wen⁴** ～問 *v.* complain
  ~**⁴ tang⁴** ～當 *n.* pawnshop

~**wu⁴** ~物 *n.* security pledge

~**ya¹** ~押 *v.* pledge security

CHIH² 執 *v.* hold, grasp, seize, arrest

~**chao⁴** ~照 *n.* license (document)

~**cheng⁴** ~政 *v.* manage the government

~**hsing²** ~行 *v.* execute, carry out; *n.* performance of duty

~**hsing² wei² yüan² hui⁴** ~行委員會 *n.* executive committee

~**niu⁴** ~拗 *a.* obstinate

~**wen⁴** ~問 *n.* inquiry

CHIH³ 指 *n.* finger; *v.* point.   ~¹ **chia³** ~甲 *n.* fingernail

~³ **chai¹** ~摘 *v.* denounce

~**chiao⁴** ~教 *v.* ask for advice

~**huan²** ~環 *n.* ring finger

~**hui¹** ~揮 *v.* command, order

~**hui¹ kuan¹** ~揮官 *n.* commander

~**nan²** ~南 *n.* guidebook

~**nan² chen¹** ~南針 *n.* compass

~**piao¹** ~標 *n.* target

~**shih⁴** ~示 *v.* indicate, show

~**tao⁴** ~導 *v.* direct, lead, instruct

~**ting⁴** ~定 *v.* appoint, designate

CHIH³ 只 *adv.* only, merely, just

CHIH³ 止 *v.* stop, cease; *n.* cessation

~**hsüeh⁴ yao⁴** ~血藥 *n.* styptic

~**pu⁴** ~步 *v.* halt

~**t'ung⁴ yao⁴** ~痛藥 *n.* anodyne

CHIH⁴ 至 *v.* reach, arrive at; *prep.* to, until; *conj.* until

~**chin¹** ~今 *adv.* up to the present time

~**ch'eng²** ~誠 *a.* most sincere

~**ch'in¹** ~親 *a.* most intimate

~**shao³** ~少 *adv.* at least

~**to¹** ~多 *adv.* at most

CHIH⁴ 致 *v.* cause

CHIH⁴ 製 *v.* manufacture

~**tsao⁴** ~造 *v.* manufacture

~**tsao⁴ ch'ang³** ~造廠 *n.* factory

~**tsao⁴ p'in³** ~造品 *n.* manufacture goods

22

CHIH⁴ 制 *n.* rule, system ; *v.* control, regulate
~**e⁴** ~扼 *v.* pin down
~**fu²** ~服 *n.* uniform
~**k'ung¹ ch'uan²** ~空權 *n.* air superiority
~**shih⁴ chiao⁴ lien⁴** ~式教練 *n.* drill
~**ting⁴** ~定 *v.* regulate, enact
~**tu⁴** ~度 *n.* system
~**t'u² ch'ih³** ~圖尺 *n.* pantograph
~**ya¹** ~壓 *v.* neutralize by fire

CHIH⁴ 治 *v.* govern, regulate, cure ; *a.* peaceful
~**an¹** ~安 *n.* public safety
~**li³** ~理 *v.* manage
~**liao²** ~療 *v.* cure
~**wai⁴ fa³ ch'uan²** ~外法權 *n.* extraterritoriality

CHIH⁴ 置 *v.* let go, put aside, arrange

CHIH⁴ 志 *n.* ambition, aim, intention
~**hsiang⁴** ~向 *n.* ambition
~**shih⁴** ~士 *n.* patriot
~**yüan⁴** ~願 *n.* will
~**yüan⁴ ping¹** ~願兵 *n.* volunteer
~**yüan⁴ shu¹** ~願書 *n.* written agreement

CHIN¹ 今 *adv.* now ; *n.* present, modern
~**hou⁴** ~後 *adv.* henceforth, hereafter
~**nien²** ~年 *n.* this year
~**t'ien¹** ~天 *n.* today
~**tsao³** ~早 *n.* this morning
~**yeh⁴** ~夜 *n.* tonight

CHIN¹ 巾 *n.* towel, napkin, handkerchief
~**kuo¹** ~幗 *n.* womankind
~**kuo¹ ying¹ hsiung²** ~幗英雄 *n.* heroine

CHIN¹ 金 *n.* gold, metal ; *a.* golden
~**chi¹ na⁴ shuang¹** ~鷄納霜 *n.* quinine
~**jung²** ~融 *n.* finance
~**kang¹ tsuan⁴** ~剛鑽 *n.* diamond
~**pen³ wei⁴** ~本位 *n.* gold standard
~**pi⁴** ~幣 *n.* gold coin
~**se⁴** ~色 *a.* golden
~**tzu⁴ t'a³** ~字塔 *n.* pyramid
~**t'iao²** ~條 *n.* gold bar
~**yin² hua¹** ~銀花 *n.* woodbine
~**yü²** ~魚 *n.* goldfish

CHIN¹ 津 *n.* ferry, ford, saliva
~t'ieh¹ ~貼 *n.* allowance
CHIN¹ 斤 *n.* Chinese weight for 604.79 grams
~liang³ ~兩 *n.* weight
CHIN¹ 筋 *n.* sinew
~jou⁴ ~肉 *n.* muscle
~li⁴ ~力 *n.* sinew (strength)
CHIN³ 緊 *a.* urgent, important; *v.* bind tight
~chang¹ ~張 *n.* physical tension
~chi² ~急 *a.* urgent; *n.* emergency
~chi² ching³ pao⁴ hsin¹ hao⁴ ~急警報信號 *n.* air raid danger signal
~chi² shih² ch'i¹ ~急時期 *n.* state of emergency
~ts'ou⁴ ~湊 *a.* close tight
CHIN³ 僅 *adv.* only, merely, hardly, scarcely
CHIN⁴ 近 *a.* near, close
~chan⁴ ~戰 *n.* close combat
~chiao¹ ~郊 *n.* suburb
~chü² li² sou¹ so³ ~距離搜索 *n.* close reconnaissance
~hu¹ ~乎 *adv.* approximately
~lai² ~來 *adv.* recently
~lin² ~鄰 *n.* neighborhood
~p'o⁴ ~迫 *v.* make ready to sap
~shih⁴ ~世 *a.* modern
~shih⁴ ~視 *a.* near-sighted
~shih⁴ yen³ ~視眼 *n.* near-sighted
~tai⁴ shih³ ~代史 *n.* modern history
~tan⁴ ~彈 *n.* short-sighted
~ti⁴ ~地 *n.* vicinity
~tung¹ ~東 *n.* Near East
CHIN⁴ 進 *v.* enter, advance
~chan³ ~展 *n.* progress, gain
~ch'ang³ teng¹ ~場燈 *n.* approach light
~hua⁴ ~化 *n.* evolution
~hua⁴ lun⁴ ~化論 *n.* theory of evolution
~hsing² ~行 *v.* proceed
~hsing² chien⁴ she⁴ ~行建設 *v.* proceed with construction**
~hsing² ch'ü³ ~行曲 *n.* march music
~hsing² hsüan¹ ch'uan² ~行宣傳 *v.* conduct

propaganda**

~hsing² tzu⁴ wo³ p'i¹ p'ing² ～行自我批評 *v.* make self-criticism**

~ju⁴ chen⁴ ti⁴ ～入陣地 *v.* enter a position

~kung¹ ～攻 *v.* attack

~kung⁴ ～貢 *v.* send tribute

~k'ou³ huo⁴ ～口貨 *n.* import

~k'ou³ shui⁴ ～口稅 *n.* import duty

~k'uan³ ～款 *n.* income

~lu⁴ ～路 *n.* avenues of approach

~pu⁴ ～步 *v.* progress

CHIN⁴ 盡 *a.* all, finished; *adv.* entirely; *v.* exhaust, end; *n.* the last

~hsin¹ ～心 *v.* devote

~li⁴ ～力 *v.* try one's best

~t'ou² ～頭 *n.* end

CHIN⁴ 禁 *v.* forbid, prohibit, restrain, keep off

~chih³ ～止 *v.* forbid, prohibit

~chih³ ju⁴ nei⁴ ～止入內 *v.* keep out

~ling⁴ ～令 *n.* prohibition order

~yen¹ ～煙 *n.* no smoking

CHING¹ 京 *n.* capital

~ch'eng² ～城 *n.* national capital

CHING¹ 經 *n.* classics; *v.* pass through

~chi⁴ ～濟 *a.* economical; *n.* economy

~chi⁴ chu³ i⁴ ～濟主義 *n.* economism

~chi⁴ feng¹ so³ ～濟封鎖 *n.* economic blockade

~chi⁴ ho² suan⁴ chih⁴ ～濟核算制 *n.* economic accounting system**

~chi⁴ hsüeh² ～濟學 *n.* economics

~chi⁴ hsüeh² chia¹ ～濟學家 *n.* economist

~chi⁴ jen² ～紀人 *n.* broker, agent

~chi⁴ k'ung³ huang¹ ～濟恐慌 *n.* economic horror

~chi⁴ pu⁴ ～濟部 *n.* Ministry of Economics*

~ch'ang² ～常 *a.* constant; *adv.* usually

~fei⁴ ～費 *n.* fund

~hsien⁴ ～線 *n.* meridian of longitude

~kuo⁴ ～過 *v.* pass

~li³ ～理 *n.* logistics, manager

~shang¹ ～商 *v.* trade

25

  ~**shih³ fa³** ~始法 *n.* lay-out method (*engin.*)

  ~**tien³** ~典 *n.* classics

  ~**tu⁴** ~度 *n.* longitude

  ~**wei³ tu⁴** ~緯度 *n.* map coordinates

  ~**yen⁴** ~驗 *n.* experience

  ~**yen⁴ lun⁴** ~驗論 *n.* "empiricism"**

  ~**yu²** ~由 *prep.* via

CHING¹ 精 *a.* skillful, fine, delicate

  ~**chi‘ao³** ~巧 *a.* skillful

  ~**ch‘ung²** ~蟲 *n.* sperm cell

  ~**ch‘üeh⁴** ~確 *a.* accurate

  ~**hua²** ~華 *n.* essence

  ~**jui⁴ pu⁴ tui⁴** ~銳部隊 *n.* crack units

  ~**li⁴** ~力 *n.* energy, vigor

  ~**shen²** ~神 *a.* spiritual; *n.* spirit

  ~**shen² ping⁴** ~神病 *n.* insanity

  ~**tu⁴** ~度 *n.* accuracy

  ~**yeh⁴** ~液 *n.* semen, sperm, seminal fluid

CHING¹ 驚 *v.* fear; *a.* afraid, frightened, terrified

  ~**ch‘i²** ~奇 *a.* surprised, marvelous

  ~**hsia⁴** ~嚇 *v.* scare

  ~**hsien³** ~險 *a.* dangerous, adventurous

  ~**jen²** ~人 *a.* surprising, astonishing, amazing

  ~**tung⁴** ~動 *v.* disturb

CHING³ 景 *n.* view, scenery

  ~**chih⁴** ~緻 *n.* scenery

  ~**hsiang⁴** ~象 *n.* sight

  ~**k‘uang⁴** ~況 *n.* condition, circumstance

  ~**se⁴** ~色 *n.* landscape

  ~**yang³** ~仰 *v.* admire

CHING³ 井 *n.* well

  ~**jan²** ~然 *a.* orderly

CHING³ 警 *n.* police; *v.* warn, stimulate

  ~**chieh⁴** ~戒 *n.* defensive security

  ~**chieh⁴** ~界 *n.* police circles

  ~**chung¹** ~鐘 *n.* alarm bell

  ~**ch‘a²** ~察 *n.* police

  ~**ch‘a² chü²** ~察局 *n.* police bureau

  ~**kao⁴** ~告 *v.* warn; *n.* admonition

  ~**pao⁴** ~報 *n.* alarm, air raid alarm

  ~**pei⁴** ~備 *v.* alert

CHING⁴ 竟 *v.* search; *adv.* finally

CHING⁴ 境 *n.* frontier, boundary, region, district, condition
 ~**chieh⁴** ~界 *n.* boundary
 ~**k'uang⁴** ~況 *n.* condition

CHING⁴ 敬 *v.* respect, honor
 ~**ai⁴** ~愛 *v.* love and respect deeply, revere
 ~**chung⁴** ~重 *v.* respect
 ~**ch'i³** ~啓 *v.* inform
 ~**feng⁴** ~奉 *v.* worship
 ~**li³** ~禮 *v.* salute

CHING⁴ 競 *v.* struggle, quarrel
 ~**cheng¹** ~爭 *n.* competition
 ~**chi⁴** ~技 *n.* game
 ~**sai⁴** ~賽 *n.* match (contest)

CHING⁴ 靜 *a.* quiet, still, repose, silent
 ~**chih³** ~止 *n.* rest (absence of motion)
 ~**mo⁴** ~脈 *n.* vein
 ~**tien⁴** ~電 *n.* static electricity
 ~**yang³** ~養 *v.* rest

CHING⁴ 淨 *a.* pure, spotless, neat; *v.* wash; *adv.* only
 ~**k'uei¹** ~虧 *n.* net loss
 ~**li⁴** ~利 *n.* net profit
 ~**liang⁴** ~量 *n.* net weight

CHING⁴ 勁 *a.* strong, unyielding
 ~**lü³** ~旅 *n.* crack units

CHIU¹ 究 *v.* investigate, inquire
 ~**ching⁴** ~竟 *adv.* finally, at last
 ~**ch'a²** ~查 *v.* examine, investigate
 ~**fa²** ~罰 *v.* punish
 ~**pan⁴** ~辦 *v.* prosecute
 ~**wen⁴** ~問 *v.* investigate; *n.* investigation

CHIU¹ 糾 *v.* impeach, collect, correct
 ~**cheng⁴** ~正 *v.* correct; *n.* correction
 ~**fen¹** ~紛 *n.* quarrel

CHIU³ 久 *a.* lasting, permanent, long; *adv.* lastingly, permanently, long
 ~**liu²** ~留 *v.* stay long
 ~**pieh²** ~別 *a.* long separated
 ~**yüan³** ~遠 *adv.* forever

27

CHIU³ 酒 *n.* wine, liquor, spirits

~**ching¹** ~精 *n.* alcohol

~**lou²** ~樓 *n.* restaurant

~**pa¹ chien¹** ~吧間 *n.* bar room

~**pei¹** ~杯 *n.* wine glass

~**tien¹** ~店 *n.* bar room, tavern, saloon

~**tsui⁴** ~醉 *a.* drunk, intoxicated

CHIU³ 九 *n. & a.* nine

~**che²** ~折 *n.* ten-per cent discount

~**san¹ hsüeh² she⁴** ~三學社 *n.* Chiu San Socie-ty**

~**yüeh⁴** ~月 *n.* September

CHIU⁴ 就 *v.* go to, follow; *adv.* immediately

~**chih²** ~職 *n.* inauguration

~**ch'in³** ~寢 *v.* go to bed

~**shih⁴** ~是 *adv.* namely

~**ti⁴ shen³ p'an⁴** ~地審判 *n.* on-the-spot trial**

CHIU⁴ 救 *v.* rescue, save

~**chi²** ~急 *n.* first aid

~**chi² yao⁴ pao¹** ~急藥包 *n.* first-aid packet

~**hu⁴ ch'e¹** ~護車 *n.* ambulance

~**huo³ chi¹** ~火機 *n.* fire engine

~**sheng¹ ch'uan²** ~生船 *n.* lifeboat

~**sheng¹ tai⁴** ~生帶 *n.* life belt

CHIU⁴ 舊 *a.* old, ancient; *adv.* formerly

~**chi⁴** ~跡 *n.* ruins

~**li⁴** ~例 *n.* precedent

~**shih⁴** ~式 *n.* old style; *a.* old-fashioned

~**yüeh¹** ~約 *n.* Old Testament

CHO¹ 桌 *n.* table, desk

~**pu⁴** ~布 *n.* tablecloth

~**tzu¹** ~子 *n.* table

CHO¹ 捉 *v.* catch, arrest

~**mi² ts'ang²** ~迷藏 *n.* hide-and-seek

~**pu³** ~捕 *v.* arrest, catch

CHOU¹ 周 *n.* revolutionary movement, circum-ference

~**chi⁴** ~濟 *v.* bestow

~**ch'üan²** ~全 *adv.* completely

~**tao⁴** ~到 *adv.* completely

~**wei²** ~圍 *n.* surroundings

28

CHOU¹ 週 *n.* week, cycle; *adv.* weekly
　~**ch'i¹ hsing⁴** ~期性 *a.* periodic
　~**k'an¹** ~刊 *n.* weekly magazine
　~**nien²** ~年 *n.* anniversary
　~**wei²** ~圍 *n.* surroundings
　~**yu²** ~遊 *v.* travel
CHOU¹ 州 *n.* prefecture, State (U.S.)
CHU¹ 豬 *n.* pig
　~**jou⁴** ~肉 *n.* pork
CHU¹ 朱 *n.* red, vermilion; *a.* scarlet
　~**hung²** ~紅 *a.* scarlet
　~**sha¹** ~砂 *n.* cinnabar
CHU¹ 珠 *n.* pearl
　~**pao³** ~寶 *n.* jewel, gem
　~**pao³ shang¹** ~寶商 *n.* jeweler
　~**suan⁴** ~算 *n.* abacus
CHU² 竹 *n.* bamboo
　~**kan¹** ~竿 *n.* bamboo cane
　~**mu⁴** ~幕 *n.* bamboo curtain
CHU² 築 *v.* build
CHU³ 主 *n.* lord, master, owner, host; *a.* principal, main
　~**chang¹** ~張 *n.* assertion, advocacy; *v.* advocate
　~**chiao⁴** ~教 *n.* bishop
　~**ch'ih²** ~持 *v.* have charge of
　~**ch'üan²** ~權 *n.* sovereignty
　~**fan⁴** ~犯 *n.* law principal
　~**fu⁴** ~婦 *n.* housewife
　~**hsi²** ~席 *n.* chairman
　~**i⁴** ~義 *n.* principle, doctrine, theory
　~**jen²** ~人 *n.* master, owner, employer, host
　~**jen⁴** ~任 *n.* director (of general office), committee chairman
　~**jen⁴ wei³ yüan²** ~任委員 *n.* committee chairman
　~**jih⁴ hsüeh² hsiao⁴** ~日學校 *n.* Sunday school
　~**ku⁴** ~顧 *n.* customer
　~**kuan¹** ~觀 *n.* subjectivity
　~**kuan¹ hsing⁴** ~觀性 *n.* subjectivism**
　~**li⁴ chien⁴** ~力艦 *n.* capital ship
　~**pi³** ~筆 *n.* chief editor

29

~wei⁴ ~位 *n.* host's seat, subjective case

~yao⁴ ~要 *n.* importance, essence

CHU³ 煮 *v.* boil

~fu² ~沸 *v.* boil

CHU⁴ 住 *v.* dwell, live

~chai² ~宅 *n.* home, residence, house

~chih³ ~址 *n.* mail address

~so³ ~所 *n.* dwelling

CHU⁴ 注 *v.* pour, instill

~chung⁴ ~重 *v.* emphasize

~i⁴ ~意 *n.* attention ; *v.* pay attention

~ju⁴ ~入 *v.* pour

~mu⁴ ~目 *v.* gaze

~she⁴ ~射 *n.* injection

~she⁴ ch'i⁴ ~射器 *n.* injector

~shih⁴ ~視 *v.* gaze

CHU⁴ 柱 *n.* pillar

CHU⁴ 祝 *v.* pray, celebrate

~fu² ~福 *v.* bless

~ho⁴ ~賀 *v.* congratulate

CHU⁴ 助 *v.* help, assist ; *n.* help

~chiao⁴ ~教 *n.* assistant professor

~kung¹ ~攻 *n.* secondary attack

~li³ ~理 *n.* assistant

~shou³ ~手 *n.* assistant

~tung⁴ tz'u² ~動詞 *n.* auxiliary verb

CHUA¹ 抓 *v.* scratch

~ch'ü³ ~取 *v.* choose, select

~yang³ ~癢 *v.* scratch an itchy place

CHUAN¹ 專 *a.* single, particular

~chia¹ ~家 *n.* expert

~chih⁴ ~制 *n.* absolutism, despotism

~hsin¹ ~心 *v.* pay attention

~k'o¹ ~科 *n.* academy

~mai⁴ ch'üan² ~賣權 *n.* monopoly

~mai⁴ p'in³ ~賣品 *n.* commercial monopoly

~men² ~門 *n.* specialty

~shih³ ~使 *n.* special representative

CHUAN¹ 磚 *n.* brick, tile

CHUAN³ 轉 *v.* transmit, forward. **~⁴** *v.* turn around ; *n.* motor revolutions

~³ chi¹ ~機 *n.* turning point

~chiao¹ ~交 *adv.* in care of

~chin⁴ ~進 *v.* make a retrograde movement

~shun⁴ ~瞬 *v.* wink

~t'a³ ~塔 *n.* turret

~yün⁴ ~運 *v.* transport

CHUAN⁴ 賺 *v.* gain, earn

~ch'ien² ~錢 *v.* earn money

CHUAN⁴ 傳 *see* CH'UAN²

CHUANG¹ 裝 *v.* pack, contain, decorate

~chia³ ~甲 *a.* armor plated, armored

~chia³ ch'e¹ ~甲車 *n.* armored car

~chia³ ping¹ hsüeh² hsiao⁴ ~甲兵學校 *n.* Armored Force School*

~chia³ ping¹ lü³ ~甲兵旅 *n.* armored brigade

~chia³ pu⁴ tui⁴ ~甲部隊 *n.* armored force

~huang² ~璜 *n.* decoration

~hsiang¹ ~箱 *v.* pack; *n.* packing

~pei⁴ ~備 *n.* equipment, kit

~ping⁴ ~病 *v.* malinger

~p'ei⁴ ~配 *v.* assembly

~shih⁴ ~飾 *v.* adorn, decorate

~shih⁴ p'in³ ~飾品 *n.* ornament

~shu⁴ ~束 *v.* dress

~ting⁴ ~訂 *v.* bind sheets of paper

~t'ien⁴ ~塡 *v.* load ammunition

~tsai⁴ ~載 *v.* load

~yang² ~佯 *v.* pretend

~yao⁴ ~藥 *n.* powder charge

~yün⁴ ~運 *v.* transport

CHUANG¹ 莊 *n.* village, farm, agriculture, store

~hu⁴ ~戶 *n.* farmer

~yen² ~嚴 *a.* stately

CHUANG⁴ 壯 *a.* strong, healthy

~chien⁴ ~健 *a.* able-bodied, strong and healthy

~chih⁴ ~志 *a.* strong-minded

~li⁴ ~麗 *a.* magnificent, grand, stately

~nien² ~年 *n.* manhood

~ting¹ ~丁 *n.* able-bodied man

CHUANG⁴ 狀 *n.* shape, form, petition, warrant

~k'uang⁴ p'an⁴ tuan⁴ ~況判斷 *n.* estimate of

31

the situation

~t'ai⁴ ~態 *n.* condition, state

CHUI¹ 追 *v.* follow, chase, pursuit

~chiu¹ ~究 *v.* investigate

~ch'iu² ~求 *v.* chase, hunt

~hui⁴ ~悔 *v.* repent

~kan³ ~趕 *v.* pursuit

~ssu¹ ~思 *v.* recall

~tao⁴ hui⁴ ~悼會 *n.* memorial service

CHUN³ 準 *n.* standard, accuracy; *a.* right, accurate

~ch'üeh⁴ ~確 *a.* accurate, exact; *n.* accuracy

~pei⁴ ~備 *v.* prepare; *n.* preparation

~pei⁴ chin¹ ~備金 *n.* reserve funds

~shih² ~時 *a.* punctual

~tu⁴ ~度 *n.* accuracy

CHUN³ 准 *v.* allow, permit, grant, approve

~chiang⁴ ~將 *n.* brigadier general, commodore

~hsü³ ~許 *v.* authorize

~ju⁴ ~入 *v.* let in

CHUNG¹ 鐘 *n.* bell, clock

~lou² ~樓 *n.* bell-tower

~pai³ ~擺 *n.* pendulum

~piao³ chiang⁴ ~錶匠 *n.* watchmaker

~tien³ ~點 *n.* hour

CHUNG¹ 中 *a.* middle, central; *n.* center; *prep.* between, among, within, in. **~⁴** *v.* hit

~chiang⁴ ~將 *n.* lieutenant general, vice admiral

~chien¹ ~間 *a.* middle, central; *prep.* between, among

~chih³ ~止 *n.* cessation

~hua² ch'üan² kuo² hsüeh² sheng¹ lien² ho² hui⁴ ~華全國學生聯合會 *n.* All-China Students' Federation**

~hua² ch'üan² kuo² min² chu³ ch'ing¹ nien² lien² ho² tsung³ hui⁴ ~華全國民主青年聯合總會 *n.* All-China Federation of Democratic Youth**

~hua² ch'üan² kuo² min² chu³ fu⁴ nü³ lien² ho² hui⁴ ~華全國民主婦女聯合會 *n.* All-China Democratic Women's Federation**

~hua² ch'üan² kuo² tsung³ kung¹ hui⁴ 華全國總公會 *n*. All-China Federation of Labor**

~hua² ch'üan² kuo² wen² hsüeh² i⁴ shu⁴ chieh⁴ lien² ho² hui⁴ 華全國文學藝術界聯合會 *n*. All-China Federation of Literary and Art Circles**

~hua² min² kuo² ~華民國 *n*. Republic of China

~hua² min² kuo² hsien⁴ fa³ 華民國憲法 *n*. Constitution of the Republic of China*

~hsiao⁴ ~校 *n*. lieutenant colonel, commander

~hsin¹ ~心 *n*. center

~hsing⁴ ~性 *n*. neuter

~hsüeh² hsiao⁴ ~學校 *n*. high school

~ku³ ~古 *n*. Middle Ages

~kung⁴ ~共 *n*. Chinese Communist Party**

~kung¹ chung¹ yang¹ ~共中央 *n*. Central Committee of the Chinese Communist Party**

~kung⁴ ch'i¹ chieh⁴ san¹ chung¹ ch'üan² hui⁴ ~共七屆三中全會 *n*. Third Plenary Session of the Central Committee elected by the Seventh Party Congress**

~kuo² ~國 *n*. China

~kuo² chih⁴ kung¹ tang³ ~國致公黨 *n*. China Chih Kung Tang**

~kuo² ch'ing¹ nien² fan³ kung⁴ chiu⁴ kuo² t'uan² ~國青年反共救國團 *n*. China Youth Anti-Communist National Salvation Corps*

~kuo² fu² li⁴ hui⁴ ~國福利會 *n*. China Welfare Institute**

~kuo² hua⁴ ~國話 *n*. Chinese, spoken Chinese

~kuo² hung² shih² tzu⁴ hui⁴ ~國紅十字會 *n*. Red Cross Society of China**

~kuo² hsin¹ min² chu³ chu³ i⁴ ch'ing¹ nien² t'uan² ~國新民主主義青年團 *n*. China New Democratic Youth League**

~kuo² jen² ~國人 *n*. Chinese

~kuo² jen² min² cheng⁴ chih⁴ hsieh² shang¹ hui⁴ i⁴ ch'üan² kuo² wei³ yüan² hui⁴ ~國人民政治協商會議全國委員會 *n*. National Committee of Chinese People's Political Consultative Conference**

33

~**kuo² jen² min² cheng⁴ chih⁴ hsieh² shang¹ hui⁴ i⁴ ch'üan² t'i³ hui⁴ i⁴** ~國人民政治協商會議全體會議 *n.* Plenary Session of Chinese People's Political Consultative Conference**

~**kuo² jen² min² chieh³ fang⁴ chün¹** ~國人民解放軍 *n.* Chinese People's Volunteers**

~**kuo² jen² min² hang² k'ung¹ kung¹ ssu¹** ~國人民航空公司 *n.* National Civil Aviation Company**

~**kuo² jen² min² pao³ wei⁴ shih⁴ chieh⁴ ho² p'ing² fan³ tui⁴ mei³ kuo² ch'in¹ lüeh⁴ wei³ yüan² hui⁴** ~國人民保衛世界和平反對美國侵略委員會 *n.* Chinese People's Committee for World Peace and Against American Aggression**

~**kuo² jen² min² wai⁴ chiao¹ hsüeh² hui⁴** ~國人民外交學會 *n.* Chinese People's Institute of Foreign Affairs**

~**kuo² kung⁴ ch'an³ tang³** ~國共産黨 *n.* Chinese Communist Party**

~**kuo² kuo² min² tang³ ko² ming⁴ wei² yüan² hui⁴** ~國國民黨革命委員會 *n.* Revolutionary Committee of the Kuomintang**

~**kuo² min² chu³ t'ung² meng²** ~國民主同盟 *n.* China Democratic League**

~**kuo² min² chu³ ts'u⁴ chin⁴ hui⁴** ~國民主促進會 *n.* China Association for Promoting Democracy**

~**kuo² nung² kung¹ min² chu³ tang³** ~國農工民主黨 *n.* Chinese Peasants and Workers Democratic Party**

~**kuo² yin² hang²** ~國銀行 *n.* Bank of China

~**li⁴** ~立 *n.* neutrality

~**su¹ yu³ hao³ hsieh² hui⁴** ~蘇友好協會 *n.* Sino-Soviet Friendship Association**

~**su¹ yu³ hao³ t'ung² meng² hu⁴ chu⁴ t'iao² yüeh¹** ~蘇友好同盟互助條約 *n.* Sino-Soviet Treaty of Friendship, Alliance and Mutual Assistance**

~**shan¹ fu²** ~山服 *n.* Sun Yat-Sen Uniform

~**shih⁴** ~士 *n.* sergeant first class (army)

~**teng³** ~等 *n.* average

~teng³ chiao⁴ yü⁴ 等教育 *n.* secondary education

~tuan⁴ ~斷 *v.* discontinue

~t'u² ~途 *n.* midway, halfway

~wei⁴ ~尉 *n.* first lieutenant, lieutenant junior grade

~wen² ~文 *n.* Chinese language

~yang¹ ~央 *a.* central, middle

~yang¹ cheng⁴ fu³ ~央政府 *n.* Central Government

~yang¹ jen² min² cheng⁴ fu³ wei⁵ yüan² hui⁴ ~央人民政府委員會 *n.* Central People's Government Council**

~yang¹ jih⁴ pao⁴ ~央日報 *n.* Central Daily News*

~yang¹ she⁴ ~央社 *n.* Central News Agency*

~yang¹ tang³ pu⁴ ~央薰部 *n.* Central Kuomintang Headquarters

~yang¹ yin² hang² ~央銀行 *n.* Central Bank of China

~yung¹ ~庸 *n.* mean

~⁴ feng¹ ~風 *n.* apoplexy

~shu³ ~暑 *v.* suffer a heat stroke; *n.* sunstroke

~tu² ~毒 *n.* infection

CHUNG¹ 忠 *a.* loyal, faithful; *n.* loyalty

~hou⁴ ~厚 *a.* trustworthy, reliable

~hsiao⁴ ~孝 *a.* loyal

~hsin⁴ ~信 *a.* faithful

~i⁴ ~義 *a.* honest and righteous

~kao⁴ ~告 *v.* advise; *n.* advice

~shih² ~實 *a.* honest; *n.* honesty

CHUNG¹ 終 *n.* end; *adv.* finally; *v.* die

~chieh² ~結 *n.* conclusion

~chü² ~局 *n.* conclusion

CHUNG³ 種 *n.* seed, kind. **~⁴** *v.* plant, cultivate

~³ lei⁴ ~類 *n.* kind, class, sort, variety

~tsu² ~族 *n.* race, tribe

~tzu³ ~子 *n.* seed

~⁴ chih² ~植 *v.* plant

~tou⁴ ~痘 *v.* vaccinate; *n.* vaccination

CHUNG⁴ 重 *a.* heavy, severe; *n.* weight. **CH'-**

UNG² *n.* fold, repetition
~hsin⁴ ~心 *n.* center of gravity
~shui⁴ ~税 *n.* heavy tax
~yao⁴ ~要 *a.* important
~yin¹ ~音 *n.* accent
ch'ung² fu⁴ ~複 *n.* repetition
~hun¹ ~婚 *n.* bigamy
~hsiu¹ ~修 *v.* repair
~ting⁴ te¹ ~訂的 *a.* revised
CHUNG⁴ 衆 *a.* all, many, numerous
CHÜ¹ 居 *n.* dwelling, abode; *v.* dwell, live
~chu⁴ ~住 *v.* live, dwell
~ch'u⁴ ~処 *n.* residence, abode
~liu² ~留 *v.* sojourn
~min² ~民 *n.* inhabitant, resident
CHÜ² 局 *n.* bureau (office)
~chang³ ~長 *n.* chief of a bureau
~mien⁴ ~面 *n.* situation
~pu⁴ ~部 *a.* local
~shih⁴ ~勢 *n.* situation, condition
~wai⁴ jen² ~外人 *n.* outsider
CHÜ³ 舉 *v.* raise, lift up, begin
~chien⁴ ~薦 *v.* recommend personnel
~chung⁴ ~重 *n.* weight lifting
~kuo² ~國 *n.* whole country
~shou³ ~手 *v.* raise a hand
~shou³ li³ ~手禮 *n.* hand salute
~tung⁴ ~動 *n.* behavior
CHÜ⁴ 句 *n.* sentence
~fa³ ~法 *n.* syntax
~tien³ ~點 *n.* punctuation
CHÜ⁴ 據 *n.* evidence; *v.* rely upon; *adv.* according to
~cheng⁴ ~證 *n.* proof, evidence
~ling³ ~領 *v.* occupy
~tien³ ~點 *n.* key point
CHÜ⁴ 聚 *v.* collect, gather, assemble
~ho² ~合 *v.* unite
~tu³ ~賭 *v.* assemble for gambling
~ts'an¹ ~餐 *v.* dine together
CHÜ⁴ 具 *n.* tool

36

~ch'eng² ~呈 *v.* submit a petition

~ling³ ~領 *v.* receive

~pao⁴ ~報 *v.* submit a report

~t'i³ te¹ ~體的 *a.* concrete

CHÜ⁴ 劇 *n.* play; *v.* add; *a.* severe, strong; *adv.* very, more

~chung¹ jen² ~中人 *n.* cast (actors)

~lieh⁴ ~烈 *a.* violent; *n.* violence

~pen³ ~本 *n.* drama

~tao⁴ ~盜 *n.* highwayman

~yüan⁴ ~院 *n.* theater

CHÜ⁴ 拒 *v.* oppose, refuse

~chüeh² ~絕 *v.* reject, refuse

~pu³ ~捕 *v.* resist arrest

~ti² ~敵 *v.* resist an enemy

CHÜAN¹ 捐 *v.* contribute

~ch'i⁴ ~棄 *v.* abandon

~ch'ü¹ ~軀 *v.* sacrifice one's life

~k'uan³ ~款 *n.* contribution

~shui⁴ ~稅 *n.* taxation

CHÜAN³ 捲 *v.* curl, roll up, pack up

~hsin¹ ts'ai⁴ ~心菜 *n.* cabbage

~t'ao² ~逃 *v.* abscond

~yen¹ ~煙 *n.* cigarette

CHÜEH² 決 *v.* decide, sentence; *adv.* decidedly

~lieh⁴ ~裂 *n.* breach (quarrel)

~pu⁴ ~不 *adv.* never, by no means

~ting⁴ ~定 *v.* decide, determine; *n.* decision, determination; *a.* decided, determined

~tou⁴ ~鬥 *n.* duel; *v.* fight a duel

~tuan⁴ ~斷 *n.* decision

CHÜEH² 絕 *v.* break off, sever; *adv.* extremely, very

~chi⁴ ~跡 *v.* cease

~chiao¹ ~交 *v.* sever friendship

~pi⁴ ~壁 *n.* precipice, cliff

~ting³ ~頂 *n.* summit

~tui⁴ ~對 *a.* absolute

~wang⁴ ~望 *v.* despair

~yüan² ~緣 *n.* insulation

~yüan² t'i³ ~緣體 *n.* insulator

CHÜEH² 覺 v. feel, understand, discover

~**t'ung⁴** ~痛 v. feel pain

~**wu⁴** ~悟 v. understand

CHÜN¹ 均 a. equal, even, uniform, all

~**i¹** ~一 a. same, equal

~**shih⁴** ~勢 n. balance of power

~**t'an¹** ~攤 v. share equally

CHÜN¹ 軍 n. army, troop, soldier; v. station, banish (units)

~**chang³** ~長 n. army commander

~**cheng⁴ wei³ yüan² hui⁴** ~政委員會 n. Military and Administrative Committee**

~**chi⁴** ~紀 n. military discipline

~**chieh⁴** ~界 n. military circles

~**chien⁴** ~艦 n. warship

~**chuang¹** ~裝 n. uniform

~**fa²** ~閥 n. warlord

~**fa³** ~法 n. military law

~**fa³ chü²** ~法局 n. Judge Advocate General*

~**fei⁴** ~費 n. military expenditure

~**hao⁴** ~號 n. army bugle

~**huo³** ~火 n. munitions, ordnance materiel

~**hsiang³** ~餉 n. army pay

~**hsieh⁴ pao³ yang³ hsün⁴ lien⁴ pan¹** ~械保養訓練班 n. Ordnance Maintenance Training Class*

~**hsü¹** ~需 n. military supplies, quartermaster

~**hsü¹ hsün⁴ lien⁴ pan¹** ~需訓練班 n. Quartermaster Training Class*

~**i¹** ~醫 n. medical officer

~**jen²** ~人 n. soldier, military personnel

~**kuan¹** ~官 n. line officer

~**liang²** ~糧 n. military provisions

~**pei⁴** ~備 n. armament

~**tui⁴** ~隊 n. troop

~**ying²** ~營 n. military camp

~**yu² chü²** ~郵局 n. army post officer

~**yung⁴ chi¹** ~用機 n. military plane

~**yung⁴ p'iao¹** ~用票 n. Military Payment Certificate (MPC)

~**yung⁴ tien⁴ hua⁴** ~用電話 n. army telephone

38

~**yüeh⁴ tui⁴** ~樂隊 *n.* military band
CHÜN⁴ 菌 *n.* bacteria

CH'

CH'A¹ 差 *n.* difference, distinction. **CH'AI¹** *n.* legate ; *v.* send
~**pieh²** ~別 *n.* difference ; *v.* differ
~**pu⁴ to¹** ~不多 *adv.* almost
~**wu⁴** ~誤 *n.* error, mistake
ch'ai¹ ch'ien³ ~遣 *v.* send, dispatch
~**i⁴** ~役 *n.* public servant
~**shih⁴** ~事 *n.* business, employment
CH'A¹ 插 *v.* stick in, insert, pierce
~**ch'ü³** ~曲 *n.* musical interlude
~**ju⁴** ~入 *v.* insert
~**k'ou³** ~口 *v.* interrupt
CH'A² 茶 *n.* tea
~**ch'ih²** ~匙 *n.* teaspoon
~**fang²** ~房 *n.* restaurant waiter
~**hu²** ~壺 *n.* tea kettle, teapot
~**hua¹** ~花 *n.* camellia
~**hua⁴ hui⁴** ~話會 *n.* tea party
~**kuan³** ~館 *n.* tea shop
~**pei¹** ~杯 *n.* teacup
~**tien³** ~點 *n.* refreshment
~**tien⁴** ~店 *n.* tea shop
CH'A² 查 *v.* examine, search
~**chang⁴** ~帳 *v.* audit
~**chiu¹** ~究 *v.* investigate
~**wen⁴** ~問 *v.* question, examine
~**yen⁴** ~驗 *v.* examine
CH'A² 察 *v.* examine, investigate
~**chiu¹** ~究 *v.* investigate, examine
CH'AI¹ 差 *see* **CH'A¹**
CH'AI² 柴 *n.* firewood
CH'AN³ 產 *v.* produce, bear ; *n.* production
~**ch'u¹ liang⁴** ~出量 *n.* output
~**fu⁴** ~婦 *n.* confined woman
~**k'o¹** ~科 *n.* midwifery

~k'o¹ hu⁴ shih⁴ ~科護士 *n.* maternity nurse

~k'o¹ i¹ yüan⁴ ~科醫院 *n.* maternity hospital

~sheng¹ ~生 *v.* produce, bear

~wu⁴ ~物 *n.* product

~yeh⁴ ~業 *n.* estate

CH'ANG¹ 倡 *v.* promote; *n.* promotion

~tao³ ~導 *v.* promote

CH'ANG² 常 *a.* constant, regular, frequent; *adv.* always, usually

~ch'ang² ~常 *adv.* always, often

~kuei¹ ~規 *n.* routine

~pei⁴ chün¹ ~備軍 *n.* standing army

~shih⁴ ~識 *n.* common sense

~wu⁴ wei³ yüan² ~務委員 *n.* standing committee member

~wu⁴ wei³ yüan² hui⁴ ~務委員會 *n.* standing committee

CH'ANG² 腸 *n.* intestines

~ping⁴ ~病 *n.* intestinal malady

CH'ANG² 長 *see* CHANG³

CH'ANG³ 場 *n.* yard, open place

CH'ANG³ 廠 *n.* factory, manufacturing, workshop

CH'ANG⁴ 唱 *v.* sing

~ko¹ ~歌 *v.* sing songs

~ko¹ pan¹ ~歌班 *n.* choir

CH'AO¹ 吵 *n.* bawl, quarrel, uproar

~nao⁴ ~鬧 *v.* quarrel

CH'AO¹ 超 *v.* step over, surpass

~e² wan² ch'eng² ~額完成 *n.* over-fulfillment**

~fan²⁾ ~凡 *a.* unusual

~jen² ~人 *a.* superhuman

~kuo⁴ ~過 *v.* surpass, exceed, excel

~teng³ ~等 *a.* excellent

CH'AO² 朝 *n.* court, dynasty, Korea; *v.* face; *prep.* toward. CHAO¹ *n.* morning

~tai⁴ ~代 *n.* dynasty

~t'ing² ~廷 *n.* court

CH'E¹ 車 *n.* automobile, carriage, vehicle

~chan⁴ ~站 *n.* station (railroad, bus)

~chang³ ~掌 *n.* streetcar conductor

~chia⁴ ~架 *n.* vehicle chassis

~**chou²** ~軸 *n.* vehicle axle
~**ch'uang²** ~床 *n.* lathe
~**fu¹** ~夫 *n.* chauffeur, driver, coachman
~**liang⁴** ~輛 *n.* vehicle
~**lun²** ~輪 *n.* vehicle wheel
~**p'iao⁴** ~票 *n.* transportation ticket
~**t'ai¹** ~胎 *n.* tire

CH'EN² 陳 *a.* ancient, old; *v.* arrange, exhibit, state
~**chiu⁴** ~舊 *a.* old, out-of-date
~**fu³** ~腐 *a.* old-fashioned
~**lieh⁴** ~列 *v.* display
~**lieh⁴ p'in³** ~列品 *n.* exhibit objects
~**she⁴** ~設 *v.* arrange
~**shu⁴** ~述 *v.* state, explain

CH'EN² 晨 *n.* morning, dawn
~**pao⁴** ~報 *n.* morning paper

CH'EN⁴ 趁 *v.* go to, avail of
~**shih⁴** ~勢 *v.* take advantage

CH'ENG¹ 稱 *v.* weigh, call, praise. ~⁴ *a.* fit; *n.* balance
~**¹ hu¹** ~呼 *v.* call, style, name
~**hsieh⁴** ~謝 *v.* thank
~**yang²** ~揚 *v.* praise
~**⁴ hsin¹** ~心 *a.* satisfied

CH'ENG² 成 *v.* finish, succeed
~**chi¹** ~績 *n.* efficiency, school record
~**jen²** ~仁 *v.* die for a noble cause
~**kung¹** ~功 *n.* success, achievement
~**li⁴** ~立 *v.* establish, constitute (a new unit)
~**pen³** ~本 *n.* cost

CH'ENG² 城 *n.* city
~**ch'iang²** ~牆 *n.* city wall
~**pao⁰** ~堡 *n.* castle
~**shih⁴** ~市 *n.* city, town
~**shih⁴ mai¹ pan³ chieh¹ chi²** ~市買辦階級 *n.* comprador class in the cities**

CH'ENG² 程 *n.* measure, route, rule, journey
~**hsü⁴** ~序 *n.* procedure, order
~**tu⁴** ~度 *n.* standard

CH'ENG² 誠 *a.* sincere, true, real

41

~i⁴ ~意 *a.* sincere

~k'en³ ~懇 *a.* sincere

~shih² ~實 *a.* honest

CH'ENG² 乘 *v.* ride, multiply. ~⁴ *n.* chariot, annals

~chi¹ ~機 *v.* take advantage of

~ch'uan² ~船 *v.* board a ship

~fa³ ~法 *n.* multiplication

~huo³ ch'e¹ ~火車 *v.* board a train

~k'o⁴ ~客 *n.* passenger

~liang² ~涼 *v.* enjoy the cool air

~ma³ ~馬 *v.* ride a horse; *n.* riding horse

~yüan² ~員 *n.* crew

CH'ENG² 承 *v.* support, uphold, receive, consent

~chi⁴ ~繼 *v.* adopt

~chi⁴ jen² ~繼人 *n.* successor

~jen⁴ ~認 *v.* acknowledge, recognize

~lan³ ~攬 *v.* contract

~no⁴ ~諾 *v.* promise

~shou⁴ ~受 *v.* receive

~tsu¹ ~租 *v.* rent from

CH'ENG² 盛 *see* **SHENG⁴**

CH'I¹ 七 *n. & a.* seven

~hsien² ch'in² ~絃琴 *n.* lyre

~yüeh⁴ ~月 *n.* July

CH'I¹ 期 *v.* expect; *n.* period

~chien¹ ~間 *n.* duration

~hsien⁴ ~限 *n.* a limit of time

~p'iao⁴ ~票 *n.* promissory note

~wang⁴ ~望 *v.* expect, hope

CH'I¹ 妻 *n.* wife, better-half

CH'I¹ 欺 *v.* cheat

~meng² ~朦 *v.* fool

~p'ien⁴ ~騙 *v.* cheat

~wu³ ~侮 *v.* insult

CH'I² 齊 *n.* harmony, order; *v.* equalize; *a.* even, uniform

~cheng³ ~整 *a.* orderly, neat

~chi² ~集 *v.* gather, collect

~ch'üan² ~全 *a.* complete

~hsin¹ ~心 *adv.* unanimously

~**pei⁴** 備 *a.* all ready

~**she⁴** ~射 *n.* salvo fire

CH'I² 騎 *v.* ride, sit astride

~**ma³** ~馬 *v.* mount a horse

~**ping⁴** ~兵 *n.* cavalry

~**shih¹** ~師 *n.* skilled horseman

~**shih⁴** ~士 *n.* knight

~**shu⁴** ~術 *n.* horsemanship

CH'I² 奇 *a.* strange, wonderful, marvelous

~**chen¹** ~珍 *n.* rare treasure

~**chi⁴** ~跡 *n.* miracle

~**ch'iao³** ~巧 *a.* wonderful

~**i⁴** ~異 *a.* remarkable

~**shu⁴** ~數 *n.* odd number

~**t'an²** ~談 *n.* strange talk

~**ts'ai²** ~才 *n.* remarkable talents

CH'I² 其 *pron.* they, he, she, it ; *a.* this, that

~**shih²** ~實 *adv.* in fact

~**yü²** ~餘 *n.* rest

CH'I² 旗 *n.* flag, banner

~**chien⁴** ~艦 *n.* flagship

~**chih⁴** ~幟 *n.* flag

~**kan¹** ~竿 *n.* flagpole

~**yü³** ~語 *n.* flag semaphore

CH'I³ 起 *v.* stand up, rise, start

~**chung⁴ chi¹** ~重機 *n.* crane, jack, hoist

~**ch'uang² hao⁴** ~床號 *n.* reveille

~**fei¹** ~飛 *v.* take off (airplane)

~**fu² ti⁴** ~伏地 *n.* rolling terrain

~**huo³** ~火 *v.* catch fire

~**huo⁴ tan¹** ~貨單 *n.* bill of lading

~**kao³** ~稿 *v.* draft

~**lai²** ~來 *v.* get up, arise

~**li⁴** ~立 *v.* stand up

~**mao²** ~錨 *v.* weigh anchor

~**su⁴** ~訴 *v.* accuse

~**su⁴ jen²** ~訴人 *n.* suitor (lawsuit)

~**shen¹** ~身 *v.* arise

~**tien³** ~點 *n.* starting point

~**ts'ao³** ~草 *v.* draft

CH'I³ 啓 *v.* open, begin, announce, notice, explain

~**fa**¹ ~發 *v.* instruct
~**meng**² ~蒙 *a.* elementary; *n.* beginning
~**shih**⁴ ~事 *n.* notice

CH'I⁴ 器 *n.* utensil, vessel
~**chü**⁴ ~具 *n.* apparatus, furniture
~**kuan**¹ ~官 *n.* organ
~**min**³ ~皿 *n.* utensil, vessel
~**ts'ai**² ~材 *n.* materiel (weapons and equipment)

CH'I⁴ 汽 *n.* steam
~**ch'e**¹ ~車 *n.* automobile, motor car
~**ch'uan**² ~船 *n.* steamboat, steamship
~**ti**² ~笛 *n.* steam whistle
~**yu**² ~油 *n.* gasoline

CH'I⁴ 氣 *n.* steam, air, breath
~**ch'iu**² ~球 *n.* balloon
~**ch'uan**³ ~喘 *n.* asthma; *a.* asthmatic
~**hou**⁴ ~候 *n.* climate
~**hsiang**⁴ **hsüeh**² ~象學 *n.* meteorology
~**hsiang**⁴ **t'ai**² ~象臺 *n.* observatory
~**kuan**³ ~管 *n.* windpipe, trachea
~**li**⁴ ~力 *n.* energy, strength
~**se**⁴ ~色 *n.* complexion
~**t'i**³ ~體 *n.* gas
~**ya**¹ ~壓 *n.* air pressure
~**wei**⁴ ~味 *n.* smell, odor
~**yen**⁴ ~焰 *n.* flame

CH'IA⁴ 恰 *adv.* just, exactly
~**ch'iao**³ ~巧 *adv.* fortunately

CH'IANG¹ 槍 *n.* lance. [Same as 鎗] gun, rifle
~**liu**² **tan**⁴ ~榴彈 *n.* rifle grenade
~**shang**¹ ~傷 *n.* bullet wound
~**shen**¹ ~身 *n.* gun barrel
~**tan**⁴ ~彈 *n.* bullet, cartridge
~**t'ang**² ~膛 *n.* barrel bore

CH'IANG² 強 *a.* strong. ~³ *v.* force
~² **tao**⁴ ~盜 *n.* robber
~**ying**⁴ ~硬 *a.* unyielding
~³ **to**² ~奪 *v.* seize (by force)

CH'IANG² 牆 *n.* wall
CH'IANG³ 搶 *v.* rob, plunder

~**chieh²** ~劫 *n.* plunder
~**chieh² che³** ~劫者 *n.* robber
~**to² tsui⁴** ~奪罪 *n.* burglary

CH'IAO² 瞧 *v.* look on, consider

CH'IAO² 橋 *n.* bridge
~**liang²** ~樑 *n.* bridge
~**p'ai² hsi⁴** ~牌戲 *n.* bridge (card game)
~**tung⁴** ~洞 *n.* arch of bridge
~**t'ou² pao³** ~頭堡 *n.* bridgehead

CH'IAO³ 巧 *a.* cunning, clever, ingenious
~**chi⁴** ~計 *n.* ingenuity
~**miao⁴** ~妙 *a.* ingenious, skillful
~**yü⁴** ~遇 *v.* meet by chance

CH'IEH¹ 切 *v.* cut
~¹ **hsien⁴** ~線 *n.* tangent
~**k'ai¹** ~開 *v.* cut apart, mince, slice
~⁴ **chi⁴** ~忌 *a.* prohibitive, prohibitory
~**shih²** ~實 *a.* real, true; *adv.* really, truly
~**wang³** ~望 *a.* eager

CH'IEH³ 且 *adv.* also, moreover, besides

CH'IEN¹ 千 *n.* & *a.* thousand

CH'IEN¹ 牽 *v.* pull, haul, connect
~**chih⁴** ~制 *v.* hold (the enemy)
~**ch'iang²** ~強 *n.* halter, tie rope
~**lien²** ~連 *v.* involve

CH'IEN¹ 簽 *n.* paper slip, signature; *v.* sign, endorse
~**cheng⁴** ~證 *n.* visa
~**ming²** ~名 *n.* signature
~**t'iao²** ~條 *n.* paper slip, label
~**tzu⁴** ~字 *n.* signature

CH'IEN² 前 *n. prep.* before, in front of, in advance of, ahead of; *adv.* formerly, previously; *a.* previous, front
~**chih⁴ tz'u²** ~置詞 *n.* preposition
~**chin⁴** ~進 *v.* move forward, advance
~**fang¹** ~方 *n.* front (opposite of rear)
~**feng¹** ~鋒 *n.* vanguard
~**hsien⁴** ~綫 *n.* front (line of battle)
~**jen⁴** ~任 *n.* predecessor
~**men²** ~門 *n.* front door

45

~**mien⁴** ~面 n. front

~**shao⁴** ~哨 n. outpost

~**t'u²** ~途 n. chance of future success

~**wei⁴** ~衛 n. advance guard

~**yüan²** ~緣 n. leading edge

CH'IEN² 錢 n. money, current coin, wealth

~**hsiang¹** ~箱 n. till

~**pi⁴** ~幣 n. money, current coin, currency

~**tai⁴** ~袋 n. purse

CH'IEN³ 淺 a. shallow, superficial; v. run a-ground

~**hsüeh²** ~學 a. shallow, superficial

~**i⁴** ~易 a. easy

~**po²** ~薄 a. shallow

CH'IEN⁴ 欠 v. owe

~**chai⁴** ~債 v. owe debt

~**ch'üeh¹** ~缺 a. insufficient

~**shen¹** ~伸 v. yawn

CH'IH¹ 吃 v. eat

~**chin³** ~緊 a. critical, dangerous

~**ching¹** ~驚 v. be frightened

~**fan⁴** ~飯 v. take meals

~**k'uei¹** ~虧 v. suffer a loss

~**li⁴** ~力 a. difficult

~**ts'u⁴** ~醋 v. be jealous

CH'IH² 池 n. pool, pond

~**t'ang²** ~塘 n. pond

CH'IH² 持 v. hold, maintain

~**chiu³ chan⁴** ~久戰 n. delaying resistance

~**chiu³ hsing⁴** ~久性 a. persistent

~**chiu³ li⁴** ~久力 n. endurance

CH'IH² 遲 n. delay; v. defer; a. slow, late

~**tao⁴** ~到 a. late

~**yen²** ~延 v. delay

CH'IH³ 尺 n. Chinese linear measure for 14.1 inches

~**² ts'un⁴** ~寸 n. size

~**³ tu²** ~牘 n. letter writing

CH'IH³ 恥 a. ashamed

~**hsiao⁴** ~笑 v. ridicule

~**ju⁴** ~辱 n. shame, disgrace

46

CH'IH³ 齒 *n.* teeth, age
~**lun²** ~輪 *n.* gear (mechanical)

CH'IN¹ 親 *n.* relation; *v.* love, approach, kiss; *a.* dear, close, own
~**ai⁴ te¹** ~愛的 *a.* dear
~**ch'i¹** ~戚 *n.* relative
~**mi⁴** ~密 *a.* intimate; *n.* intimacy
~**shan⁴** ~善 *a.* kind, close
~**tsui³** ~嘴 *n.* & *v.* kiss
~**tzu⁴** ~自 *adv.* personally

CH'IN¹ 侵 *v.* invade
~**chan⁴** ~佔 *v.* occupy
~**ch'e⁴ li⁴** ~徹力 *n.* force of penetration
~**lüeh⁴** ~略 *v.* invade; *n.* invasion
~**shih²** ~蝕 *n.* erosion
~**t'un¹** ~吞 *v.* squeeze

CH'IN² 勤 *a.* diligent, industrious; *n.* diligence
~**chien³** ~儉 *a.* diligent and frugal
~**hsüeh²** ~學 *v.* study hard
~**k'u³** ~苦 *a.* toilsome, laborious
~**lao²** ~勞 *a.* toilsome, laborious

CH'ING¹ 輕 *a.* light, easy, low, unimportant
~**chi¹ kuan¹ ch'iang¹** ~機關槍 *n.* light machine gun
~**chien⁴** ~賤 *a.* low, mean
~**ch'i¹ ch'iu²** ~氣球 *n.* hydrogen balloon
~**fu²** ~浮 *a.* unsteady, flimsy
~**hsin⁴** ~信 *v.* believe recklessly
~**i⁴** ~易 *a.* easy
~**kung¹ yeh⁴ pu⁴** ~工業部 *n.* Ministry of Light Industry**
~**k'uai⁴** ~快 *a.* nimble
~**k'uang²** ~狂 *a.* frivolous
~**ping¹ ch'i⁴** ~兵器 *n.* light arms
~**po²** ~薄 *a.* disrespectful
~**shang¹ che³** ~傷者 *n.* walking wounded
~**shih⁴** ~視 *v.* despise
~**yin¹ yüeh⁴** ~音樂 *n.* light music

CH'ING¹ 清 *v.* purify, pure; *a.* pure, clear
~**chieh²** ~潔 *n.* cleanness
~**ching⁴** ~淨 *a.* clean

~**ch'u³** ~楚 *a.* clear
~**hsiang¹** ~香 *a.* fragrant
~**hsien²** ~閒 *adv.* leisurely
~**hsiu⁴** ~秀 *a.* pretty
~**lang³** ~朗 *a.* clear
~**li³** ~理 *v.* settle
~**lien²** ~廉 *n.* integrity
~**po²** ~白 *n.* innocence
~**sao³** ~掃 *v.* clear (field of fire)
~**suan⁴** ~算 *v.* liquidate; *n.* liquidation
~**tang³** ~黨 *n.* purge (from a party)
CH'ING¹ 青 *a.* green
~**ch'un¹** ~春 *n.* youth; *a.* juvenile, youthful
~**ch'un¹ ch'i¹** ~春期 *n.* adolescence
~**nien²** ~年 *n.* youth, young man
~**nien² hui⁴** ~年會 *n.* Young Men's Christian Association
~**wa¹** ~蛙 *n.* frog
CH'ING² 情 *n.* passion, affection, emotion, circumstance, fact
~**ai⁴** ~愛 *n.* affection, love
~**chieh²** ~節 *n.* plot (of a play)
~**hsing²** ~形 *n.* condition, situation, state
~**hsü⁴** ~緒 *n.* emotion
~**i²** ~誼 *n.* friendship
~**jen²** ~人 *n.* lover, sweetheart
~**kan³** ~感 *n.* emotion; *a.* sentimental, emotional
~**li³** ~理 *n.* reason
~**pao⁴** ~報 *n.* intelligence, information (*mil.*)
~**pao⁴ tsung³ shu³** ~報總署 *n.* Information Administration**
~**shu¹** ~書 *n.* love letter
~**yüan⁴** ~願 *a.* willing
CH'ING² 晴 *n.* a clear sky
~**t'ien¹** ~天 *n.* fine weather
~**yü³ piao³** ~雨表 *n.* barometer
CH'ING³ 請 *v.* beg, request, invite
~**chin⁴** ~進 *v.* come in (please)
~**ch'iu²** ~求 *n. & v.* request
~**k'o⁴** ~客 *v.* invite guests

~t'ieh³ ~帖 *n.* invitation card
~tso⁴ ~坐 *v.* sit down (please)
~yüan⁴ ~願 *n.* petition
CH'ING⁴ 慶 *v.* congratulate
~chu⁴ ~祝 *v.* celebrate; *n.* celebration
~ho⁴ ~賀 *v.* congratulate; *n.* congratulations
CH'IU¹ 秋 *n.* autumn, fall
~chi⁴ ~季 *n.* autumn, fall
~shou¹ ~收 *n.* harvest
CH'IU² 求 *v.* beg, ask, request
~chien⁴ ~見 *v.* request an interview
~chu⁴ ~助 *v.* ask for help
~ch'ing² ~情 *v.* ask a favor
~hun¹ ~婚 *v.* woo, court
~hsüeh² ~學 *v.* learn, study
CH'IU² 球 *n.* ball, globe
~ch'ang³ ~場 *n.* playground
~hsing² ~形 *n.* sphere, globe
~men² ~門 *n.* goal (sports)
CH'IUNG² 窮 *a.* poor, exhausted
~jen² ~人 *n.* poor people
~k'un⁴ ~困 *a.* impoverished
CH'OU¹ 抽 *v.* draw
~chin¹ ~筋 *n.* spasm
~ch'ien¹ ~籤 *v.* draw lots
~hsiang⁴ ~象 *n.* abstraction
~hsien² ~閒 *v.* take a little leisure
~shui⁴ ~稅 *v.* levy taxes
~shui³ t'ung³ ~水筒 *n.* water pump
~t'i⁴ ~屜 *n.* drawer (furniture)
CH'OU² 酬 *v.* entertain, repay
~hsieh⁴ ~謝 *v.* return thanks
~lao² ~勞 *n.* & *v.* reward
~pao⁴ ~報 *v.* remunerate; *n.* remuneration
~wu⁴ ~物 *n.* gratuity
CH'OU² 籌 *n.* lot, ticket; *v.* calculate
~chieh⁴ ~借 *v.* raise money
~hua⁴ ~劃 *v.* plan
~pei⁴ ~備 *v.* prepare
CH'OU² 綢 *n.* silk cloth
~i¹ ~衣 *n.* silk garment

CH'OU² 仇 *n.* enmity, hate
~**hen⁴** ~恨 *n.* enmity, hate
~**jen²** ~人 *n.* enemy
~**ti²** ~敵 *n.* enemy

CH'OU² 愁 *a.* sad; *n.* sorrow
~**men⁴** ~悶 *a.* sorry, sad

CH'OU⁴ 臭 *a.* stench, stink
~**ch'i⁴** ~氣 *n.* stink
~**ch'ung²** ~蟲 *n.* bedbug
~**ming²** ~名 *n.* bad reputation
~**shui³** ~水 *n.* carbonic acid

CH'U¹ 出 *v.* go out, produce, pay
~**chung⁴** ~衆 *a.* noteworthy
~**ch'an³** ~產 *v.* produce, bear; *n.* product
~**fa¹** ~發 *v.* start, begin a journey
~**han⁴** ~汗 *v.* perspire, sweat
~**hsi⁴** ~席 *v.* attend
~**hsien⁴** ~現 *v.* appear; *n.* appearance
~**hsün²** ~巡 *v.* go in a circuit; *n.* circuit
~**k'ou³** ~口 *n.* exit
~**ming²** ~名 *a.* celebrated, famous, well-known
~**pan³** ~版 *v.* publish
~**p'in³** ~品 *n.* manufacture, product
~**tsu¹** ~租 *adv.* for rent
~**ya²** ~芽 *v.* put forth buds
~**yu²** ~遊 *v.* travel; *n.* excursion, pleasure trip

CH'U¹ 初 *a.* original, beginning
~**chi²** ~級 *a.* primary, elementary
~**chi² chiao⁴ lien⁴ chi¹** ~級教練機 *n.* primary trainer
~**hsüeh² che³** ~學者 *n.* beginner
~**liao²** ~療 *n.* first aid
~**pan³** ~版 *n.* first edition
~**pu⁴ te¹** ~步的 *a.* elementary
~**su⁴** ~速 *n.* muzzle velocity
~**teng³ chiao⁴ yü⁴** ~等教育 *n.* elementary education
~**teng³ hsüeh² hsiao⁴** ~等學校 *n.* elementary school
~**tz'u⁴** ~次 *n.* first time

CH'U² 除 *v.* exclude, divide, remove

~**ch'ü⁴** ~去 *v.* remove
~**fa³** ~法 *n.* division (mathematics)
~**fei¹** ~非 *conj.* unless
~**hsi¹** ~夕 *n.* New Year's Eve
~**ken¹** ~根 *v.* eradicate
~**ming²** ~名 *v.* dismiss; *n.* dismissal
~**tz'u³ i³ wai⁴** ~此以外 *adv.* besides
CH'U² 鋤 *n. & v.* hoe
CH'U³ 處 *v.* stay, rest, dwell, arrange, punish.
~**⁴** *n.* place, matter, condition
~**³ fa²** ~罰 *v.* punish
~**li³** ~理 *v.* manage
~**nü³** ~女 *n.* virgin, maiden
~**nü³ mo⁴** ~女膜 *n.* hymen
~**⁴ chang³** ~長 *n.* director
~**ch'u⁴** ~處 *adv.* everywhere
CH'U³ 楚 *a.* woody; *n.* pain
CH'U⁴ 畜 *n.* animal; *v.* rear, raise
~**mu⁴** ~牧 *n.* pasturage
~**sheng¹** ~牲 *n.* brute
~**yang³** ~養 *v.* rear, raise, feed
CH'UAN¹ 川 *n.* stream
~**tzu¹** ~資 *n.* traveling expenses
CH'UAN¹ 穿 *v.* penetrate, put on, pass
~**chen¹** ~針 *v.* thread a needle
~**chia³** ~甲 *n.* armor-piercing
~**hsieh²** ~鞋 *v.* put on shoes
~**i¹** ~衣 *v.* wear, put on
CH'UAN² 船 *n.* ship, boat
~**chu³** ~主 *n.* ship captain
~**fu¹** ~夫 *n.* boatman
~**ku³** ~骨 *n.* keel
~**ts'ang¹** ~艙 *n.* hold of a ship
~**wei²** ~桅 *n.* mast
~**wei³** ~尾 *n.* stern
CH'UAN² 傳 *v.* transmit, summon, pass. **CHUAN⁴**
  n. biography
~**chiao⁴** ~教 *v.* preach
~**chiao⁴ shih⁴** ~教士 *n.* priest
~**jan³** ~染 *v.* infect; *n.* infection
~**jan³ ping⁴** ~染病 *n.* infectious diseases

~**pu⁴** ~佈 *v.* spread
~**p'iao⁴** ~票 *n.* summons
~**ta²** ~達 *n.* transmission
~**tan¹** ~單 *n.* leaflet, handbill
~**ti⁴** ~遞 *v.* transmit; *n.* transmission
chuan⁴ chi⁴ ~記 *n.* biography
CH'UANG¹ 窗 *n.* window
~**hu⁴** ~戶 *n.* window
~**lien²** ~簾 *n.* window curtain
CH'UANG¹ 創 *v.* cut. ~⁴ *v.* create, begin
~**¹ shang¹ chi⁴** ~傷劑 *n.* vulnerary medicine
~**⁴ chih⁴ ch'üan²** ~制權 *n.* initiative
~**li⁴** ~立 *v.* establish
~**pan⁴ jen²** ~辦人 *n.* founder
~**shih³** ~始 *v.* begin, start
~**tsao⁴** ~造 *v.* create; *n.* creation
~**yeh⁴** ~業 *n.* set up a foundation
CH'UANG² 牀 *n.* bed
~**chia⁴** ~架 *n.* bedstead
~**ju⁴** ~褥 *n.* mattress
~**pien¹** ~邊 *n.* bedside
~**p'u⁴** ~鋪 *n.* bed, bedding
~**tan¹** ~單 *n.* bedspread
CH'UI¹ 吹 *v.* blow
~**hsü¹** ~噓 *v.* recommend; *n.* recommendation
~**k'ou³ shao⁴** ~口哨 *v.* whistle
~**niu²** ~牛 *v.* boast
CH'UI² 錘 *n.* counterweight
CH'UN¹ 春 *n.* spring
~**chi⁴** ~季 *n.* spring
~**chia⁴** ~假 n. spring vacation
~**ch'ing²** ~情 *n.* passion (sexual love)
~**ch'ing² fa¹ tung⁴ ch'i¹** ~情發動期 *n.* puberty
CH'UN² 純 *a.* pure, simple
~**cheng⁴** ~正 *a.* righteous, upright
~**chieh²** ~潔 *n.* purity, cleanness
~**hsiao⁴** ~孝 *a.* filial
~**jan²** ~然 *adv.* purely
~**li⁴** ~利 *n.* net profit
~**liang²** ~良 *a.* good
~**se⁴** ~色 *n.* pure color

52

~ts'ui⁴ ~粹 *a.* pure

CH'UNG¹ 充 *v.* fill

~chün¹ ~軍 *v.* banish

~fen⁴ te¹ ~分的 *a.* sufficient

~kung¹ ~公 *v.* confiscate ; *n.* confiscation

~man³ ~滿 *v.* fill

~shih² ~實 *n.* fulfillment

~yü⁴ ~裕 *a.* abundant

CH'UNG¹ 衝 *v.* push forward

~ch'u¹ ~出 *v.* break from encirclement

~feng¹ ~鋒 *v.* assault

~ju⁴ ~入 *v.* break in a defense

~kuo⁴ ~過 *v.* overrun a position

~p'o⁴ ~破 *v.* break in

~t'u¹ ~突 *v.* conflict

CH'UNG² 蟲 *n.* insect

CH'Ü¹ 曲 *a.* crooked, bent, twisted, curved. ~³ *n.* song, aria, air

~che² ~折 *adv.* zigzag; *a.* complicated

~chieh³ ~解 *n.* misunderstanding, distortion

~hsien⁴ ~綫 *n.* curve

~hsien⁴ mei¹ ~綫美 *n.* curve of beauty

CH'Ü¹ 區 *n.* place, district, zone

~ch'ih⁴ wei⁴ ta⁴ tui⁴ ~赤衛大隊 *n.* district Communist guards**

~ch'ü¹ ~區 *a.* small, petty, trifling

~fen¹ ~分 *n.* partition

~pieh² ~別 *v.* distinguish

~yü⁴ ~域 *n.* region

CH'Ü³ 取 *v.* take

~hsiao¹ ~消 *v.* nullify

~nuan³ ~暖 *v.* make warm

CH'Ü³ 娶 *v.* marry a wife

~ch'i¹ ~妻 *v.* marry a wife

CH'Ü⁴ 去 *v.* go

~nien² ~年 *n.* last year

CH'Ü⁴ 趣 *a.* pleasant; *v.* hasten to

~hua⁴ ~話 *n.* joke

~shih⁴ ~事 *n.* interesting story

~wei⁴ ~味 *n.* interest, taste

CH'ÜAN¹ 圈 *n.* circle, ring, snare, dot

53

~t'ao⁴ 套 *n.* snare (trap)

CH'ÜAN² 全 *a.* whole, complete, entire, perfect

~ch'üan² ~權 *n.* plenipotentiary

~kuo²　te¹ ~國的 *a.* national

~mien⁴　te¹ ~面的 *a.* overall (everything)

~neng² ~能 *a.* almighty

~t'i³ ~體 *pron.* all

~wu² ~無 *pron.* none

CH'ÜAN² 泉 *n.* fountain, spring, source

~shui³ ~水 *n.* spring water

~yüan² ~源 *n.* fountain

CH'ÜAN² 權 *n.* power, authority

~heng² ~衡 *v.* weigh (consider)

~hsien⁴ ~限 *n.* authority

~li⁴ ~利 *n.* right (privilege)

~li⁴ ~力 *n.* power (authority)

~ping³ ~柄 *n.* power

~shih⁴ ~勢 *n.* authority, influence

~wei¹ ~威 *n.* expert authority

CH'ÜAN⁴ 勸 *v.* advise, exhort, admonish

~chieh³ ~解 *v.* compromise

~chieh⁴ ~戒 *v.* advise

~mien³ ~勉 *v.* admonish

~tao³ ~導 *v.* exhort

~wei⁴ ~慰 *v.* condole

CH'ÜEH¹ 缺 *n.* defect, imperfection, lack, shortage; *a.* defective; *prep.* less

~fa² ~乏 *n.* lack, shortage

~han⁴ ~憾 *v.* disappoint

~huo⁴ ~貨 *n.* out of stock

~hsi² ~席 *a.* absent

~hsien⁴ ~陷 *n.* deficiency

~k'ou³ ~口 *n.* breach, gap

~tien³ ~點 *n.* weak point, defect

CH'ÜEH⁴ 却 *v.* withdraw, reject, decline; *adv.* still, yet

CH'ÜEH⁴ 確 *adv.* really, truly, accurate

~cheng⁴ ~證 *n.* evidence

~chih¹ ~知 *v.* be sure

~shih² ~實 *a.* real, actual, true; *adv.* really, actually, truly

~**ting⁴** ～定 *a.* certain

CH'ÜN² 群 *n.* flock, herd, crowd, group

~**chung⁴** ～衆 *n.* masses

~**chung⁴ lu⁴ hsien⁴** ～衆路線 *n.* mass line**

E

E² 俄 *a.* momentary; *adv.* suddenly, momentarily.

~**⁴** *n.* Russia

E⁴ 餓 *a.* hungry; *n.* hunger

~**ssu³** ～死 *v.* starve; *n.* starvation

E⁴ 惡 *a.* bad, evil

~**hsi²** ～習 *n.* bad habits

~**i⁴** ～意 *n.* malignity

~**kan³** ～感 *n.* bad feeling

~**kuei³** ～鬼 *n.* devil

~**tu²** ～毒 *a.* vicious

EN¹ 恩 *n.* favor, mercy, kindness

~**ai⁴** ～愛 *n.* affection

~**ch'ing²** ～情 *n.* kindness

~**feng⁴** ～俸 *n.* pension

~**hui⁴** ～惠 *n.* favor, beneficence

~**jen²** ～人 *n.* benefactor

ERH² 兒 *n.* son. ～¹ -son [a suffix]

~**hsi⁴** ～戲 *n.* puerility

~**nü³** ～女 *n.* children (your own)

~**t'ung²** ～童 *n.* children (other's)

~**t'ung² chieh²** ～童節 *n.* Children's Day

~**tzu³** ～子 *n.* son

ERH² 而 *conj.* but, also, and, yet, nevertheless, however

~**chin¹** ～今 *adv.* now

~**ch'ieh³** ～且 *adv.* moreover, also

ERH³ 耳 *n.* ear

~**lung²** ～聾 *a.* deaf

~**wen²** ～聞 *v.* hear

~**yü³** ～語 *v.* whisper

ERH⁴ 二 *n. & a.* two

~**yüeh⁴** ～月 *n.* February

F

FA¹ 發 *v.* start, issue, dispatch (documents); *n.* round of ammunition

~**chan³** ~展 *v.* develop

~**chi³** ~給 *v.* issue supplies

~**chiao⁴** ~酵 *v.* ferment; *n.* fermentation

~**ch'i³** ~起 *v.* promote (start)

~**ch'i³ jen²** ~起人 *n.* founder

~**hun¹** 昏 *v.* faint

~**hsiang³** ~餉 *v.* pay

~**hsien⁴** ~見 *v.* discover

~**hsin⁴ che³** ~信者 *n.* sender of a message

~**hsing²** ~行 *v.* publish

~**jo⁴** ~熱 *v.* have fever

~**ming²** ~明 *v.* invent

~**ming² chia¹** ~明家 *n.* inventor

~**nu⁴** ~怒 *v.* become angry

~**piao³** ~表 *v.* announce

~**p'iao⁴** ~票 *n.* invoice

~**she⁴** ~射 *v.* fire (shoot)

~**sheng¹** ~生 *v.* happen

~**shih⁴** ~誓 *v.* swear

~**tien⁴ chi¹** ~電機 *n.* generator, dynamo

~**tung⁴ chi¹** ~動機 *n.* engine, motor

~**ts'ai²** ~財 become rich

~**yen²** ~言 *v.* speak

~**yen²** ~炎 *n.* inflammation

~**yin¹ hsüeh²** ~音學 *n.* phonetics

FA² 罰 *n.* punishment, penalty, fine; *v.* punish

~**hsin¹** ~薪 *n.* forfeiture of pay

~**k'uan³** ~款 *n.* & *v.* fine

~**tse²** ~則 *n.* penal regulations

FA³ 法 *n.* law, process, method; *a.* legal

~**chih⁴ wei³ yüan² hui⁴** ~制委員會 *n.* Commission of Legislative Affairs**

~**hsüeh² yüan⁴** ~學院 *n.* college of law

~**kuan¹** ~官 *n.* judge

~**ling⁴** ~令 *n.* law

56

~**lü⁴** ~律 *n.* law

~**t'ing²** ~庭 *n.* court, tribunal (law)

~**yüan⁴** ~院 *n.* law court

FA³ 髮 *n.* hair

~**shua¹** ~刷 *n.* hair-brush

~**yu²** ~油 *n.* pomade, hair tonic

FAN¹ 翻 *v.* turn over, upset

~**i⁴** ~譯 *v.* translate, interpret

~**i⁴ yüan²** ~譯員 *n.* translator, interpreter

~**ken¹ tou³** ~筋斗 *n.* somersault

~**shen¹** ~身 *v.* turn over to**

~**yin⁴** ~印 *v.* reprint

FAN² 凡 *a.* all, every; *prep.* whatever

~**jen²** ~人 *n.* mankind, laity

~**li⁴** ~例 *n.* example

~**su²** ~俗 *a.* vulgar

~**shih⁴** ~事 *pron.* everything

FAN² 煩 *v.* trouble

~**jao³** ~擾 *v.* annoy

~**men⁴** ~悶 *a.* sad

~**nan²** ~難 *a.* difficult

~**nao³** ~惱 *n.* worry

FAN³ 反 *v.* reverse, revolt, rebel

~**fu⁴** ~復 *n.* repetition

~**hui³** ~悔 *v.* repent

~**hsiang³** ~響 *n.* response, reaction

~**hsing² hui⁴** ~行賄 *n.* anti-bribery**

~**hsing³** ~省 *n.* introspection

~**kuan¹ liao² chu³ i⁴** ~官僚主義 *n.* anti-bureaucracy**

~**kung⁴ i⁴ shih⁴** ~共義士 *n.* anti-Communist patriots

~**kung⁴ k'ang⁴ e⁴** ~共抗俄 *v.* fight against the Communists and Russians

~**k'ang⁴** ~抗 *v.* oppose, resist

~**lang⁴ fei⁴** ~浪費 *n.* anti-waste**

~**pi³ li⁴** ~比例 *n.* inverse proportion

~**p'an⁴** ~叛 *v.* rebel

~**she⁴** ~射 *v.* reflect

~**tao⁴ ch'ieh⁴ kuo² chia¹ ching¹ chi⁴ ch'ing² pao⁴** ~盜竊國家經濟情報 *n.* anti-stealing of eco-

57

nomic information from government sources for private speculation**

~tao⁴ ch'ieh⁴ kuo² chia¹ tzu¹ ts'ai² 盜竊國家資財 *n.* anti-theft of state property**

~tung⁴ ~動 *n.* reaction (political)

~t'an¹ wu¹ ~貪污 *n.* anti-corruption**

~t'ou¹ kung¹ chien³ liao⁴ ~偷工減料 *n.* anti-cheating on government contracts**

~t'ou¹ shui⁴ lou⁴ shui⁴ ~偷稅漏稅 *n.* anti-tax evasion**

~ying⁴ ~應 *n.* reaction (*chem.*)

FAN⁴ 飯 *n.* meal

~tien⁴ ~店 *n.* restaurant

FAN⁴ 犯 *n.* prisoner, criminal; *v.* offend, violate

~fa³ ~法 *v.* offend against the law

~jen² ~人 *n.* prisoner, criminal

~tsui⁴ ~罪 *n.* crime

~tsui⁴ hsüeh² ~罪學 *n.* criminology

FAN⁴ 範 *n.* pattern

~ch'ou² ~疇 *n.* category

~pen³ ~本 *n.* pattern, model

~wei² ~圍 *n.* limit, scope

FANG¹ 方 *n.* direction, square; *a.* square quadrangular

~chang⁴ ~丈 *n.* abbot

~chen¹ ~針 *n.* aim, objective, direction

~ch'eng² shih⁴ ~程式 *n.* equation

~fa³ ~法 *n.* method, means, way

~hsiang⁴ ~向 *n.* direction

~pien⁴ ~便 *n.* convenience; *a.* convenient

~yen² ~言 *n.* dialect

FANG² 房 *n.* house, room, chamber

~chüan¹ ~捐 *n.* house rent

~ch'an³ ~産 *n.* estate, landed property

~k'o⁴ ~客 *n.* tenant

~shih⁴ ~事 *n.* venery (sexual)

~tung¹ ~東 *n.* landlord, landlady

~tsu¹ ~租 *n.* rent

~wu¹ ~屋 *n.* house

FANG² 防 *n.* defense, protection; *v.* defend, guard against

58

~k‘ung¹ ~空 *n.* ground air defense

~k‘ung¹ hsüeh² hsiao⁴ ~空學校 *n.* Anti-Air Raid School*

~k‘ung¹ tung² ~空洞 *n.* air-raid shelter

~k‘ung¹ yen³ hsi² ~空演習 *n.* air-raid drill

~shou³ ~守 *v.* defend

~yü hsien⁴ ~禦線 *n.* line of defense

FANG² 妨 *v.* hinder, obstruct

~hai⁴ ~害 *v.* harass

FANG³ 訪 *v.* visit, search out, inquire into

~k‘o⁴ ~客 *n.* visitor

~wen⁴ ~問 *v.* interview

FANG³ 紡 *v.* spin (material)

~chih¹ ~織 *v.* spin and weave

~ch‘e¹ ~車 *n.* reel

~ch‘ui² ~錘 *n.* spindle

~sha¹ ~紗 *n.* cotton spinning

~sha¹ ch‘ang³ ~紗廠 *n.* spinning mill

FANG⁴ 放 *v.* set free, exile, place, put

~chang⁴ ~賑 *v.* give credit

~chia⁴ ~假 *n.* holiday, vacation

~chu² ~逐 *v.* exile

~ch‘i⁴ ~棄 *v.* abandon

~ch‘i⁴ ~氣 *n.* deflation (of object)

~huo³ tsui⁴ ~火罪 *n.* arson

~hsiang³ ~餉 *v.* hand out the pay

~hsüeh² ~學 *v.* let out school

~jen⁴ ~任 *n.* laissez faire

~sung¹ ~鬆 *v.* untie, loosen

~ssu⁴ ~肆 *a.* impudent, impolite

~ta⁴ ~大 *v.* enlarge

~ta⁴ ching⁴ ~大鏡 *n.* magnifying lens

~tang⁴ ~蕩 *a.* profligate, wanton

FEI¹ 飛 *v.* fly; *n.* flight

~chi¹ ~機 *n.* airplane, aircraft

~chi¹ chih⁴ tsao⁴ ch‘ang³ ~機製造廠 *n.* airplane factory

~chi¹ ch‘ang³ ~機場 *n.* airdrome, airport

~ch‘in² ~禽 *n.* bird

~ch‘uan² ~船 *n.* airship

~hsing² ~行 *n.* flight (flying)

59

~**hsing² chia¹** ~行家 *n.* pilot, aviator

~**hsing² shu⁴** ~行術 *n.* aviation

~**hsing² yüan²** ~行員 *n.* pilot, aviator

~**pen¹** ~奔 *v.* gallop

~**tan²** ~彈 *n.* wild shot

~**yen⁴** ~雁 *n.* wild-goose

FEI¹ 非 *adv.* no, not, wrong; *a.* no, wrong

~**chan⁴ chu³ i⁴ che³** ~戰主義者 *n.* conscientious objector

~**cheng⁴ shih⁴** ~正式 *a.* informal

~**chin¹ shu³** ~金屬 *n.* non-metal

~**ch'ang²** ~常 *adv.* exceedingly; *a.* extraordinary, unusual

~**fa³** ~法 *a.* illegal

~**li³** ~禮 *a.* indecent

~**wu³ chuang¹ ch'ü¹** ~武裝區 *n.* demilitarized zone

FEI² 肥 *a.* fat, stout

~**chuang⁴** ~壯 *a.* fat and strong

~**jou⁴** ~肉 *n.* fat meat

~**jun⁴** ~潤 *a.* glossy

~**liao⁴** ~料 *n.* fertilizer, manure

~**ni⁴** ~膩 *a.* greasy

~**p'ang⁴** ~胖 *a.* fat

~**ta⁴** ~大 *a.* stout

~**tsao⁴** ~皂 *n.* soap

~**wo⁴** ~沃 *a.* fertile

FEI³ 匪 *n.* bandit, highwayman, robber

~**tang³** ~黨 *n.* bandit clique

~**t'u²** ~徒 *n.* bandit

FEI⁴ 費 *v.* use, spend, waste; *n.* fee, fare

~**shih²** ~時 *v.* waste time

~**yung⁴** ~用 *n.* expenditure, expense

FEI⁴ 肺 *n.* lung

~**chieh² ho² ping⁴** ~結核病 *n.* pulmonary tuberculosis

~**yen²** ~炎 *n.* pneumonia

FEI⁴ 廢 *a.* useless, wasteful, ruined; *v.* abandon

~**chih³** ~紙 *n.* waste paper

~**ch'i⁴** ~棄 *v.* abandon

~**ch'u²** ~除 *v.* abolish; *n.* abolition

~**hua⁴** ～話 *n.* verbiage
~**jen²** ～人 *n.* cripple, disabled person
~**wu⁴** ～物 *n.* trash
FEN¹ 分 *n.* cent, minute, division; *v.* divide, separate
  ~**chieh³** ～解 *v.* analyze; *n.* analysis
  ~**hua⁴** ～化 *n.* differentiation
  ~**hsi¹** ～析 *v.* analyze; *n.* analysis
  ~**ko¹** ～割 *n.* partition
  ~**kung¹** ～工 *n.* division of labor
  ~**lei⁴** ～類 *n. & v.* classify; *n.* classification
  ~**li²** ～離 *n. & v.* separate, depart
  ~**pi⁴** ～泌 *v.* secrete; *n.* secretion
  ~**pieh²** ～別 *v.* separate, distinguish
  ~**pu⁴** ～佈 *v.* spread, scatter, distribute
  ~**p'ai⁴** ～派 *v.* distribute
  ~**p'ei⁴** ～配 *n.* distribution
  ~**san⁴** ～散 *n. & v.* disperse, scatter
  ~**shu⁴** ～數 *n.* grade, rating, fraction
  ~**tien⁴** ～店 *n.* branch store
  ~**tzu³** ～子 *n.* molecule, member
  ~**wan³** ～娩 *n.* confinement
FEN¹ 紛 *a.* confused; *n.* disorder
  ~**ch'i²** ～岐 *a.* different, discrepant
  ~**luan⁴** ～亂 *n.* disorder
FEN³ 粉 *n.* flour, powder
  ~**hung²** ～紅 *n.* pink
  ~**pi³** ～筆 *n.* chalk
  ~**sui⁴** ～碎 *n.* smash
  ~**shih⁴** ～飾 *v.* paint, adorn
  ~**ssu¹** ～糸 *n.* vermicelli
FEN⁴ 奮 *v.* arouse, strike; *a.* zealous
  ~**mien³** ～勉 *v.* encourage
  ~**tou⁴** ～鬥 *n. & v.* struggle
  ~**yung³** ～勇 *a.* courageous, brave
FEN⁴ 糞 *n.* stool, excrement, dung
FENG¹ 封 *v.* seal, close, blockade
  ~**chien⁴ chih⁴ tu⁴** ～建制度 *n.* feudal system
  ~**chien⁴ she⁴ hui⁴** ～建社會 *n.* feudal society
  ~**chien⁴ shih⁴ li⁴** ～建勢力 *n.* feudal influence
  ~**chien⁴ ssu¹ hsiang³** ～建思想 *n.* feudalism

~**chien⁴ te¹** ~建的 *a.* feudal

~**pi⁴** ~閉 *v.* close

~**so³** ~鎖 *n.* & *v.* blockade

~**t'iao²** ~條 *n.* label

FENG¹ 風 *n.* wind, breeze

~**cheng¹** ~箏 *n.* kite

~**ching³** ~景 *n.* scenery, landscape

~**ch'in²** ~琴 *n.* musical organ

~**ch'ing²** ~情 *n.* climate

~**hsiang¹** ~箱 *n.* bellows

~**su²** ~俗 *n.* custom

~**shan⁴** ~扇 *n.* electric fan

~**shih¹ ping⁴** ~溼病 *n.* rheumatism

~**ya³** ~雅 *a.* refined

~**yü³ piao³** ~雨表 *n.* barometer

FENG¹ 豐 *a.* copious, plentiful, abundant

~**fu⁴** ~富 *a.* copious, rich

~**man³** ~滿 *a.* plentiful, rich

~**shou¹** ~收 *n.* ample harvest

FENG² 縫 *v.* sew, mend.　~⁴ *n.* crack, split

~² **chen¹** ~針 *n.* sewing needle

~**i¹** ~衣 *v.* stitch clothes

~**jen⁴** ~紉 *n.* needlework, sewing

~**jen⁴ chi¹** ~紉機 *n.* sewing machine

~**jen⁴ hsien⁴** ~紉線 *n.* sewing thread

FOU³ 否 *a.* negative; *adv.* no, not

~**chüeh²** ~決 *v.* vote down

~**jen⁴** ~認 *v.* deny; *n.* denial

~**tse²** ~則 *adv.* otherwise

FU¹ 夫 *n.* husband

~**fu⁴** ~婦 *n.* couple, husband and wife

~**jen²** ~人 *n.* madam, lady, wife

FU² 服 *n.* clothes, dress; *v.* dress, obey, be submissive

~**shih⁴** ~飾 *n.* adornment

~**shih⁴** ~式 *n.* costume

~**shih⁴** ~侍 *v.* serve

~**tu²** ~毒 *v.* take poison purposely

~**ts'ung²** ~從 *v.* obey; *n.* obedience; *a.* obedient

~**wu⁴** ~務 *v.* serve; *n.* service

~**yao⁴** ~藥 *v.* take medicine

FU² 伏 *v.* prostrate, surrender, ambush
~**luan³** ~卵 *v.* hatch
~**ping¹** ~兵 *n.* ambush
~**wo⁴** ~臥 *v.* lie down flat
FU² ~扶 *v.* aid, help
~**chu⁴** ~助 *v.* aid, assist
~**ch'ih²** ~持 *v.* support
~**yang³** ~養 *v.* support, rear (family)
FU² 福 *n.* good fortune, felicity, blessing
~**ch'i⁴** ~氣 *n.* good fortune
FU³ 府 *n.* prefecture, residence, mansion
FU³ 腐 *a.* rotten, spoiled, putrid; *n.* decay
~**hua⁴** ~化 *a.* putrid (food)
~**hua⁴ fen⁴ tzu³** ~化份子 *a.* corrupt elements
~**lan⁴** ~爛 *a.* rotten, corrupt, decayed
~**pai²** ~敗 *a.* corrupt
~**shih²** ~蝕 *n.* corrosion
FU³ 斧 *n.* hatchet, axe
~**yüeh⁴** ~鉞 *n.* halberd
FU⁴ 父 *n.* father, daddy, papa, pop
~**mu³** ~母 *n.* parent
FU⁴ 婦 *n.* woman, lady
~**ju²** ~孺 *n.* women and children
~**nü³** ~女 *n.* woman, lady
~**tao⁴** ~道 *n.* womanhood (character)
~**te²** ~德 *n.* woman's virtue
FU⁴ 富 *a.* rich, abundant, wealthy
~**ch'iang²** ~強 *a.* rich and strong
~**li⁴** ~麗 *a.* splendid
~**weng¹** ~翁 *n.* millionaire
FU⁴ 負 *n.* defeat, lose; *v.* fail, lose; *a.* negative
~**chai⁴** ~債 *v.* owe money
~**chung⁴** ~重 *n.* heavy burden
~**hsin¹** ~心 *a.* ungrateful
~**tan¹** ~擔 *n.* burden
~**yüeh¹** ~約 *v.* break one's promise
FU⁴ 付 *v.* pay; *n.* payment
~**ch'i⁴** ~訖 *a.* paid
~**ch'ing¹** ~清 *v.* pay in full
~**ch'u¹** ~出 *v.* pay
~**huan²** ~還 *v.* pay back

~hsien⁴ ~現 *v.* pay in cash

~k'an¹ ~刊 *v.* be published

FU⁴ 附 *v.* attach, subjoin, enclose

~chi⁴ ~記 *n.* remarks

~chia¹ shui⁴ ~加税 *n.* surtax

~chin⁴ ~近 *a.* near, adjacent

~lu⁴ ~錄 *n.* appendix

~shu³ ~屬 *a.* dependent, accessory

~shu³ p'in³ ~屬品 *n.* accessory

~yung¹ kuo² ~庸國 *n.* satellite nation

FU⁴ 副 *v.* aid ; *n.* assistant, second

~chien¹ ch'a² chang³ ~檢察長 *n.* Deputy Procurator-General

~chu³ hsi² ~主席 *n.* vice-chairman

~chu³ jen⁴ ~主任 *n.* vice-chairman

~chu³ jen⁴ wei³ yüan² ~主任委員 *n.* vice-chairman

~fei¹ hsing² yüan² ~飛行員 *n.* co-pilot

~hang² chang³ ~行長 *n.* assistant managing director

~kuan¹ ~官 *n.* adjutant, personal aide

~ling³ shih⁴ ~領事 *n.* vice-consul

~mi⁴ shu¹ chang³ ~祕書長 *n.* assistant secretary-general

~pen³ ~本 *n.* duplicate copy

~pu⁴ chang³ ~部長 *n.* vice-minister

~shu³ chang³ ~署長 *n.* vice-pirector

~tsung³ li³ ~總理 *n.* vice-premier

~tsung³ t'ung³ ~總統 *n.* vice-president

~yüan⁴ chang³ ~院長 *n.* vice-president

FU⁴ 復 *v.* reply, restore, return ; *adv.* again

~chih² ~職 *v.* rehabilitate (former rank)

~ch'ou² ~仇 *n.* revenge

~huo² chieh² ~活節 *n.* Easter

~hsing¹ ~興 *v.* revive

~sung⁴ ~誦 *v.* repeat a message

~yüan² ~元 *n.* recovery (health)

~yüan² ~原 *v.* recover from illness

~yüan² ~員 *n.* demobilization

FU⁴ 複 *a.* double

~hsüan³ ~選 *n.* indirect vote

64

~li⁴ ～利 *n.* compound interest
~shu⁴ ～數 *n.* plural number
~tsa² ～雜 *a.* complicated, complex

H

HA¹ 哈 [an exclamation]
HAI² 孩 *n.* child
~t'ung² ～童 *n.* child
HAI³ 還 *see* HUAN²
HAI³ 海 *n.* sea
~an⁴ ～岸 *n.* coast
~an⁴ fang² yü⁴ ～岸防禦 *n.* coast defense
~an⁴ hsien⁴ ～岸線 *n.* coastline
~chün¹ ～軍 *n.* Navy
~chün¹ chi¹ hsieh⁴ hsüeh² hsiao⁴ ～軍機械學
校 *n.* Navy Mechanics School*
~chün¹ chi¹ ti⁴～ ～軍基地 *n.* naval base
~chün¹ chih³ hui¹ ts'an¹ mou² hsüeh² hsiao⁴
～軍指揮參謀學校 *n.* Navy Command and Staff
College*
~chün¹ chün¹ kuan¹ hsüeh² hsiao⁴ ～軍軍官
學校 *n.* Navy Academy*
~chün¹ lu⁴ chan⁴ tui⁴ ～軍陸戰隊 *n.* marines
~chün¹ pu⁴ ～軍部 *n.* Department of the Navy
(*U.S.*)
~chün¹ shih⁴ ping¹ hsüeh² hsiao⁴ ～軍士兵學
校 *n.* Navy Petty Officers and Seamen School*
~chün¹ tsao⁴ ch'uan² ch'ang³ ～軍造船廠 *n.*
navy yard
~chün¹ tsung³ ssu¹ ling⁴ pu⁴ ～軍總司令部 *n.*
Navy Headquarters*
~chün¹ wu³ kuan¹ ～軍武官 *n.* naval attache
~fang² ～防 *n.* coast guard
~hsia² ～峽 *n.* strait
~kang³ ～港 *n.* seaport, harbor
~kuan¹ ～關 *n.* custom house
~k'ou³ ～口 *n.* seaport, port, harbor
~li³ ～里 *n.* nautical mile
~pa² ～拔 *n.* above sea level (height)

~**pin¹** ～濱 *n.* seashore

~**p'ing² mien⁴** ～平面 *n.* sea level

~**shang⁴ pao³ hsien¹** ～上保險 *n.* marine insurance

~**shui³ yü⁴** ～水浴 *n.* swimming

~**tao³** ～島 *n.* island

~**tao⁴** ～盜 *n.* pirate

~**ti³ tien⁴ hsien⁴** ～底電線 n. cablegram

~**t'an¹** ～灘 *n.* beach

~**wai⁴ yüan³ cheng¹** ～外遠征 *n.* overseas expedition

~**wan¹** ～灣 *n.* bay

~**yang²** ～洋 *n.* ocean

~**yüan²** ～員 *n.* seaman

~**yün⁴** ～運 *n.* sea transportation

HAI⁴ 害 *v.* injure, hurt, harm; *n.* disadvantage

~**hsiu¹** ～羞 *a.* bashful, shy

~**ping³** ～病 *v.* suffer from sickness

~**p'a⁴** ～怕 *a.* afraid

HAN² 寒 *a.* cold, chilly, poor

~**leng³** ～冷 *a.* cold

~**shu³ piao³** ～暑表 *n.* thermometer

~**tai⁴** ～帶 *n.* Frigid Zone

HAN² 含 *v.* contain, hold

~**hu²** ～糊 *a.* vague, ambiguous

~**hsiu¹** ～羞 *a.* bashful, shy

~**yüan¹** ～冤 *v.* have a grievance

HAN³ 喊 *v.* cry, call

HAN⁴ 汗 *n.* perspiration, sweat

~**hsien⁴** ～腺 *n.* sweat gland

~**shan¹** ～衫 *n.* undershirt

HAN⁴ 旱 *n.* drought; *a.* rainless, dry

~**tsai¹** ～災 *n.* drought

HAN⁴ 漢 *n.* ancient Chinese dynasty, Chinese

~**jen²** ～人 n. Chinese people

~**tsu²** ～族 *n.* Chinese race

~**wen²** ～文 *n.* Chinese writing

HANG² 航 *v.* navigate, sail

~**ch'eng²** ～程 *n.* course (way)

~**hai³** ～海 *n.* navigation

~**hai³ chia¹** ～海家 *n.* navigator

~**hsien⁴** ~線 *n.* sea route, air line route

~**k'ung¹** ~空 *n.* aviation, air navigation

~**k'ung¹ chan⁴** ~空站 *n.* airdrome

~**k'ung¹ chi¹** ~空機 *n.* aircraft

~**k'ung¹ hsüeh²** ~空學 *n.* aeronautics

~**k'ung¹ mu³ chien⁴** ~空母艦 *n.* aircraft carrier

~**k'ung¹ tui⁴** ~空隊 *n.* air fleet

~**yün⁴** ~運 *n.* air transportation

HANG² 行 *see* **HSING²**

HAO³ 好 *a.* good, fine, well, right; *adv.* well. ~⁴ *v.* be fond of

~³ **ch'ih¹** ~吃 *a.* palatable. ~⁴ *a.* gluttonous

~**hsiao⁴** ~笑 *a.* funny

~**k'an⁴** ~看 *a.* beautiful, pretty, handsome

~**yün⁴** ~運 *n.* good luck

~⁴ **se⁴** ~色 *v.* be fond of beauty

HAO⁴ 號 *n.* sign, mark, title, bugle, signal, order, name, firm; *v.* cry, call

~**chao⁴** ~召 *v.* summon

~**k'u¹** ~哭 *v.* cry

~**ma³** ~碼 *n.* number

~**ping¹** ~兵 *n.* bugler

~**wai⁴** ~外 *n.* newspaper extra

HEI¹ 黑 *n. & a.* black, dark

~**an⁴** ~暗 *a.* dark; *n.* darkness

~**jen²** ~人 *n.* negro

~**mei²** ~莓 *n.* blackberry

~**ming² tan¹** ~名單 *n.* black list

~**pan³** ~板 *n.* blackboard

~**se⁴** ~色 *n.* black

~**shih⁴** ~市 *n.* black market

HEN³ 很 *adv.* very, quite

~**hao³** ~好 *a.* very good

HEN⁴ 恨 *v.* hate; *n.* hate, hatred

HENG² 橫 *a.* horizontal. ~⁴ *a.* perverse, wicked; *adv.* crosswise

~² **hsing²** ~行 *n.* bad conduct

~⁴ **huo⁴** ~禍 *n.* unexpected calamity

~**pao⁴** ~暴 *a.* perverse

~**ssu³** ~死 *n.* unnatural death

~**ts'ai²** ~財 *n.* windfall (unexpected profit)

67

HO¹ 喝 *v.* drink. ~⁴ *v.* shout

~¹ **chiu³** ~酒 *v.* drink wine

~**ch'a²** ~茶 *v.* drink tea

~⁴ **ts'ai³** ~采 *v.* applaud

HO² 何 *pron.* who, which, what; *adv.* how, why

~**i³** ~以 *adv.* why

~**jen²** ~人 *pron.* who

~**ku⁴** ~故 *adv.* why

~**shih²** ~時 *adv.* when

~**shih⁴** ~事 *pron.* what

~**ti⁴** ~地 *adv.* where

HO² 河 *n.* river

~**an⁴** ~岸 *n.* bank

~**ch'uan¹ chan⁴** ~川戰 *n.* river warfare

~**ch'uang²** ~床 *n.* river bed

~**liu²** ~流 *n.* stream

~**tao⁴** ~道 *n* river course

HO² 合 *v.* shut, close, enclose; *a.* suitable, accordant

~**chin¹** ~金 *n.* alloy

~**fa³** ~法 *a.* legal

~**ko²** ~格 *a.* qualified

~**li³** ~理 *a.* reasonable

~**suan⁴** ~算 *v.* add; *a.* profitable

~**t'ung²** ~同 *n.* contract, agreement

~**tso⁴** ~作 *v.* cooperate; *n.* cooperation

~**tso⁴ hua⁴** ~作化 *n.* co-operativisation**

~**tso⁴ nung² ch'ang³** ~作農場 *n.* Co-operative Farm**

HO² 和 *conj.* and; *a.* friendly

~**ai³** ~藹 *a.* genial

~**chieh³** ~解 *v.* compromise

~**ch'i⁴** ~氣 *a.* kind

~**feng¹** ~風 *n.* breeze

~**hao³** ~好 *v.* reconcile

~**hsieh²** ~諧 *a.* harmonious; *n.* harmony

~**nuan³** ~暖 *a.* warm

~**p'ing²** ~平 *a.* peaceful; *n.* peace

~**p'ing² hui⁴ i⁴** ~平會議 *n.* peace conference

~**p'ing² t'an² p'an⁴** ~平談判 *n.* peace negotiations

~**shang⁴** ~尚 *n.* monk
~**yüeh¹** ~約 *n.* peace treaty
HO⁴ 賀 *v.* congratulate
~**hsi³** ~喜 *v.* congratulate
~**hsin¹ nien²** ~新年 *v.* offer New Year's greetings
HOU¹ 喉 *n.* throat
~**t'ung⁴** ~痛 *n.* sore throat
HOU⁴ 候 *v.* wait
~**ch'e¹ shih⁴** ~車室 *n.* waiting room (station)
~**pu³** ~補 *n.* candidacy
~**pu³ che³** ~補者 *n.* candidate
~**shen³** ~審 *v.* wait trial
HOU⁴ 後 *prep.* after, behind; *a.* future, late; *adv.* afterwards
~**fang¹** ~方 *n.* zone of the interior, rear
~**fang¹ i¹ yüan⁴** ~方醫院 *n.* base hospital
~**fu⁴** ~父 *n.* stepfather
~**hui³** ~悔 *v.* regret
~**jen⁴** ~任 *n.* successor
~**lai²** ~來 *adv.* afterwards
~**mu³** ~母 *n.* stepmother
~**pu⁴** ~部 *n.* back
~**tso⁴ li⁴** ~座力 *n.* force of recoil
~**wei⁴** ~衛 *n.* rear guard
~**yüan²** ~緣 *n.* trailing edge
~**yüan² chün¹** ~援軍 *n.* re-enforcement
HOU⁴ 厚 *n.* thickness, density; *a.* thick
~**ch'ing²** ~情 *a.* friendly
~**tai⁴** ~待 *v.* treat kindly
~**tao⁴** ~道 *a.* generous
~**yen²** ~顏 *a.* shameless
HU¹ 呼 *v.* call, exclaim, cry
~**han³** ~喊 *n. & v.* shout
~**hao⁴** ~號 *v.* yell
~**hsi¹** ~吸 *v.* breathe
HU¹ 忽 *a.* careless; *v.* neglect
~**jan²** ~然 *adv.* suddenly; *a.* sudden
~**lüeh⁴** ~略 *a.* careless, neglectful, negligent
HU² 湖 *n.* lake
HU² 胡 *a.* arbitrary; *adv.* recklessly; *n.* northern barbarians

69

~chiao¹ ~椒 *n.* pepper
~ch'in² ~琴 *n.* Chinese violin
~kua¹ ~瓜 *n.* cucumber
~luan⁴ ~亂 *a.* confused
~shuo¹ ~說 *n.* nonsense
~t'ao² ~桃 *n.* walnut
~t'ung² ~同 *n.* lane
HU² 壺 *n.* kettle, pot
HU³ 虎 *n.* tiger
~lieh⁴ la¹ ~列拉 *n.* cholera
HU⁴ 互 *adv.* mutually, each other
~ai⁴ ~愛 *v.* love each other
~chu⁴ ~助 *n.* mutual assistance
~chu⁴ hsiao³ tsu³ ~助小組 *n.* mutual aid team**
~hsiang¹ ~相 *adv.* mutually, each other
~hsiang¹ ho² tso⁴ ~相合作 *n.* cooperation**
~hsiang¹ i¹ lai⁴ ~相依賴 *n.* interdependence**
~hsiang¹ kuan⁴ t'ung¹ ~相貫通 *n.* interpenetration**
~hsiang¹ lien² lo⁴ ~相聯絡 *n.* interconnection**
~hsiang¹ shen⁴ t'ou⁴ ~相滲透 *n.* interpermeation**
HU⁴ 戶 *n.* door, family
~k'ou³ ~口 *n.* population
~k'ou³ chien³ ch'a² ~口檢查 *n.* census
~wai⁴ yün⁴ tung⁴ ~外運動 *n.* outdoor sports
HU⁴ 護 *v.* protect, guard; *n.* protection
~chao⁴ ~照 *n.* passport
~chiu⁴ ~救 *v.* rescue
~hang² tui⁴ ~航隊 *n.* convoy
~ping¹ ~兵 *n.* private bodyguard
~sung⁴ ~送 *v.* convoy
~wei⁴ ~衞 *v.* defend, protect
HUA¹ 花 *n.* flower
~ch'iu² ~球 *n.* bouquet
~ch'üan¹ ~圈 *n.* garland, wreath
~fang² ~房 *n.* greenhouse, hothouse
~fei⁴ ~費 *v.* spend, expend
~fen³ ~粉 *n.* pollen
~hung² ~紅 *n.* bonus
~jui³ ~蕊 *n.* bud

~**kang¹ shih²** ～岡石 *n.* granite
~**kuan¹** ～冠 *n.* flower petals
~**lan²** ～籃 *n.* flower basket
~**liu³ ping⁴** ～柳病 *n.* venereal disease
~**ming² ts'e⁴** ～名册 *n.* roll (list of names)
~**pan⁴** ～瓣 *n.* petal
~**p'ing²** ～瓶 *n.* vase
~**yang⁴** ～樣 *n.* pattern
~**yüan²** ～園 *n.* garden

HUA² 華 *n.* China, flower, glory; *a.* stately, beautiful
~**ch'iao²** ～僑 *n.* overseas Chinese
~**ch'iao² shih⁴ wu⁴ wei³ yüan² hui⁴** ～僑事務委員會 *n.* Commission of Overseas Chinese Affairs**
~**li⁴** ～麗 *a.* pompous
~**pei³ hsing² cheng⁴ wei³ yüan² hui⁴** ～北行政委員會 *n.* North China Administrative Committee**
~**pei³ jen² min² ko² ming⁴ ta⁴ hsüeh²** ～北人民革命大學 *n.* North China People's Revolutionary University**
~**tan⁴** ～誕 *n.* birthday

HUA² 劃 *v.* divide, mark, cut
~² **fen¹** ～分 *v.* divide
~**p'o⁴** ～破 *v.* scratch
~⁴ **i¹** ～一 *a.* uniform

HUA⁴ 話 *n.* word, speech, spoken language

HUA⁴ 化 *v.* change, alter, melt, convert, dissolve
~**ho² wu⁴** ～合物 *n.* compound (*chem.*)
~**hsüeh²** ～學 *n.* chemistry
~**hsüeh² chan⁴** ～學戰 *n.* chemical warfare
~**shih²** ～石 *n.* fossil
~**yu² ch'i⁴** ～油器 *n.* carburetor

HUA⁴ 畫 *v.* draw, paint; *n.* picture, drawing
~**chia¹** ～家 *n.* painter, artist
~**chia⁴** ～架 *n.* picture easel
~**fang³** ～舫 *n.* excursion barge
~**pu⁴** ～布 *n.* painting canvas

HUAI² 懷 *n.* bosom; *v.* conceal, think of
~**hen⁴** ～恨 *v.* hate

~**i²** ~疑 *v.* doubt, suspect; *a.* skeptical

~**nien⁴** ~念 *v.* think of

~**pao⁴** ~抱 *n.* bosom; *v.* cherish, nestle

~**yün⁴** ~孕 *a.* pregnant; *n.* pregnancy

HUAI⁴ 壞 *a.* vicious, corrupt; *v.* destroy, ruin, spoil

~**ch'u⁴** ~處 *n.* defect

~**ch'uan²** ~船 *n.* wreck

~**jen²** ~人 *n.* bad man

~**yün⁴** ~運 *n.* bad luck

HUAN¹ 歡 *v.* rejoice, like; *n.* joy, delight; *a.* merry, jolly

~**hsi³** ~喜 *n.* joy, delight, happiness

~**ying²** ~迎 *v.* welcome

~**ying² hui⁴** ~迎會 *n.* reception (party)

HUAN² 還 *v.* return, repay, compensate. **HAI²** *adv.* still

HUAN² 環 *n.* ring, loop, coil, eye, eyelet, bracelet; *v.* surround

~**chi¹** ~擊 *v.* return fire

~**ching⁴** ~境 *n.* surroundings

~**jao⁴** ~繞 *v.* surround, circle

~**shih⁴** ~視 *v.* look around

HUAN⁴ 換 *v.* change, exchange, replace

~**ch'i⁴** ~氣 *v.* ventilate

~**ch'ien²** ~錢 *v.* exchange money

~**nao³** ~腦 *n.* brain-changing**

HUANG¹ 慌 *a.* nervous

~**chang¹** ~張 *a.* nervous, excited

~**luan⁴** ~亂 *n.* disorder

~**mang²** ~忙 *a.* hurried

HUANG¹ 荒 *a.* barren, wild; *n.* famine

~**liang²** ~涼 *a.* desert

~**lin²** ~林 *n.* wildwood

~**miu⁴** ~謬 *a.* absurd

~**nien²** ~年 *n.* famine

~**p'i⁴** ~僻 *a.* desolate

~**tan⁴** ~誕 *a.* fabulous

~**wu²** ~蕪 *a.* weedy

~**yin²** ~淫 *a.* dissipated

HUANG² 黃 *n. & a.* yellow

72

~**chin¹** ～金 *n.* gold ; *a.* golden
~**chin¹ shih² tai⁴** ～金時代 *n.* golden age
~**chung⁸** ～種 *n.* yellow race
~**feng¹** ～蜂 *n.* wasp
~**ho²** ～河 *n.* Yellow River
~**hun¹** ～昏 *n.* dusk
~**huo⁴** ～禍 *n.* yellow peril
~**kua¹** ～瓜 *n.* cucumber
~**la⁴** ～臘 *n.* wax
~**se⁴** ～色 *n.* yellow
~**se⁴ yao⁴** ～色藥 *n.* picric acid, trinitrophenol
~**shu¹ lang²** ～鼠狼 *n.* weasel
~**tan³ ping⁴** ～胆病 *n.* jaundice
~**tou⁴** ～豆 *n.* soy bean
~**t'ung²** ～銅 *n.* brass
~**ying¹** ～鶯 *n.* chaffinch
HUANG² 蝗 *n.* locust
HUI¹ 灰 *n.* ash, dust, lime, mortar ; *a.* gray
~**ch'en²** ～塵 *a.* dusty
~**se⁴** ～色 *n.* & *a.* gray
HUI¹ 揮 *v.* move, shake, rouse, wag
~**huo⁴** ～霍 *v.* squander
~**shou³** ～手 *v.* wave the hand
HUI² 回 *n.* turn, time ; *v.* return
~**chia¹** ～家 *v.* return home
~**chiao⁴** ～教 *n.* Mohammedanism
~**chiao⁴ kuo²** ～教國 *n.* Moslem states
~**chiao⁴ t'ang²** ～教堂 *n.* Mosque
~**chiao⁴ t'u²** ～教徒 *n.* Mohammedan, Moslem
~**ch'ü⁴** ～去 *v.* return
~**i⁴** ～憶 *v.* recall, remember
~**i⁴ lu⁴** ～憶錄 *n.* memoirs
~**kuei¹ hsien⁴** ～歸線 *n.* Tropics
~**kuei¹ je⁴** ～歸熱 *n.* relapsing fever
~**sheng¹** ～聲 *n.* echo
~**ta²** ～答 *n.* & *v.* answer
~**tsui³** ～嘴 *v.* retort
~**yung⁴** ～佣 *n.* commission (money)
HUI³ 悔 *v.* repent ; *n.* repentance
~**kai³** ～改 *v.* repent
~**kuo⁴** ～過 *v.* repent

~tsui⁴ ~罪 *v.* repent

HUI³ 毀 *v.* injure, break, spoil

~huai⁴ ~壞 *v.* destroy; *n.* destruction

~mieh⁴ ~滅 *v.* destroy

~pang⁴ ~謗 *v.* slander

~shang¹ ~傷 *v.* injure, hurt

HUI⁴ 會 *v.* meet together, assemble, know. **K'UAI⁴** *v.* calculate; *n.* society, guild

~chan⁴ ~戰 *n.* war battle

~chien⁴ ~見 *n.* interview

~ch'ang³ ~場 *n.* place of meeting

~ho² ~合 *v.* meet together

~hua⁴ ~話 *n.* conversation

~i⁴ ~議 *n.* conference

~k'o⁴ shih⁴ ~客室 *n.* drawing room, parlor

~shang¹ ~商 *v.* consult, confer

~shih¹ ~師 *n.* join forces (*mil.*)

k'uai⁴ chi⁴ ~計 *n.* accountant

~chi⁴ hsüeh² ~計學 *n.* accounting

~chi⁴ yüan² ~計員 *n.* accountant

HUN¹ 婚 *v.* marry; *n.* marriage, wedding

~li³ ~禮 *n.* wedding

~yin¹ ~姻 *n.* marriage

~yin¹ fa³ ~姻法 *n.* Marriage Law**

~yin¹ tzu⁴ yu² ~姻自由 *n.* freedom of marriage

HUN⁴ 混 *a.* mingled, mixed, confused

~chan⁴ ~戰 *n.* dog fight

~ho² ~合 *v.* mix

~ho² wu⁴ ~合物 *n.* compound

~luan⁴ ~亂 *n.* chaos

HUNG¹ 轟 *n.* roar, boom

~cha⁴ ~炸 *v.* bomb; *n.* bombardment

~cha⁴ chi¹ ~炸機 *n.* bomber

~chi¹ ~擊 *v.* shell; *n.* bombardment

HUNG² 紅 *n.* red, scarlet

~chün¹ ~軍 *n.* Communist Army

~ch'a² ~茶 *n.* black tea

~hsüeh⁴ ch'iu² ~血球 *n.* red blood corpuscle

~li⁴ ~利 *n.* bounus

~pao³ shih² ~寶石 *n.* ruby

~se⁴ ~色 *n.* red

74

~shih² tzu⁴ hui⁴ ~十字會 *n.* Red Cross

~shih² tzu⁴ i¹ yüan² ~十字醫院 *n.* Red Cross Hospital

HUO² 活 *n.* living, livelihood

~ch'i¹ ts'un² k'uan³ ~期存款 *n.* checking account

~p'o¹ ~潑 *a.* active, lively

~tung⁴ ~動 *n.* activity; *a.* active, movable

HUO³ 火 *n.* fire

~chi¹ ~雞 *n.* turkey

~chien⁴ ~箭 *n.* rocket

~chiu³ ~酒 *n.* alcohol

~ch'ai² ~柴 *n.* match

~ch'e¹ ~車 *n.* train

~ch'e¹ t'ou² ~車頭 *n.* locomotive

~fu¹ ~夫 *n.* fireman

~hsien³ ~險 *n.* fire insurance

~hsien⁴ ~線 *n.* firing line

~hsing¹ ~星 *n.* Mars (planet)

~lu² ~爐 *n.* stove

~pa³ ~把 *n.* torch

~shan¹ ~山 *n.* volcano

~shih² ~石 *n.* flint

~t'ui³ ~腿 *n.* ham

~tsai¹ ~災 *n.* conflagration

~tsang⁴ ~葬 *n.* cremation

~yao⁴ ~藥 *n.* gunpowder, powder

~yen⁴ ~燄 *n.* flame

~yen⁴ fang⁴ she⁴ ch'i⁴ ~焰放射器 *n.* flame thrower

HUO³ 伙 *n.* companion, furniture

~pan⁴ ~伴 *n.* companion, partner

~shih² ~食 *n.* food

HUO⁴ 貨 *v.* deal (business); *n.* goods, merchandise, cargo (for sale)

~chan⁴ ~棧 *n.* warehouse

~ch'e¹ ~車 *n.* wagon, truck

~pi⁴ ~幣 *n.* money

~tan¹ ~單 *n.* invoice

~wu⁴ ~物 *n.* merchandise, goods, cargo

~wu⁴ chiao¹ huan⁴ ~物交換 *n.* barter

75

~yang⁴ ~樣 *n.* samples of goods
HUO⁴ 禍 *n.* misfortune, calamity
~hai⁴ ~害 *n.* damage, injury
~huan⁴ ~患 *n.* misfortune
~luan⁴ ~亂 *n.* disturbance
HUO⁴ 或 *adv.* perhaps, maybe, possibly
~che³ ~者 *adv.* perhaps
HUO⁴ 獲 *v.* catch, obtain, get
~li⁴ ~利 *v.* make profit
~sheng⁴ ~勝 *v.* win
~te² ~得 *v.* obtain
~tsui⁴ ~罪 *v.* commit a crime

HS

HSI¹ 西 *n.* west; *a.* west, western
~fang¹ ~方 *a.* western
~jen² ~人 *n.* Westerner, foreigner
~kua¹ 瓜 *n.* watermelon
~nan² fang¹ ~南方 *a.* southwestern
~yu² chi⁴ ~遊記 *n.* Pilgrimage to the West
(Chinese novel)
HSI¹ 希 *a.* rare, few, strange; *adv.* rarely, seldom
~ch'i² ~奇 *a.* wonderful, curious, strange
~han³ ~罕 *a.* rare; *adv.* seldom, rarely
~wang⁴ ~望 *n. & v.* hope
HSI¹ 稀 *a.* rare, few, seldom, scarce
~fan⁴ ~飯 *n.* rice gruel
~pao² ~薄 *a.* this
~shao³ ~少 *a.* rare; *adv.* seldom
~shu¹ ~疏 *a.* sparse
HSI¹ 吸 *v.* inhale, suck, attract
~li⁴ ~力 *n.* attraction
~mo⁴ chih³ ~墨紙 *n.* blotter, blotting paper
~shou¹ ~收 *n.* absorption
~t'ieh³ shih² ~鉄石 *n.* loadstone
~yin³ ~引 *n.* attraction
HSI² 習 *n.* custom, usage; *v.* practise, learn
~ch'ang² ~常 *a.* common, usual
~kuan⁴ ~慣 *n.* habit, custom

76

~**su²** ~俗 *n.* custom, usage

~**t'i²** ~題 *n.* problem

~**tzu⁴ t'ieh³** ~字帖 *n.* copybook

HSI² 惜 *v.* pity, be sympathetic, spare, care for

HSI² 息 *v.* cease, stop, rest

HSI² 席 *n.* mat, seat, banquet

HSI² 錫 *n.* tin, gifts; *v.* give

~**chiang⁴** ~匠 *n.* tinsmith

~**ch'i⁴** ~器 *n.* tinware

~**po²** ~箔 *n.* tin foil

HSI³ 喜 *n.* joy, delight; *a.* glad, cheerful

~**chiu³** ~酒 *n.* wedding feast

~**chü⁴** ~劇 *n.* comedy

~**ch'iao¹** ~鵲 *n.* magpie

~**huan¹** ~歡 *v.* like; *a.* happy

~**hsin⁴** ~信 *n.* happy news

~**le⁴** ~樂 *a.* joy

~**yüeh⁴** ~悦 *a.* pleasant

HSI³ 洗 *v.* wash, cleanse

~**ch'ing** ~清 *v.* make clean

~**i¹ chi¹ ch'i⁴** ~衣機器 *n.* washing machine

~**i¹ tso⁴** ~衣作 *n.* laundry

~**li³** ~禮 *n.* baptism

~**nao³** ~腦 *n.* brain-washing**

~**shou³** ~手 *v.* wash hands

~**shou³ chien¹** ~手間 *n.* washroom

~**t'ou²** ~頭 *v.* shampoo

~**tsao³** ~澡 *v.* bathe; *n.* bath

~**ts'a¹** ~擦 *v.* wash

HSI⁴ 細 *a.* fine, thin, slender, delicate; *adv.* carefully

~**ch'ang²** ~長 *a.* spindling, slender

~**hsiao³** ~小 *a.* small

~**hsin¹** ~心 *a.* careful

~**pao¹** ~胞 *n.* cell (living matter)

~**tse²** ~則 *n.* regulation

~**yü³** ~雨 *n.* drizzle

HSI⁴ 戲 *n.* drama, play; *v.* play, joke

~**chü⁴** ~劇 *n.* drama

~**chü⁴ chia¹** ~劇家 *n.* dramatist

~**t'ai²** ~臺 *n.* theater stage

~**yen**² ~言 *v.* joke

~**yüan**⁴ ~院 *n.* theater

HSI⁴ 系 *n.* connection, university department, system

~**p'u**³ ~譜 *n.* genealogy

~**shu**⁴ ~數 *n.* joint agent

~**t'ung**³ ~統 *n.* system, clique

HSI⁴ 係 *v.* belong to

HSIA¹ 瞎 *a.* blind, heedless; *adv.* blindly, heedlessly

~**nao**⁴ ~閙 *n.* nonsense

~**shuo**¹ ~說 *n.* lie

~**tzu**¹ ~子 *n.* blinder

HSIA⁴ 下 *n.* bottom; *adv.* below, down, under; *a.* inferior, mean, low; *v.* descend, go down

~**chi**² ~級 *n.* inferior, junior, low grade

~**chien**⁴ ~賤 *a.* mean, base

~**ch'e**¹ ~車 *v.* get out of a car

~**ch'i**² ~棋 *v.* play chess

~**ch'uan**² ~船 *v.* disembark

~**hsüeh**² ~學 *n.* elementary study

~**hsüeh**³ ~雪 *v.* snow

~**jen**² ~人 *n.* servant, attendant

~**k'ou**³ **ling**⁴ ~口令 *v.* give commands (in drill)

~**lou**² ~樓 *v.* come downstairs

~**mao**² ~錨 *v.* anchor

~**pan**¹ ~班 *v.* go off duty

~**pan**⁴ **ch'i**² ~半旗 *v.* half-mast a flag

~**shen**¹ ~身 *n.* lower part of the body, privates

~**shih**⁴ ~士 *n.* sergeant (army)

~**shu**³ ~屬 *n.* subordinates

~**teng**³ ~等 *n.* inferior (quality)

~**t'a**⁴ ~榻 *v.* lodge

~**ts'eng**² **she**⁴ **hui**⁴ ~層社會 *n.* lower class

~**tz'u**⁴ ~次 *n.* next time

~**wu**³ ~午 *n.* afternoon

~**wu**⁴ ~霧 *a.* foggy

~**yu**² ~游 *adv.* & *a.* downstream

~**yüeh**⁴ ~月 *n.* next month

HSIA⁴ 夏 *n.* summer

~**chi**⁴ ~季 *n.* summer

~**chih⁴** ~至 *n.* summer solstice

HSIANG¹ 香 *n.* incense; *a.* fragrant

~**chiao¹** ~蕉 *n.* banana

~**chün¹** ~菌 *n.* mushroom

~**ch'i⁴** ~氣 *n.* perfume, fragrance

~**k'o⁴** ~客 *n.* pilgrim

~**liao⁴** ~料 *n.* spice

~**lu²** ~炉 *n.* censer

~**pin¹ chiu³** ~檳酒 *n.* champagne

~**shui³** ~水 *n.* perfume

~**yen¹** ~煙 *n.* cigarette

HSIANG¹ 箱 *n.* box, chest

~**tzu¹** ~子 *n.* suitcase, trunk

HSIANG¹ 相 *a.* reciprocal

~**cheng¹** ~爭 *v.* quarrel

~**chu⁴** ~助 *v.* help each other

~**ch'ih²** ~持 *n.* stalemate

~**fan³** ~反 *a.* opposite

~**fu²** ~符 *v.* correspond

~**hui⁴** ~會 *v.* meet

~**hsin⁴** ~信 *v.* believe

~**i¹** ~依 *a.* interdependent

~**lien²** ~連 *v.* connect

~**pi³** ~比 *v.* compare

~**shih⁴** ~識 *n.* acquaintance

~**ssu⁴** ~似 *a.* alike, similar

~**teng³** ~等 *a.* equal; *n.* equality

~**tui⁴ lun⁴** ~對論 *n.* theory of relativity

~**t'ung²** ~同 *a.* same

~**mao⁴** ~貌 *n.* appearance

~**p'ien⁴** ~片 *n.* photograph

HSIANG¹ 鄉 *n.* village, country

~**ch'ih⁴ wei⁴ tui⁴** ~赤衛隊 *n.* township Communist guards**

~**hsia⁴** ~下 *n.* country, rural district

~**ts'un¹** ~村 *n.* village

~**ts'un¹ chiao⁴ yü⁴** ~村教育 *n.* rural education

~**ts'un¹ hao² shen¹ chieh¹ chi²** ~村豪紳階級 *n.* landed gentry in the countryside**

HSIANG² 詳 *v.* report, examine; *adv.* minutely

HSIANG² 降 *see* **CHIANG⁴**

79

HSIANG³ 想 *v.* think about, reflect, consider

~**chia¹** ~家 *a.* homesick

~**hsiang⁴** ~像 *v.* imagine; *n.* fancy imagination

~**hsiang⁴ li⁴** ~像力 *n.* imagination

~**nien⁴** ~念 *v.* think

~**tao⁴** ~到 *v.* remember

HSIANG³ 享 *v.* enjoy

~**shou⁴** ~受 *v.* enjoy

~**yu³** ~有 *v.* possess

HSIANG³ 響 *n.* sound, noise, echo; *a.* noisy

~**wei³ she²** ~尾蛇 *n.* rattlesnake

~**ying⁴** ~應 *n.* echo (response); *v.* respond

HSIANG⁴ 向 *prep.* toward

~**ch'ien²** ~前 *adv.* forward, ahead, onward

~**hou⁴** ~後 *adv.* backward, behind

~**hsia⁴** ~下 *adv.* downward, down

~**jih⁴ k'uei²** ~日葵 *n.* sunflower

~**lai²** ~來 *adv.* hitherto, until now

~**li⁴** ~例 *adv.* habitably

~**nei⁴** ~內 *adv.* inward

~**shang⁴** ~上 *adv.* upward, above

~**wai⁴** ~外 *adv.* outward, beyond

HSIANG⁴ 像 *n.* image; *v.* resemble

~**mao⁴** ~貌 *n.* appearance

~**p'ien⁴** ~片 *n.* photograph, picture

HSIANG⁴ 象 *n.* elephant

~**ch'i²** ~棋 *n.* chess

~**hsing² wen² tzu⁴** ~形文字 *n.* hieroglyphics

~**pi²** ~鼻 *n.* elephant's trunk

~**ya²** ~牙 *n.* ivory

~**ya² shan⁴** ~牙扇 *n.* ivory fan

HSIANG⁴ 項 *n.* nape, neck, kind, sort

~**ch'üan¹** ~圈 *n.* necklace

~**mu⁴** ~目 *n.* item

HSIANG⁴ 巷 *n.* lane, alley

~**chan⁴** ~戰 *n.* street fighting

HSIAO¹ 消 *v.* melt, disappear, diminish

~**chi²** ~極 *a.* passive, negative

~**ch'ien³** ~遣 *n.* pastime, amusement, recreation

~**ch'u²** ~除 *v.* remove

~**fang² tui⁴** ~防隊 *n.* fire station (place or personnel)

~**fei⁴ ho² tso⁴ she⁴** ~費合作社 *n.* post exchange (army)

~**hao⁴** ~耗 *v.* waste; *n.* ammunition expenditure

~**hao⁴ chan⁴** ~耗戰 *n.* war of attrition

~**hao⁴ p'in³** ~耗品 *n.* expendable property

~**hua⁴** ~化 *v.* digest; *n.* digestion

~**hua⁴ pu⁴ liang²** ~化不良 *n.* indigestion

~**hsi²** ~息 *n.* information, news

~**mieh⁴** ~滅 *v.* annihilate

~**shih¹** ~失 *v.* vanish, disappear

~**shou⁴** ~瘦 *a.* lean

~**tu²** ~毒 *n.* decontamination, disinfection

HSIAO¹ 削 *v.* cut, sharpen; *a.* steep

~**jo⁴** ~弱 *v.* weaken

~**pi⁴** ~壁 *n.* cliff, precipice

HSIAO³ 曉 *n.* dawn, light; *v.* know, understand

HSIAO³ 小 *a.* little, small, tiny, petty, slight, minute, young

~**chieh³** ~姐 *n.* Miss, girl, unmarried woman

~**ch'an³** ~產 *n.* abortion

~**ch'i⁴** ~氣 *a.* narrow-minded; *adv.* narrow-mindedly

~**ch'ou⁸** ~丑 *n.* clown

~**fan⁴** ~販 *n.* peddler

~**fei⁴** ~費 *n.* tip (money)

~**hsin¹** ~心 *a.* careful; *adv.* carefully

~**hsüeh² hsiao⁴** ~學校 *n.* primary school

~**kung¹** ~工 *n.* coolie

~**lu⁴** ~路 *n.* small path

~**mai⁴** ~麥 *n.* rye

~**pien⁴** ~便 *v.* urinate; *n.* urine

~**shu⁴** ~數 *a. & n.* decimal

~**shuo¹** ~說 *n.* fiction, novel, story

~**t'uan² t'i³ chu³ i⁴** ~団體主義 *n.* cliquism**

~**tzu¹ ch'an³ chieh¹ chi²** ~資産階級 *n.* petty bourgeoisie**

HSIAO⁴ 效 *v.* imitate; *n.* result

~**fa³** ~法 *v.* imitate

~**lü⁴** ~率 *n.* efficiency, proficiency

~**yung⁴** ~用 *n.* utility

HSIAO⁴ 笑 *v.* smile, laugh, ridicule
　~**hua⁴** ~話 *n.* joke
　~**ping³** ~柄 *n.* laughingstock
HSIAO⁴ 校 *see* CHIAO⁴
HSIEH¹ 些 *a.* little, few; *adv.* slightly
　~**wei¹** ~微 *adv.* slightly
HSIEH¹ 歇 *v.* rest, stop
HSIEH² 鞋 *n.* shoe
　~**chiang⁴** ~匠 *n.* shoemaker
　~**ken¹** ~跟 *n.* shoe heel
　~**pa²** ~拔 *n.* shoehorn
　~**shua¹** ~刷 *n.* shoe brush
　~**tai⁴** ~帶 *n.* shoelace, shoestring
　~**ti³** ~底 *n.* shoe sole
HSIEH² 協 *n.* agreement, mutual help
　~**ho²** ~和 *v.* harmonize; *n.* harmony
　~**hui⁴** ~會 *n.* association
　~**li⁴** ~力 *v.* cooperate
　~**shang¹** ~商 *v.* negotiate, discuss; *n.* negotiation
　~**ting⁴** ~定 *n.* agreement
　~**t'iao²** ~調 *v.* coordinate
　~**t'ung²** ~同 *v.* cooperate; *n.* cooperation
HSIEH² 斜 *a.* transverse, oblique, irregular
　~**chiao³** ~角 *n.* oblique angle
　~**mien⁴** ~面 *n.* slope
　~**p'o¹** ~坡 *n.* ramp, slope
　~**she⁴** ~射 *n.* oblique fire
HSIEH³ 寫 *v.* write
　~**hsin⁴** ~信 *v.* write a letter
　~**i⁴** ~意 *a.* comfortable
　~**sheng¹** ~生 *v.* draw a picture
　~**shih² chu³ i⁴** ~實主義 *n.* realism (art)
　~**shih² p'ai⁴** ~實派 *n.* realist (art)
　~**tso⁴** ~作 *v.* write (literature)
　~**tzu⁴ chien¹** ~字間 *n.* office
HSIEH⁴ 謝 *v.* thank
　~**chüeh²** ~絕 *v.* refuse
　~**tsui⁴** ~罪 *v.* apologize; *n.* apology
　~**wei¹** ~萎 *v.* fade; *a.* faded
HSIEH⁴ 械 *n.* arm, weapon, tool

82

~**tou⁴** ~鬪 *v.* fight with weapons

HSIEN¹ 仙 *n.* fairy, cent

  ~**ching⁴** ~境 *n.* fairyland

  ~**nü³** ~女 *n.* fairy

HSIEN¹ 先 *prep. adv. & conj.* before; *a.* previous

  ~**chao⁴** ~兆 *n.* omen

  ~**chien⁴** ~見 *n.* foresight

  ~**chih¹** ~知 *n.* prophet

  ~**ch'i¹** ~期 *a.* premature, advance (ahead of time)

  ~**ch'ü¹** ~驅 *n.* forerunner, herald

  ~**feng¹** ~鋒 *n.* pioneer, vanguard, spearhead

  ~**hou⁴** ~後 *adv.* in succession, one after another

  ~**li⁴** ~例 *n.* example, precedent

  ~**sheng¹** ~生 *n.* teacher

  ~**t'ou² pu⁴ tui⁴** ~頭部隊 *n.* leading elements of column

HSIEN¹ 鮮 *a.* fresh, new. ~³ *a.* rare, few

  ~**hua¹** ~花 *n.* fresh flower

  ~**kuo³** ~果 *n.* fresh fruit

  ~**mei³** ~美 *n.* fresh and delicious

  ~**yen⁴** ~艷 *a.* attractive

HSIEN² 嫌 *v.* dislike, loathe

  ~**ch'i⁴** ~棄 *v.* reject

  ~**i²** ~疑 *a.* suspicious; *n.* suspicion

  ~**i² fan⁴** ~疑犯 *n.* suspect

  ~**wu⁴** ~惡 *v.* dislike

HSIEN² 閒 *a.* vacant, idle; *n.* leisure

  ~**hsia²** ~暇 *n.* leisure

  ~**t'an²** ~談 *n.* gossip

HSIEN³ 險 *n.* danger; *a.* dangerous

  ~**cha⁴** ~詐 *a.* treacherous; *n.* treachery

  ~**e⁴** ~惡 *a.* vicious

HSIEN³ 顯 *v.* display, show; *a.* apparent, clear, glorious

  ~**ho⁴** ~赫 *a.* prominent

  ~**ming²** ~明 *a.* apparent

  ~**shih⁴** ~示 *v.* show

  ~**wei¹ ching⁴** ~微鏡 *n.* microscope

HSIEN⁴ 現 *v.* appear, display; *adv.* now; *a.* visible

  ~**chin¹** ~金 *n.* cash

~chuang⁴ ~狀 *n.* status quo

~ch'u¹ ~出 *v.* appear

~hsiang⁴ ~象 *n.* phenomena

~i⁴ ~役 *n.* active service, active duty

~k'uan³ chiao¹ i⁴ ~款交易 *n.* cash sale

~shih² chu³ i⁴ ~實主義 *n.* realism

~tsai⁴ ~在 *adv.* now, present

HSIEN⁴ 限 *n. & v.* limit; *n.* limitation

~chih⁴ ~制 *v.* limit; *n.* limitation

~ch'i¹ ~期 *n.* deadline

HSIEN⁴ 縣 *n.* district, country

~ch'ih⁴ wei⁴ tsung³ tui³ ~赤衛總隊 *n.* County Communist Guards**

HSIEN⁴ 線 *n.* thread, yarn, cord, line

~chou² ~軸 *n.* spool

~so³ ~索 *n.* clue

HSIEN⁴ 獻 *v.* offer, give, present

~chi⁴ ~計 *v.* give advice

~chi⁴ ~祭 *v.* sacrifice

~chin¹ ~金 *n.* monetary contribution

~hua⁴ ~花 *v.* present a bouquet

HSIN¹ 心 *n.* heart

~ai⁴ ~愛 *a.* beloved

~chiao¹ ~焦 *n.* worried

~fu⁴ ~腹 *a.* intimate

~hsüeh⁴ ~血 *n.* lifeblood

~li³ chan⁴ cheng¹ ~理戰爭 *n.* psychological warfare

~li³ hsüeh² ~理學 *n.* psychology; *a.* psychological

~ling² ~靈 *n.* soul

~luan⁴ ~亂 *a.* confused

~t'iao⁴ ~跳 *n.* pulse

~t'ung⁴ ~痛 *n.* heartache

~yüan⁴ ~願 *n.* hope, desire

HSIN¹ 新 *a.* new, fresh, modern, recent

~chin⁴ 近 *adv.* recently

~hsien¹ ~鮮 *a.* fresh

~lang² ~郎 *n.* bridegroom

~min² chu³ chu³ i⁴ ~民主主義 *n.* New Democracy**

~**niang²** ~娘 *n.* bride
~**nien²** ~年 *n.* New Year
~**ping¹** ~兵 *n.* recruit
~**sheng¹ huo² yün⁴ tung⁴** ~生活運動 *n.* New Life Movement*
~**shih⁴** ~式 *n.* new style
~**ssu⁴ chün¹** ~四軍 *n.* New Fourth Army**
~**wen²** ~聞 *n.* press, news
~**wen² chi⁴ che³** ~聞記者 *n.* journalist, news-man
~**wen² tsung³ shu³** ~聞總署 *n.* Press Administration**
~**yüeh¹** ~約 *n.* New Testament

HSIN¹ 辛 *a.* pungent, toilsome, grievous
~**ch'in²** ~勤 *a.* toilsome, laborious
~**la⁴** ~辣 *a.* peppery, hot
~**lao²** ~勞 *a.* industrious, diligent

HSIN⁴ 信 *v.* believe, trust; *n.* letter, information; *a.* faithful
~**cha²** ~札 *n.* letter
~**chien¹** ~箋 *n.* letter-paper
~**ch'ai¹** ~差 *n.* mailman, postman
~**feng¹** ~封 *n.* envelope
~**hao⁴** ~號 *n.* signal
~**hao⁴ ch'iang¹** ~號鎗 *n.* pyrotechnics projector
~**hao⁴ tan⁴** ~號彈 *n.* signal shells, pyrotechnics
~**hsi²** ~息 *n.* news, information
~**hsiang¹** ~箱 *n.* mailbox
~**jen⁴** ~任 *v.* trust, believe
~**kuan³** ~管 *n.* fuze
~**t'iao²** ~條 *n.* creed
~**t'u²** ~徒 *n.* disciple, follower
~**wu⁴** ~物 *n.* pledge, security
~**yang³** ~仰 *n.* belief
~**yung⁴** ~用 *n.* credit

HSING¹ 興 *n.* fashion; *v.* rise; *a.* flourishing. ~⁴ *n.* high spirits
~¹ **fen⁴** ~奮 *a.* excited
~**fen⁴ chi⁴** ~奮劑 *n.* stimulant
~**lung²** ~隆 *a.* flourishing; *n.* prosperity
~⁴ **ch'ü⁴** ~趣 *n.* interest

85

HSING¹ 星 *n.* star
 ~**ch'i¹** ~期 *n.* week
 ~**ch'i¹ erh⁴** ~期二 *n.* Tuesday
 ~**ch'i¹ i¹** ~期一 *n.* Monday
 ~**ch'i¹ jih⁴** ~期日 *n.* Sunday
 ~**ch'i¹ liu⁴** ~期六 *n.* Saturday
 ~**ch'i¹ san¹** ~期三 *n.* Wednesday
 ~**ch'i¹ ssu⁴** ~期四 *n.* Thursday
 ~**ch'i¹ wu³** ~期五 *n.* Friday
 ~**hsiang⁴ chia¹** ~相家 *n.* fortuneteller
 ~**kuang¹** ~光 *n.* starlight
 ~**su⁴** ~宿 *n.* constellation

HSING² 行 walk, act; *n.* conduct, behavior.
 HANG² *n.* row, line, store
 ~**cheng⁴** ~政 *n.* administration
 ~**cheng⁴ yüan⁴** ~政院 *n.* Executive Yuan*
 ~**hui⁴** ~賄 *n.* bribery
 ~**hsing¹** ~星 *n.* planet
 ~**li³** ~李 *n.* baggage
 ~**li³** ~禮 *v.* salute
 ~**lieh⁴** ~列 *n.* array, procession
 ~**tz'u⁴** ~刺 *v.* assassinate, murder
 ~**wei²** ~爲 *n.* conduct, behavior
 hang² chang³ ~長 *n.* managing director (bank)

HSING² 形 *n.* shape, form, figure
 ~**chuang⁴** ~狀 *n.* shape, form
 ~**erh² shang⁴ hsüeh²** ~而上学 *n.* metaphysics
 ~**jung²** ~容 *v.* modify, describe
 ~**jung² tz'u²** ~容詞 *n.* adjective
 ~**shih⁴** ~勢 *n.* situation, condition
 ~**shih⁴** ~式 *n.* form, shape
 ~**shih⁴ chu³ i⁴** ~式主義 *n.* formalism

HSING³ 醒 *v.* wake up, awake, make sober; *a.* awake, sober
 ~**mu⁴** ~目 *a.* clear, attractive
 ~**wu⁴** ~悟 *v.* become aware

HSING³ 省 *see* **SHENG³**

HSING⁴ 姓 *n.* surname
 ~**ming²** ~名 *n.* name
 ~**ming² chieh¹ chi²** ~名階級 *n.* personnel identity (*mil.*)

86

~**p‘u³** ~譜 *n.* genealogy

HSING⁴ 性 *n.* sex, nature, temper

~**chi²** ~急 *a.* hot-tempered

~**chiao¹** ~交 *n.* sexual intercourse

~**chih²** ~質 *n.* quality

~**ch‘ing²** ~情 n. temper

~**kan³** ~感 *a.* sexy

~**ming⁴** ~命 *n.* life

~**pieh²** ~別 *n.* sex

~**ping⁴** ~病 *n.* venereal disease

~**yü⁴** ~慾 *n.* sexuality

HSING⁴ 幸 *n.* luck; *a.* lucky, fortunate

~**erh²** ~而 *adv.* fortunately

~**fu²** ~福 *n.* fortune

~**yün⁴** ~運 *n.* good luck, fortune

HSIU¹ 休 *v.* rest, resign, retire, divorce, cease

~**chan⁴** ~戰 *n.* armistice, truce

~**ch‘i⁴** ~棄 *v.* divorce a wife

~**hsi²** ~息 *n.* rest (after work)

~**yeh⁴** ~業 *n.* recess

HSIU¹ 修 *v.* repair, mend

~**cheng⁴** ~正 *v.* amend

~**kai³** ~改 *v.* correct, revise

~**li³** ~理 *v.* repair

~**shih⁴** ~飾 *v.* decorate

~**tao⁴ yüan⁴** ~道院 *n.* monastery

~**yang³** ~養 *n.* tolerance

~**yeh⁴ cheng⁴ shu¹** ~業證書 *n.* certificate of attendance

HSIU¹ 羞 *v.* blush, feel ashamed; *n.* viand, delicacy

~**ch‘ih³** ~恥 *n.* shame

~**ch‘üeh⁴** ~怯 *a.* shy; *adv.* shyly

~**ju³** ~辱 *v.* insult

~**k‘uei⁴** ~愧 *a.* ashamed

HSIU⁴ 秀 *a.* elegant, fair, pretty

~**li⁴** ~麗 *a.* beautiful

~**ya³** ~雅 *a.* graceful; grace

HSIU⁴ 袖 *n.* sleeve

~**k‘ou³** ~口 *n.* cuff

HSIUNG¹ 兄 *n.* older brother

87

~**ti⁴** ~弟 *n.* brother

HSIUNG¹ 兇 *a.* fierce, savage, cruel, wild

~**ch'i⁴** ~器 *n.* weapon

~**e⁴** ~惡 *a.* malignant

~**meng³** ~猛 *n.* violence

~**shou³** ~手 *n.* murderer

HSIUNG¹ 胸 *n.* chest

~**chin¹** ~襟 *n.* mind, feeling

~**pi⁴ t'eng²** ~壁疼 *n.* pleurodynia

~**t'ang²** ~膛 *n.* thorax

HSIUNG² 雄 *a.* brave, masculine; *n.* male, hero

~**chuang⁴** ~壯 *a.* strong

~**hsin¹** ~心 *n.* ambition

~**pien⁴** ~辯 *n.* eloquence

~**pien⁴ chia¹** ~辯家 *n.* debater

~**te¹** ~的 *a.* male

HSÜ¹ 須 *a.* necessary; *v. aux.* must, ought

HSÜ¹ 虛 *a.* empty, vacant, vain, weak, useless

~**hsin¹** ~心 *a.* humble (feeling)

~**jo⁴** ~弱 *a.* weak

~**wei⁴** ~僞 *a.* false loyalty

HSÜ¹ 需 *n. & v.* need, demand; *n.* necessity

~**ch'iu²** ~求 *n. & v.* demand

~**yao⁴** ~要 *v.* need; *n.* necessity; *a.* necessary

HSÜ³ 許 *a.* a few; *v.* grant, permit, promise

~**chiu³** ~久 *n.* a long time

~**k'o³** ~可 *v.* promise

~**no⁴** ~諾 *v.* grant, allow

~**to¹** ~多 *a.* many, numerous

HSÜ⁴ 續 *v.* continue, succeed

~**chia⁴** ~假 *v.* extend leave

~**yin⁴** ~印 *v.* reprint

HSÜ⁴ 序 *n.* introduction, preface

~**wen²** ~文 *n.* preface

~**yen²** ~言 *n.* preface, introduction

HSÜAN¹ 宣 *v.* declare, announce, make known

~**chan⁴** ~戰 *v.* declare war; *n.* declaration of war

~**ch'uan²** ~傳 *v.* propagandize, propagate by propaganda

~**ch'uan² kung¹ tso⁴** ~傳工作 *n.* propaganda work

~**pu⁴** ~布 v. announce; n. announcement
~**shih⁴** ~誓 v. swear
~**tu²** ~讀 v. read
~**yang²** ~揚 v. make known
~**yen²** ~言 v. declare; n. declaration

HSÜAN³ 選 v. elect, select, choose
~**chü³** ~舉 v. elect; n. election
~**chü³ ch'üan²** ~舉權 n. suffrage
~**chü³ p'iao⁴** ~舉票 n. ballot
~**k'o¹** ~科 n. selective course
~**tse²** ~擇 v. select; n. selection

HSÜEH² 學 v. learn, study
~**che³** ~者 n. scholar
~**chih⁴** ~制 n. system of education
~**ch'ao²** ~潮 n. student's strike
~**ch'i¹** ~期 n. school term
~**fei⁴** ~費 n. tuition
~**hsi²** ~習 n. & v. study; v. learn
~**hsiao⁴** ~校 n. school, academy, college,
~**k'o¹** ~科 n. course, curriculum (school)
~**sheng¹** ~生 n. pupil, student
~**shu⁴** ~術 n. learning
~**shuo¹** ~説 n. tenet
~**t'u²** ~徒 n. apprentice
~**wei⁴** ~位 n. college degree
~**wen⁴** ~問 n. knowledge
~**yeh⁴** ~業 n. studies
~**yu³** ~友 n. schoolmate, classmate
~**yüan²** ~員 n. student-officer
~**yüan⁴** ~院 n. college

HSÜEH³ 雪 n. snow
~**ching³** ~景 n. snow scenery
~**ch'e¹** ~車 n. sleigh
~**ch'ieh² yen¹** ~茄煙 n. cigar
~**ch'iu²** ~球 n. snowball
~**hua¹** ~花 n. snowflake
~**hua¹ kao¹** ~花膏 n. vanishing cream
~**hsieh²** ~鞋 n. snowshoe
~**jen²** ~人 n. snowman
~**li²** ~犁 n. snowplow
~**⁴ ch'ih³** ~恥 v. revenge

~pai² ~白 *a.* snow-white
HSÜEH⁴ 血 *n.* blood
  ~ch'ing¹ ~清 *n.* serum
  ~ch'iu² ~球 *n.* corpuscle
  ~hsing² ~型 *n.* blood type, blood group
  ~i⁴ ~液 *n.* blood
  ~kuan³ ~管 *n.* blood vessel
  ~k'u⁴ ~庫 *n.* blood bank
  ~mo⁴ ~脈 *n.* pulse
  ~t'ung³ ~統 *n.* blood relation
  ~ya¹ ~壓 *n.* blood pressure
HSÜN² 尋 *v.* find
  ~chao³ ~找 *v.* find
  ~ch'ang² ~常 *a.* common, usual, ordinary, deferred message
  ~ch'iu² ~求 *v.* search
  ~fang³ ~訪 *v.* visit
  ~ssu¹ ~思 *v.* consider
  ~ssu³ ~死 *v.* commit suicide
HSÜN⁴ 訓 *v.* teach, instruct, advise; *n.* precept, advice, training
  ~chieh⁴ ~戒 *v.* warn, admonish
  ~hua⁴ ~話 *v.* give a speech (*off.*)
  ~lien⁴ ~練 *n.* training; *v.* train
  ~ling⁴ ~令 *n.* letter of instruction
  ~shih⁴ ~示 *v.* instruct; *n.* instruction
HSÜN⁴ 訊 *n.* trial, message
  ~wen⁴ ~問 *v.* interrogate prisoners; *n.* interrogation
  ~wen⁴ ch'u⁴ ~問處 *n.* information office

I

I¹ 一 *a.* a, an, one; *n.* one
  ~chi⁴ ~季 *n.* one fourth of a year
  ~chih⁴ hsing⁴ ~致性 *n.* coincidence**
  ~ch'u¹ hsi⁴ ~齣戲 *n.* play (drama)
  ~hsin¹ ~心 *adv.* heartily
  ~kai⁴ ~概 *n.* all; *adv.* entirely, all
  ~lan³ piao³ ~覽表 *n.* list, table, schedule

~lü⁴ ~律 *a.* uniform; *adv.* uniformly

~pan⁴ ~半 *n.* one half

~pien¹ tao³ ~邊倒 *n.* leaning to one side**

~tao⁴ ts'ai⁴ ~道菜 *n.* course (meal)

~ting⁴ ~定 *adv.* certainly, surely, decidedly

~yang⁴ ~樣 *a.* same; *adv.* alike, similarly

I¹ 衣 *n.* clothing, clothes

~chia⁴ ~架 *n.* hanger

~ch'u² ~櫥 *n.* clothes closet

~fu² ~服 *n.* clothing, clothes, garment

I¹ 依 *v.* trust, rely; *prep.* according to

~chao⁴ ~照 *adv.* according to

~fu⁴ ~附 *v.* adhere

~jan² ~然 *adv.* as before

~lai⁴ ~賴 *v.* depend upon

~t'zu⁴ ~次 *adv.* by order

~ts'ung² ~從 *v.* follow

I¹ 醫 *n.* doctor; *v.* heal, cure

~chih⁴ ~治 *v.* cure

~hsüeh² ~學 *n.* medical science

~hsüeh² po² shih⁴ ~學博士 *n.* medical doctor

~hsüeh² sheng¹ ~學生 *n.* medical student

~hsüeh² yüan⁴ ~學院 *n.* medical college

~sheng¹ ~生 *n.* doctor, practitioner

~yao⁴ ~藥 *n.* medicine

~yüan⁴ ~院 *n.* hospital

I² 宜 *a.* suitable, fit

I² 疑 *n.* suspicion; *v.* doubt, suspect

~huo⁴ ~惑 *v.* suspect; *n.* suspicion; *a.* suspicious

~i⁴ ~義 *n.* ambiguity

~wen⁴ ~問 *n.* question (doubt)

I² 姨 *n.* aunt

~fu⁴ ~父 *n.* husband of mother's sister (uncle)

~mu³ ~母 *n.* mother's sister (aunt)

I² 移 *v.* remove, shift, influence

~chiao¹ ~交 *v.* turn over an office to

~chih² ~植 *v.* transplant

~chü¹ ~居 *v.* change residence

~min² ~民 *v.* emigrate

~min² cheng⁴ ts'e⁴ ~民政策 *n.* emigration policy

~tung⁴ ~動 *v.* move, remove

I³ 乙 *v.* mark; *a. & n.* second

~teng³ ~等 *a.* second-class, grade B

I³ 以 *v.* do, use; *prep.* because of, with, by

~chan⁴ chih³ chan⁴ ~戰止戰 *n.* " war to end war "

~ch'ien² ~前 *adv.* ago, before

~hou⁴ ~後 *adv.* afterward

~hsia⁴ ~下 *adv. & prep.* below

~lai² ~來 *prep.* since

~mien³ ~免 *v.* avoid

~nei⁴ ~內 *prep.* within

~shang⁴ ~上 *adv. & prep.* above

~t'ai⁴ ~太 *n.* ether

~wai⁴ ~外 *prep.* besides

~wei² ~爲 *v.* consider, think

I³ 已 *adv.* already, yet; *a.* finished, passed

~ching¹ ~經 *adv.* already

~wang³ ~往 *a. & n.* past

I⁴ 益 *n.* benefit. advantage

I⁴ 異 *a.* different, strange, heterodox

~chiao⁴ ~教 *n.* paganism

~ch'ang² ~常 *a.* abnormal

~tuan¹ ~端 *n.* heresy

~yü⁴ ~域 *n.* foreign country

I⁴ 芸 *n.* handicraft, art

~neng² ~能 *n.* handicraft

~shu⁴ ~術 *n.* art; *a.* artistic

~shu⁴ chia¹ ~術家 *n.* artist

~shu⁴ huo² tung⁴ ~術活動 *n.* artistic activity

~shu⁴ hsüeh² yüan⁴ ~術學院 *n.* art college

I⁴ 義 *n.* righteousness, justice, meaning

~ch'i⁴ ~氣 *n.* heroism, chivalry

~ho² t'uan² yün⁴ tung⁴ ~和圍運動 *n.* Boxer Movement

~shih⁴ ~士 *n.* patriot

~wu⁴ ~務 *n.* obligation, duty

~wu⁴ chiao⁴ yü⁴ ~務教育 *n.* free education

I⁴ 議 *v.* consider, deliberate upon, discuss, negotiate

~an⁴ ~案 *n.* bill (proposed law)

92

~**chang³** ~長 *n.* Speaker
~**chüeh²** ~決 *v.* resolve by vote
~**chüeh² an⁴** ~決案 *n.* resolution (solution)
~**ho²** ~和 *v.* negotiate peace
~**yüan²** ~員 *n.* senator, congressman
~**yüan⁴** ~院 *n.* Congress (*U.S.*), British Parliament
I⁴ 意 *n.* thought, idea, intention, wish
~**chien⁴** ~見 *n.* opinion, idea
~**chih⁴** ~志 *n.* will
~**hsiang⁴** ~向 *n.* intention
~**i⁴** ~義 *n.* meaning
~**i⁴** ~譯 *n.* free translation
~**liao⁴** ~料 *v.* guess
~**shih⁴** ~識 *n.* consciousness
~**wai⁴** ~外 *n.* accident; *a.* accidental
~**wai⁴ te¹** ~外的 *a.* accidental
I⁴ 易 *v.* change; *a.* easy
~**jan²** ~燃 *a.* inflammable
I⁴ 疫 *n.* plague, epidemic

J

JAN² 然 *adv.* however, but, so, thus
JAN³ 染 *v.* dye, stain, infect
~**fang¹** ~坊 *n.* dye works
~**liao⁴** ~料 *n.* dyestuff
~**ping⁴** ~病 *v.* be sick
~**se⁴** ~色 *v.* dye
~**wu¹** ~污 *v.* stain
JANG⁴ 讓 *v.* cede, yield, give way, let
~**k'ai¹** ~開 *v.* clear for traffic
~**lu⁴** ~路 *v.* make way
~**pu⁴** ~步 *v.* give ground to
~**tu⁴** ~度 *n.* transference of property
~**wei⁴** ~位 *v.* abdicate
~**yü³** ~與 *v.* cede, give up
JAO⁴ 繞 *v.* wind, surround, avoid
~**tao⁴** ~道 *v.* go round about
JE⁴ 熱 *a.* hot, warm; *n.* heat; *v.* warm

~**cheng⁴** ~症 *n.* fever (disease)

~**ch'ing²** ~情 *n.* passion

~**hsin¹** ~心 *n.* zeal, enthusiasm

~**li⁴** ~力 *n.* heat power

~**tai⁴** ~帶 *n.* Tropics

~**tu⁴** ~度 *n.* fever

JEN² 人 *n.* person, people, human beings

~**chung³** ~種 *n.* race

~**ch'üan²** ~權 *n.* human rights

~**ko²** ~格 *n.* personality

~**k'ou³** ~口 *n.* population

~**lei⁴** ~類 *n.* mankind, human being, human race, humankind

~**li⁴ ch'e¹** ~力車 *n.* jinricksha, rickshaw

~**min²** ~民 *n.* people, subject

~**min² cheng⁴ fu³** ~民政府 *n.* People's Government**

~**min² chieh³ fang⁴ chün¹** ~民解放軍 *n.* People's Liberation Army**

~**min² chien¹ ch'a² wei³ yüan² hui⁴** ~民監察委員會 *n.* Committee of People's Control**

~**min² fa³ t'ing²** ~民法廷 *n.* People's Tribunals**

~**min² ko² ming⁴ chün¹ shih⁴ wei³ yüan² hui⁴** ~民革命軍事委員會 *n.* People's Revolutionary Military Council**

~**min² min² chu³ chuan¹ cheng⁴** ~民民主專政 *n.* People's Democratic Dictatorship**

~**min² p'ei² shen³ chih⁴** ~民陪審制 *n.* people's jury system**

~**min² pi⁴** ~民幣 *n.* people's currency**

~**min² yin² hang²** ~民銀行 *n.* People's Bank of China**

~**sheng¹ kuan** ~生觀 *n.* philosophy of life, view of life

~**shih⁴ pu⁴** ~事部 *n.* Ministry of Personnel**

~**tao⁴** ~道 *n.* humanity (being humane)

JEN⁴ 認 *v.* recognize, know, confess

~**k'o³** ~可 *v.* consent

~**shih⁴** ~識 *v.* know, recognize; *n.* recognition

~**tsui⁴** ~罪 *v.* apologize; *n.* apology

JEN⁴ 任 *v.* appoint, assign, undertake, employ;

n. office

~**hsing⁴** ～性 *a.* obstinate, headstrong

~**i⁴** ～意 *a.* arbitrary

~**ming⁴** ～命 *n.* appointment, assignment

~**wu⁴** ～務 *n.* mission, role

~**yung⁴** ～用 *v.* employ

JENG² 仍 *adv.* still, as before

~**chiu⁴** ～舊 *adv.* as before, as usual

JIH⁴ 日 *n.* sun, day, daytime ; *adv.* daily

~**chi⁴** ～記 *n.* diary

~**ch'i²** ～期 *n.* date

~**kuang¹** ～光 *n.* sunlight, sunshine

~**kuei¹** ～規 *n.* sundial

~**li⁴** ～曆 *n.* calender

~**pao⁴** ～報 n. daily newspaper

~**tzu¹** ～子 *n.* day

~**yung⁴ p'in³** ～用品 *n.* daily necessities

JO⁴ 弱 *a.* weak, tender

~**tien³** ～點 *n.* weak point

JOU² 柔 *a.* soft, tender, gentle, flexible

~**jo⁴** ～弱 *a.* tender

~**juan³** ～軟 *a.* soft

~**juan³ t'i⁴ ts'ao¹** ～軟体操 *n.* calisthenics

~**tao⁴** ～道 *n.* judo

JOU⁴ 肉 *n.* meat, flesh

~**t'i³** ～體 *n.* body

~**yü⁴** ～慾 *n.* lust (sex)

JU² 如 *conj.* as if ; *a.* like, similar

~**chin¹** ～今 *adv.* now, at present

~**ho²** ～何 *adv.* how

~**hsia⁴** ～下 *adv.* as follows

~**t'zu³** ～此 *adv.* so, thus

JU⁴ 入 *v.* enter, come in, step in

~**ch'ang³ ch'üan⁴** 場券 *n.* admission ticket

~**hsüeh²** ～學 *v.* enter a school

~**hsüeh² k'ao³ shih⁴** ～學考試 *n.* entrance examination

~**k'ou³** ～口 *n.* import, importation, entry

~**k'ou³ huo⁴** ～口貨 *n.* imported goods

~**tang³** ～黨 *v.* join a party, side

JUAN³ 軟 *a.* soft, pliable, yielding

~jo⁴ 弱 *a.* weak

JUNG² 容 *v.* contain; *n.* manner

~chi¹ ~積 *n.* volume, capacity

~i⁴ ~易 *a.* easy

~jen³ ~忍 *v.* tolerate

~mao⁴ ~貌 *n.* appearance, countenance

~na⁴ ~納 *v.* admit (have room for)

JUNG² 榮 *n.* honor, glory

~ju⁴ ~辱 *n.* honor and disgrace

~kuang¹ ~光 *n.* splendor

~yao⁴ ~耀 *n.* honor, glory

K

KAI¹ 該 *v. aux.* must, ought

~ch'ien⁴ ~欠 *v.* owe

KAI³ 改 *v.* change

~cheng⁴ ~正 *v.* correct

~chuang¹ ~裝 *v.* reconstruct, rebuild, make over

~hsüan³ ~選 *n.* re-election

~ko² ~革 *n.* reform

~kuo⁴ ~過 *v.* reform (conduct)

~liang² ~良 *v.* reform, improve

~pien¹ ~編 *v.* reorganize units

~pien⁴ ~變 *v.* alter, change

~tsao⁴ ~造 *v.* reconstruct, rebuild, make over

KAI⁴ 概 *v.* level, adjust; *adv.* generally

~k'uo⁴ ~括 *adv.* generally

~nien⁴ ~念 *n.* conception

KAI⁴ 蓋 *n.* roof, covering; *v.* cover, build; *prep.* for

~fang² ~房 *v.* build houses

~yin⁴ ~印 *v.* stamp

KAN¹ 乾 *a.* dry, clean

~ching⁴ ~淨 *a.* clean

~ch'uan² wu⁴ ~船塢 *n.* drydock

~je⁴ ~熱 *n.* dry heat

~lao⁴ ~酪 *n.* cheese

~liang² ~糧 *n.* travel ration, reserve ration,

emergency ration

~te¹ ~的 *a.* dry

~tien⁴ ~電 *n.* dry battery, dry cell

~tsao⁴ ~燥 *a.* parched

~ts'ao³ ~草 *n.* hay

KAN¹ 肝 *n.* liver

~cheng⁴ ~症 *n.* cirrhosis

KAN¹ 甘 *a.* sweet, delicious, pleasant, willing

~che⁴ ~蔗 *n.* sugar cane

~hsin¹ ~心 *a.* willing

~ts'ao³ ~草 *n.* licorice

~yen² ~言 *n.* sweet words

KAN¹ 干 *n.* a shield; *v.* offend against

~fan⁴ ~犯 *v.* violate, transgress

~ko¹ ~戈 *n.* weapon

~she⁴ ~涉 *v.* meddle, interfere

KAN³ 感 *v.* influence; *n.* feeling; *a.* affected

~chi¹ ~激 *n.* gratitude

~chüeh² ~覺 *n.* feeling, sensation

~ch'ing² ~情 *n.* emotion; *a.* sentimental

~en¹ ~恩 *n.* gratitude

~hua⁴ yüan⁴ ~化院 *n.* reformatory

~hsieh⁴ ~謝 *v.* thank

~hsing⁴ chieh¹ tuan⁴ ~性階段 *n.* perceptual stage**

~mao⁴ ~冒 *n.* head cold

~tung⁴ ~動 *a.* impressive

KAN³ 敢 *v.* dare, be bold; *a.* presumptuous

~ssu³ tui⁴ ~死隊 *n.* shock troops

KAN³ 趕 *v.* pursue, follow after, eject; *adv.* quickly

~chin³ ~緊 *adv.* quickly, speedily

~k'uai⁴ ~快 *v.* speed

~tsou³ ~走 *v.* expel

KAN³ 稈 *n.* hay, the stalk of millet

KAN⁴ 幹 *a.* capable, skillful; *n.* trunk, stem, body

~lien⁴ ~練 *a.* skillful

~pu⁴ ~部 *n.* cadre (*mil.*)

KANG¹ 剛 *a.* firm, solid, hard; *adv.* just

~chih² ~直 *a.* righteous, upright

~ch'iang² ~強 *a.* obstinate, stubborn

~i⁴ ~毅 *n.* fortitude

~**ts'ai²** ~才 *adv.* just

KANG¹ 鋼 *n.* steel; *a.* hard

~**ch'in²** ~琴 *n.* piano

~**ku³ shui³ ni²** ~骨水泥 *n.* reinforced concrete

~**k'uei¹** ~盔 *n.* steel helmet

~**pan³** ~板 *n.* armor plate

~**pi³** ~筆 *n.* fountain pen

KANG¹ 缸 *n.* jar, cistern

KANG³ 港 *n.* harbor, port

~**fang²** ~防 *n.* harbor defense

~**k'ou³** ~口 *n.* harbor

KAO¹ 高 *a.* high, tall

~**ao⁴** ~傲 *a.* proud

~**chi² chung¹ hsüeh²** ~級中學 *n.* senior middle school

~**hsing⁴** ~興 *a.* happy

~**kuei⁴** ~貴 *n.* dignity; *a.* noble

~**shang⁴** ~尚 *a.* high-minded

~**she⁴ p'ao⁴** ~射礮 *n.* anti-aircraft gun

~**sheng¹** ~聲 *a.* loud

~**tu⁴** ~度 *n.* height

~**ya¹** ~壓 *v.* press

~**yüan²** ~原 *n.* plateau

KAO¹ 糕 *n.* sweets, cake, pastry

~**ping³** ~餅 *n.* cake, pastry

KAO³ 稿 *n.* straw, sketch, draft

~**chien⁴** ~件 *n.* manuscript, draft

KAO³ 搞 *v.* handle, make, execute

~**huai⁴** ~壞 *v.* spoil, get out of order; *n.* break down

~**t'ung¹** ~通 *v.* have understood

~**t'ung¹ ssu¹ hsiang³** ~通思想 *v.* thoroughly understand and accept Communist policy**

KAO⁴ ~告 *v.* tell, inform, accuse

~**chia⁴** ~假 *adv.* on leave

~**chuang⁴** ~狀 *n.* lawsuit

~**fen⁴ yung³** ~奮勇 *v.* volunteer

~**pieh²** ~別 *v.* say good-bye

~**su⁴** ~訴 *v.* tell, inform

~**shih⁴** ~示 *n.* bulletin

~**t'ui⁴** ~退 *v.* leave

KEI³ 給 *v.* give. **CHI³** *v.* pay

KEN¹ 跟 *v.* follow, *n.* heel; *prep.* with
~**ts'ung² che³** ~從者 *n.* follower

KEN¹ 根 *n.* root
~**chih⁴ fa³** ~治法 *n.* radical treatment
~**chü⁴** ~據 *v.* base on
~**chü⁴ ti⁴** ~據地 *n.* base (*mil.*)
~**ch'u²** ~除 *v.* eradicate
~**pen³** ~本 *n.* foundation
~**yüan²** ~源 *n.* origin, source

KENG¹ 更 *v.* alter, change. ~⁴ *adv.* more, again
~**cheng⁴** ~正 *v.* correct
~**hsin¹** ~新 *v.* renew; *n.* renewal
~**i¹** ~衣 *v.* change clothes
~**kai³** ~改 *v.* change
~⁴ **to¹** ~多 *adv.* more

KENG¹ 耕 *v.* plow, cultivate
~**chung⁴** ~種 *v.* plow and sow
~**t'ien²** ~田 *v.* plow the field
~**tso⁴** ~作 *n.* farm

KO¹ 哥 *n.* older brother

KO¹ 歌 *n.* song; *v.* sing
~**chi⁴** ~劇 *n.* opera, operetta
~**chi⁴ yüan⁴** ~劇院 *n.* opera house
~**ch'ang⁴** ~唱 *v.* sing
~**ch'ang⁴ chia¹** ~唱家 *n.* singer
~**ch'ü³** ~曲 *n.* song
~**nü³** ~女 *n.* female vocalist
~**sung⁴** ~頌 *v.* praise with carols
~**yao²** ~謠 *n.* ballad

KO¹ 割 *v.* cut
~**chü⁴** ~據 *v.* amputate
~**jang⁴** ~讓 *n.* cession

KO² 隔 *n.* partition, shelf; *v.* interpose; *adv.* next to
~**jih⁴** ~日 *adv.* every other day
~**k'ai¹** ~開 *v.* separate, divide
~**li²** ~離 *n.* isolation, quarantine; *v.* separate
~**mo⁴** ~膜 *n.* misunderstanding, diaphragm
~**pi³** ~壁 *n.* next door, neighbor

KO² 革 *n.* leather; *v.* renew, dismiss

~chih² ~職 *v.* fire (dismiss)

~ch'u² ~除 *v.* dismiss

~hsin¹ ~新 *v.* reform

~ming⁴ ~命 *n.* revolution

~ming⁴ chün¹ ~命軍 *n.* revolutionary army

~ming⁴ tang³ ~命黨 *n.* revolutionary party

~ming⁴ tang³ yüan² ~命黨員 *n.* revolutionist

~ming⁴ yün⁴ tung⁴ ~命運動 *n.* revolutionary movement

KO² 格 *n.* grid, pattern

~shih⁴ ~式 *n.* style, form

~wai⁴ ~外 *a.* extraordinary

~yen² ~言 *n.* proverb

KO⁴ 個 *n.* unit, piece

~jen² ~人 *n.* individual

~jen² chu³ i⁴ ~人主義 *n.* individualism

~jen² chu³ i⁴ che³ ~人主義者 *n.* individualist

~pieh² ~別 *a.* individual

KO⁴ 各 *a.* each, every, all, various

~chung³ ~種 *n.* all kinds

~ch'u⁴ ~處 *adv.* everywhere

~jen² ~人 *pron.* everyone, everybody

~ti⁴ ~地 *adv.* everywhere

~yang⁴ te¹ ~樣的 *a.* various

KOU¹ 溝 *n.* drain, ditch, groove

~huo⁴ ~壑 *n.* gully

KOU³ 狗 *n.* dog

~fei⁴ ~吠 *n.* bark

KOU⁴ 够 *v.* suffice ; *a.* enough, adequate

KU¹ 估 *v.* estimate, value

~chi⁴ ~計 *v.* guess

~chia⁴ ~價 *v.* appraise, estimate value

~liang² ~量 *v.* consider

KU¹ 姑 *n.* paternal aunt

~hsi²~息 *v.* spoil

~mu³ ~母 *n.* father's sister (aunt)

~niang² ~娘 *n.* miss

~yeh² ~爺 *n.* son-in-law

KU³ 古 *n.* antiquity, oldness ; *a.* antique, ancient, old-fashioned, out-of-date

~chi⁴ ~蹟 *n.* relics, remains, ruins

~**jen²** ～人 *n.* the'ancients

~**tai⁴** ～代 *n.* antiquity

~**tien³** ～典 *n.* classics; *a.* classical

~**tung³** ～董 *n.* curio, antique

~**wen²** ～文 *n.* paleography, ancient writing

KU³ 股 *n.* thigh, share, stock. [suffix] section, branch

~**fen⁴** ～份 *n.* share, stock (company)

~**fen⁴ kung¹ ssu¹** ～份公司 *n.* stock company

~**hsi²** ～息 *n.* monetary dividend

~**pen³** ～本 *n.* capital (money)

~**p'iao⁴** ～票 *n.* stock share certificate

~**p'iao⁴ chiao¹ i⁴ so³** ～票交易所 *n.* stock exchange

~**p'iao⁴ shih⁴ ch'ang³** ～票市場 *n.* stock market

~**tung¹** ～東 *n.* shareholder, stockholder

KU³ 骨 *n.* bone

~**che²** ～折 *n.* fracture

~**chieh²** ～節 *n.* bone joint

~**kan⁴** ～幹 *n.* backbone (of an army, etc.)

~**ko²** ～骼 *n.* skeleton

~**sui³** ～髓 *n.* marrow

KU³ 鼓 *n.* drum

~**chang³** ～掌 *v.* applaud; *n.* applause

~**ch'ui¹** ～吹 *v.* inspire

~**li⁴** ～勵 *v.* encourage

~**tung⁴** ～動 *v.* stimulate

~**wu³** ～舞 *v.* inspire

KU³ 穀 *n.* grain, corn

KU⁴ 固 *a.* stable, steadfast, firm, secure

~**chieh²** ～結 *v.* consolidate

~**chih²** ～執 *a.* obstinate, stubborn

~**shou³** ～守 *v.* persist

~**ting⁴** ～定 *a.* fixed

~**t'i³** ～體 *a. & n.* solid

KU⁴ 雇 *v.* employ, hire; *n.* employment

~**chu³** ～主 *n.* employer

~**yung⁴** ～用 *v.* employ

~**yüan²** ～員 *n.* employee

KU⁴ 顧 *v.* look after, regard, consider

~**chi⁴** ～忌 *v.* fear

~**k'o⁴** ~客 *n.* customer, patron, patroness

~**nien⁴** ~念 *v.* regard

~**wen⁴** ~問 *n.* adviser

KU⁴ 故 *n.* cause, reason; *a.* late, deceased; *conj.* therefore, so

~**hsiang¹** ~鄉 *n.* native place

~**i⁴** ~意 *adv.* purposely, intentionally

~**shih⁴** ~事 *n.* story

KUA¹ 瓜 *n.* melon

~**fen¹** ~分 *v.* divide

KUA⁴ 掛 *v.* hang up, suspend

~**hao⁴** ~號 *v.* register; *n.* registration

~**hao⁴ hsin⁴ chien⁴** ~號信件 *n.* registered letter

~**kou¹** ~鈎 *n.* pintle (*mil.*)

~**nien⁴** ~念 *v.* worry

KUAI⁴ 怪 *n.* monster; *v.* blame; *a.* strange

~**i⁴** ~異 *n.* whim

~**jen²** ~人 *n.* strange fellow

~**p'i³** ~癖 *a.* queer

~**shih⁴** ~事 *n.* miracle

~**wu⁴** ~物 *n.* monster

KUAN¹ 關 *n.* barrier, custom house; *v.* shut, close

~**chieh²** ~節 *n.* bone joint

~**chieh² yen²** ~節炎 *n.* arthritis

~**hsi⁴** ~係 *n.* relation

~**hsiang³** ~餉 *v.* pay

~**hsin¹** ~心 *v.* concern

~**k'ou³** ~口 *n.* mountain pass

~**shui⁴** ~稅 *n.* tariff, customs

~**yü²** ~於 *prep.* concerning

KUAN¹ 官 *n.* officer, official

~**chang³** ~長 *n.* officer

~**chih²** ~職 *n.* rank (position)

~**fang¹** ~方 *a.* government official

~**fang¹ chan⁴ pao⁴** ~方戰報 *n.* war communique

~**liao²** ~僚 *n.* bureaucracy

~**liao² tzu¹ pen³ chieh¹ chi²** ~僚資本階級 *n.* bureaucratic-capitalist class**

~**neng²** ~能 *n.* sense

~**ssu¹** ~司 *n.* lawsuit

~**yüan²** ~員 *n.* official

KUAN¹ 觀 *v.* look, consider; *n.* view, sight
　~**chung⁴** ~衆 *n.* audience (confer)
　~**ch'a²** ~察 *v.* observe
　~**nien⁴** ~念 *n.* idea
　~**ts'e⁴** ~測 *v.* observe
KUAN³ 館 *n.* restaurant, guest house, room
KUAN³ 管 *n.* tube, pipe; *v.* govern, rule
　~**chang⁴** ~帳 *n.* cashier
　~**chih⁴** ~制 *v.* control
　~**li³** ~理 *v.* manage; *n.* administration
　~**li³ ch'üan²** ~理權 *n.* control
　~**li³ tan¹ wei⁴** ~理單位 *n.* administrative unit
　~**li³ yüan²** ~理員 *n.* manager
　~**shih⁴** ~事 *n.* steward
KUAN⁴ 慣 *a.* habitual; *adv.* usually
　~**ch'ang²** ~常 *adv.* usually, always
　~**hsing⁴** ~性 *n.* inertia
　~**li⁴** ~例 *n.* habit, custom
　~**yung⁴** ~用 *n.* usage
　~**yü²** ~於 *v.* be used to
KUANG¹ 光 *n.* light, brightness, glory
　~**fu⁴** ~復 *v.* recover by conquest
　~**hua²** ~滑 *a.* smooth
　~**hui¹** ~輝 *a.* brilliant
　~**hsien⁴** ~線 *n.* ray
　~**hsüeh²** ~學 *n.* optics
　~**jung²** ~榮 *n.* glory, honor
　~**lun²** ~輪 *n.* halo
　~**ming²** ~明 *a.* bright
　~**tse⁴** ~澤 *n.* luster; *a.* lustrous
　~**ts'ai³** ~彩 *n.* splendor
　~**yin¹** ~陰 *n.* time
KUANG³ 広 *a.* wide, broad, large
　~**kao⁴** ~告 *v.* advertise; *n.* advertisement
　~**po⁴** ~播 *n.* & *v.* broadcast
　~**po⁴ tien¹ t'ai²** ~播電臺 *n.* broadcasting station
　~**po⁴ yüan²** ~播員 *n.* announcer
　~**ta⁴** ~大 *a.* vast
KUEI¹ 規 *n.* compass, rule, custom
　~**chü⁴** ~矩 *n.* regulation
　~**ch'üan⁴** ~勸 *v.* advise

103

~**fan⁴** ~範 *n.* model, standard

~**ting⁴** ~定 *n.* regulation; *a.* authorized

~**ting⁴ fu² chuang¹** ~定服裝 *n.* prescribed uniform

KUEI¹ 歸 *v.* return, restore, belong to

~**hua⁴** ~化 *v.* naturalize; *n.* naturalization

~**shun⁴** ~順 *v.* surrender

~**t'ien¹** ~天 *v.* die; *n.* death

KUEI³ 鬼 *n.* ghost, devil

~**hua⁴** ~話 *n.* lying

~**huo³** ~火 *n.* will-o'-the-wisp, jack-o'-lantern

~**kuai⁴** ~怪 *n.* devil, demon

KUEI⁴ 貴 *a.* honorable, noble, dignified, costly, precious

~**chung⁴** ~重 *a.* precious

~**tsu²** ~族 *n.* aristocrat, noble

~**tsu² chih⁴ tu⁴** ~族制度 *n*, aristocracy, nobility

KUEI⁴ 櫃 *n.* box, case, chest

~**t'ai²** ~枱 *v.* store counter

KUN³ 滾 *v.* boil, roll, move back

~**ch'u¹ ch'ü⁴** ~出去 *v.* get out

~**k'ai¹** ~開 *v.* get away

~**shui³** ~水 *n.* boiling water

KUN⁴ 棍 *n.* stick, rowdy, club

~**pang⁴** ~棒 *n.* club, stick

~**t'u²** ~徒 *n.* rascal

~**tzu¹** ~子 *n.* stick

KUNG¹ 工 *n.* work, job, labor

~**chiang⁴** ~匠 *n.* artisan, craftsman

~**chü⁴** ~具 *n.* tool, instrument

~**ch'ang³** ~場 *n.* workshop

~**ch'ang³** ~廠 *n.* factory, plant, mill

~**ch'eng²** ~程 *n.* construction work

~**ch'eng² shih¹** ~程師 *n.* engineer

~**hui⁴** ~會 *n.* labor union

~**jen²** ~人 *n.* workman, laborer

~**jen² chieh¹ chi²** ~人階級 *n.* working class**

~**jen² yeh⁴ yü² wen² hua⁴ hsüeh⁴ hsiao⁴** ~人業餘文化學校 *n.* Workers' Spare Time Literacy School**

~**nung² hung² chün¹** ~農紅軍 *n.* Workers' and

104

Peasants' Communist Army**

~**ping¹** ～兵 *n.* engineer troops

~**ping¹ hsüeh² hsiao¹** ～兵學校 *n.* Engineering School*

~**shang¹ yeh⁴ lien² ho² hui⁴** ～商業聯合會 *n.* Federation of Industry and Commerce**

~**t'ou²** ～頭 *n.* foreman

~**tso⁴** ～作 *n.* work

~**tzu¹** ～資 *n.* wages

~**yeh⁴** ～業 *n.* industry; *a.* industrial

KUNG¹ 公 *a.* public, open

~**an¹ pu⁴** ～安部 *n.* Ministry of Public Safety**

~**chai⁴** ～債 *n.* public loan

~**chai⁴ ch'üan⁴** ～債券 *n.* bond

~**cheng¹ jen²** ～證人 *n.* notary public, notary

~**chi¹ chin¹** ～積金 *n.* reserve fund

~**chih²** ～職 *n.* public duty

~**chin¹** ～斤 *n.* kilogram

~**chu³** ～主 *n.* princess

~**chüeh²** ～爵 *n.* Duke

~**ch'an³** ～産 *n.* government property

~**fei⁴** ～費 *n.* public expenditure

~**fen¹** ～分 *n.* centimeter

~**kuan³** ～館 *n.* residence, mansion

~**kung¹** ～公 *n.* father-in-law (woman's)

~**kung⁴** ～共 *a.* common, public

~**kung⁴ ch'i⁴ ch'e¹** ～共汽車 *n.* bus

~**kung⁴ t'u² shu¹ kuan³** ～共圖書館 *n.* public library

~**kung⁴ wei⁴ sheng¹** ～共衛生 *n.* public health

~**k'ai¹ pi⁴ mi⁴** ～開祕密 *n.* open secret

~**li³** ～理 *n.* axiom

~**li³** ～里 *n.* kilometer

~**li⁴** ～例 *n.* regulation

~**lu⁴** ～路 *n.* highroad, highway

~**min²** ～民 *n.* citizen

~**pao⁴** ～報 *n.* bulletin

~**pu⁴** ～布 *v.* proclaim, declare publicly

~**p'ing²** ～平 *a.* fair

~**shih⁴** ～式 *n.* formula

~**shih⁴** ～事 *n.* official business

105

~**shih⁴** ~使 *n.* vice ambassador

~**shih⁴ kuan³** ~使館 *n.* legation

~**ssu¹** ~司 *n.* company

~**te²** ~德 *a.* public-spirited

~**wen²** ~文 *n.* official documents

~**wu⁴** ~務 *n.* public affair, official business

~**yung⁴ shih⁴ yeh⁴** ~用事業 *n.* public utility

~**yü⁴** ~寓 *n.* apartment house

~**yüan²** ~園 *n.* park

KUNG¹ 功 *n.* merit, achievement, honor; *a.* meritorious

~**k'o⁴** ~課 *n.* lesson

~**k'o⁴ piao³** ~課表 *n.* curriculum table

~**yung⁴** ~用 *n.* function, use

KUNG¹ 攻 *v.* attack

~**chi¹** ~擊 *n. & v.* attack

~**fan⁴** ~犯 *v.* invade, attack

~**tu²** ~讀 *v.* study

~**wei²** ~圍 besiege

KUNG¹ 供 *v.* supply, provide, confess. ~⁴ *v.* offer

~**¹ chi³** ~給 *v.* supply

~**chi³ chih⁴** ~給制 *n.* A system of providing free board and lodging for government officials and employees with a small amount of money for miscellaneous expenses**

~**tz'u²** ~詞 *n.* confession

~**⁴ feng⁴** ~奉 *v.* devote

~**hsien⁴** ~献 *n.* devotion, dedication

~**yang³** ~養 *v.* maintain (provide for)

KUNG⁴ 共 *v.* share; *adv.* altogether, wholly, entirely

~**ch'an³ chu³ i⁴** ~産主義 *n.* Communism

~**ch'an³ tang³** ~産黨 *n.* Communist Party

~**ch'an³ tang³ yüan²** ~産黨員 *n.* Communist

~**ho² kuo²** ~和國 *n.* republic

~**kan⁴** ~幹 *n.* Communist cadre

~**ming²** ~鳴 *n.* resonance

~**t'ung²** ~同 *adv.* together

~**t'ung² kang¹ ling³** ~同綱領 *n.* Common Programme**

KUO¹ 鍋 *n.* pot, boiler, kettle

KUO² 國 *n.* nation, state, country

~**chai⁴** ~債 *n.* national debts

~**chi²** ~籍 *n.* nationality

~**chi⁴** ~際 *a.* international

~**chi⁴ chu³ i⁴** ~際主義 *n.* internationalism

~**chi⁴ fa³ t'ing²** ~際法廷 *n.* International Court of Justice

~**chi⁴ fu⁴ nü³ chieh²** ~際婦女節 *n.* International Woman's Day

~**chi⁴ hua⁴** ~際化 *v.* internationalize

~**chi⁴ huo⁴ pi⁴ chi¹ chin¹ hui⁴** ~際貨幣基金會 *n.* international monetary fund

~**chi⁴ ko¹** ~際歌 *n.* Internationale

~**chi⁴ kuan¹ hsi⁴** ~際關係 *n.* international relations

~**chi⁴ kung¹ fa³** ~際公法 *n.* international law

~**chi⁴ lien² meng²** ~際聯盟 *n.* League of Nations

~**chi⁴ tsu³ chih¹** ~際組織 *n.* international organization

~**chi⁴ yü³** ~際語 *n.* international language

~**chia¹ chi⁴ hua⁴ wei³ yüan² hui⁴** ~家計劃委員会 *n.* State Planning Committee**

~**chia¹ chu³ i⁴** ~家主義 *n.* nationalism

~**chia¹ hua⁴** ~家化 *v.* nationalize

~**chia¹ she⁴ hui⁴ chu³ i⁴** ~家社會主義 *n.* state socialism

~**chia¹ tzu¹ pen³ chu³ i⁴** ~家資本主義 *n.* state capitalism**

~**chia¹ yin² hang²** ~家銀行 *n.* national bank

~**ch'i²** ~旗 *n.* national flag

~**fang²** ~防 *n.* national defense

~**fang² i¹ hsüeh² yüan⁴** ~防醫學院 *n.* National Defense Medical Hospital*

~**fang² pu⁴** ~防部 *n.* Department of Defense (*U.S.*)

~**fang² ta⁴ hsüeh²** ~防大学 *n.* National Defense College*

~**hui¹** ~徽 *n.* national emblem

~**hui⁴** ~會 *n.* parliament

~**ko¹** ~歌 *n.* national anthem

~k'u⁴ ~庫 n. treasury (nation)

~min² ~民 n. citizen, people

~min² cheng⁴ fu³ ~民政府 n. National Government

~min² ta⁴ hui⁴ ~民大會 n. National Assembly

~min² tang³ ~民黨 n. Kuomintang

~shih⁴ fan⁴ ~事犯 n. political criminal

~tu¹ ~都 n. national capital

~t'u³ ~土 n. territory

~wai⁴ mao⁴ i⁴ ~外貿易 n. foreign trade

~wang² ~王 n. king, ruler

~wu⁴ ch'ing¹ ~務卿 n. Secretary of State(*U.S.*)

~wu⁴ yüan⁴ ~務院 n. Department of State (*U.S.*)

~ying² nung² ch'ang³ ~營農場 n. State Farm**

~yü³ ~語 n. national language

KUO³ 果 n. fruit, result, effect; *a.* resolute

~chiang⁴ ~醬 n. jam, jelly

~jan² ~然 *adv.* surely, certainly

~shih² ~實 n. fruit

~tuan⁴ ~斷 n. decision

~yüan² ~園 n. orchard

KUO⁴ 過 *v.* pass, cross; *n.* fault, error; *adv.* too

~ch'ü⁴ ~去 n. & *a.* past

~hou⁴ ~後 *adv.* afterward, later

~shih¹ ~失 n. fault, offense

~tu⁴ ~度 *a.* excessive

~tu⁴ ch'i¹ ~度期 *n.* transition period

~yü² ~於 *prep.* over, above

K'

K'AI¹ 開 *v.* open, begin; *n.* boil

~chan⁴ ~戰 n. outbreak of war

~ch'iang¹ ~鎗 *v.* fire (gun)

~hua¹ ~花 *v.* bloom

~hua⁴ ~化 *a.* civilized

~hui⁴ ~會 *v.* hold a meeting

~hsiao³ ch'ai¹ ~小差 *v.* desert (*mil.*)

~kuan¹ ~關 n. switch (elec.)

~**k'en³** ~墾 *v.* cultivate

~**k'uang⁴** ~鑛 *v.* open mines

~**k'uo⁴ ti⁴** ~濶地 *n.* open terrain

~**she⁴** ~設 *v.* establish, open

~**shih³** ~始 *v.* begin, start; *n.* beginning

~**shih⁴** ~釋 *v.* release

~**shui³** ~水 *n.* boiled water

~**tao¹** ~刀 *n.* operation (*med.*)

~**t'ing²** ~庭 *v.* open the court

~**yao⁴ fang¹** ~葯方 *v.* prescribe (*med.*)

K'AN⁴ 看 *v.* see, look at. ~¹ *v.* watch

~¹ **hu⁴** ~護 *v.* look after

~**hu⁴ fu⁴** ~護婦 *n.* nurse

~**men²** ~門 *n.* doorkeeper, doorman

~**shou³** ~守 *v.* guard, watch

~⁴ **wang⁴** ~望 *v.* visit

K'ANG¹ 康 *n.* peace, repose, prosperity

~**chien⁴** ~健 *a.* healthy

~**le⁴** 樂 *a.* happy

~**ning²** ~寧 *n.* peaceful happiness and abundance

K'ANG⁴ 抗 *v.* resist, oppose

~**chü⁴** ~拒 *v.* resist

~**i⁴** ~議 *n.* & *v.* protest; *v.* object

~**jih⁴ min² tsu² t'ung³ i¹ chen⁴ hsien⁴** ~日民
族統一陣線 *n.* Anti-Japanese National United
Front**

~**mei³ yüan² ch'ao² yün⁴ tung⁴** ~美援朝運動 *n.*
Resist-America and Aid-Korea Movement**

~**pien⁴** ~辯 *n.* defense (lawsuit)

K'AO³ 考 *v.* test, examine; *n.* test, examination

~**cheng⁴** ~證 *v.* prove; *n.* verification

~**ch'a²** ~查 *v.* investigate

~**lü⁴** ~慮 *v.* consider

~**shih⁴** ~試 *n.* examination (test)

~**shih⁴ yüan⁴** ~試院 *n.* Examination Yuan*

K'AO⁴ 靠 *v.* lean on, trust; *a.* near to

~**chin⁴** ~近 *a.* near to

~**pu² chu⁴** ~不住 *a.* unreliable

~**te² chu⁴** ~得住 *a.* reliable, trustworthy

K'EN³ 肯 *v.* consent, agree, permit, allow

~**hsü³** ~許 *v.* assent, agree

~**ting⁴** ～定 *a.* certain, sure; *adv.* certainly, surely

K'O¹ 科 *n.* family department (biology), section, arm, branch (army)

~**fa²** ～罰 *v.* punish; *n.* punishment

~**hsüeh²** ～學 *n.* science

~**hsüeh² chia¹** ～學家 *n.* scientist

~**hsüeh² huo² tung⁴** ～學活動 *n.* scientific activity

~**hsüeh² kuan³ li³** ～學管理 *n.* scientific management

~**hsüeh² yüan⁴** ～學院 *n.* Academia Sinica**

~**yüan²** ～員 *n.* clerk

K'O¹ 刻 *v.* carve, sculpture, engrave; ～⁴ *n.* one fourth of an hour

~**⁴ k'u³** ～苦 *v.* mortify (overcome bodily desires)

~**po²** ～薄 *a.* cruel

K'O² 顆 *n.* (numerative of small round things)

K'O³ 可 *v. aux.* may, can

~**hsiao⁴** ～笑 *a.* absurd, foolish, ridiculous

~**i³** ～以 *v. aux.* & *v.* may

~**jen²** ～人 *a.* charming

~**k'ao⁴** ～靠 *a.* reliable; *n.* reliability

~**lien²** ～憐 *a.* piteous, pitiful

~**neng²** ～能 *n.* possibility; *a.* possible

~**p'a⁴** ～怕 *a.* dreadful, terrible

~**e⁴** ～惡 *a.* detestable

K'O³ 渴 *n.* thirst; *a.* thirsty

~**mu⁴** ～慕 *v.* desire earnestly

~**nien⁴** ～念 *v.* long for

~**wang⁴** ～望 *v.* expect

K'O⁴ 客 *n.* guest, visitor

~**chan⁴** ～棧 *n.* hotel, inn

~**chi¹** ～機 *n.* passenger airplane

~**ch'e¹** ～車 *n.* passenger train

~**ch'i⁴** ～氣 *a.* polite, courteous

~**jen²** ～人 *n.* guest, visitor

~**kuan¹** ～觀 *a.* objective (impersonal)

~**kuan¹ chu³ i⁴** ～觀主義 *n.* objectivism

~**t'ing¹** ～廳 *n.* parlor, sitting room

K'O⁴ 課 *n.* lesson, exercise, task

~**ch'eng²** ~程 *n.* curriculum

~**ch'eng² piao³** ~程表 *n.* curriculum table

K'O⁴ 克 *v.* overcome, conquer

~**fu²** ~服 *v.* conquer

~**fu⁴** ~復 *v.* recapture

~**nan²** ~難 *v.* conquer difficulties

K'OU³ 口 *n.* mouth, opening, gap, entrance

~**an⁴** 岸 *n.* port

~**chi¹** ~吃 *n.* & *v.* stammer

~**chiao³** ~角 *n.* & *v.* quarrel

~**ch'in²** ~琴 *n.* harmonica

~**hao⁴** ~號 *n.* slogan

~**ling⁴** 令 *n.* command, password (*mil.*)

~**shih⁴** ~試 *n.* oral examination

~**ts'ai²** ~才 *n.* eloquence

~**wei⁴** ~味 *n.* taste

K'OU⁴ 扣 *n.* button; *v.* knock, rap

~**chu⁴** ~住 *n.* fasten with buttons

~**liu²** ~留 *v.* detain; *n.* detention

~**wen⁴** ~問 *v.* ask, inquire

K'U¹ 哭 *v.* weep, cry

~**ch'i⁴** ~泣 *v.* weep

K'U³ 苦 *a.* painful; *n.* pain

~**ch'u³** ~楚 *n.* torture, distress

~**kung¹** ~工 *n.* hard work

~**li⁴** ~力 *n.* coolie

~**t'ung⁴** ~痛 *n.* pain

K'U⁴ 褲 *n.* trousers, pantaloons

K'UA³ 垮 *v.* fail, collapse, defeat

K'UAI¹ 塊 *n.* clod, lump

K'UAI⁴ 快 *a.* fast, quick, rapid, swift

~**chieh²** ~捷 *adv.* promptly

~**ch'e¹** ~車 *n.* express train

~**hsin⁴** ~信 *n.* express mail

~**le⁴** ~樂 *n.* happiness; *a.* happy

~**p'ao³** ~跑 *v.* run quickly

K'UAI⁴ 會 *see* HUI⁴

K'UAN¹ 寬 *a.* broad, large, indulgent

~**hou⁴** ~厚 *a.* kind

~**jung²** ~容 *v.* tolerate; *n.* toleration

~**shu⁴** ~恕 *v.* excuse

111

~ta⁴ ~大 *a.* wide, broad, spacious

~wei⁴ ~慰 *v.* console

~yü² ~餘 *a.* abundant

K'UAN³ 款 *n.* article, amount of money; *v.* entertain

~liu² ~留 *v.* detain

~shih⁴ ~式 *n.* style, pattern

~tai⁴ ~待 *v.* treat well

K'UANG¹ 筐 *n.* basket

K'UANG² 狂 *a.* crazy, violent, mad

~feng¹ ~風 *n.* gust, hurricane

~huan¹ chieh² ~歡節 *n.* carnival (festival)

~hsi³ ~喜 *v.* make extremely joyful

~hsiang³ ~想 *n.* extravagant thoughts

~hsiang³ ch'ü³ ~想曲 *n.* fantasia

~hsiao⁴ ~笑 *v.* laugh foolishly

~nu⁴ ~怒 *n.* fury, frenzy

~pao⁴ ~暴 *a.* violent; *n.* violence

~t'u² ~徒 *n.* profligate

~yen² ~言 *n.* nonsense

~yin³ ~飲 *v.* guzzle

K'UANG⁴ 礦 *n.* mine, ore; *a.* mineral

~hsüeh² chia¹ ~學家 *n.* mineralogist

~kung¹ ~工 *n.* miner

~k'eng¹ ~坑 *n.* mine shaft

~miao² ~苗 *n.* ore

~wu⁴ ~物 *n.* mineral

~wu⁴ hsüeh² ~物學 *n.* mineralogy

~yu² ~油 *n.* mineral oil

K'UANG⁴ 況 *adv.* moreover, also, besides, in addition

~ch'ieh³ ~且 *adv.* moreover, besides

K'UEI¹ 虧 *n.* wanting, defect; *v.* injure, harm

~ch'ien⁴ ~欠 *v.* be in debt

~hsin¹ ~心 *a.* discreditable

~k'ung¹ ~空 *n.* deficit, shortage

K'UN⁴ 困 *n.* poverty, confinement; *v.* confine; *a.* confined, fatigued

~k'u³ ~苦 *n.* poverty

~nan² ~難 *n.* difficulty

~tou⁴ ~鬪 *v.* resist desperately

K'UNG¹ 空 *a.* empty, vacant

~**chan⁴** ~戰 *n.* aerial combat

~**chien¹** ~間 *n.* space

~**chung¹ chao⁴ hsiang⁴** ~中照相 *n.* aerial photography

~**chung¹ chen¹ ch'a²** ~中偵察 *n.* air reconnaissance

~**chung¹ fang² yü⁴** ~中防禦 *n.* air defense (planes)

~**chung¹ kuan¹ ts'e⁴** ~中觀測 *n.* aerial observation

~**chung¹ kung¹ chi¹** ~中攻擊 *n.* air attack

~**chün¹ chi¹ hsieh⁴ hsüeh² hsiao⁴** ~軍機械學校 *n.* Air Force Mechanics School*

~**chün¹ chi¹ ti⁴** ~軍基地 *n.* air base

~**chün¹ chih³ hui¹ ts'an¹ mou² hsüeh² hsiao⁴** ~軍指揮參謀學校 *n.* Air Force Command and Staff College*

~**chün¹ chün¹ kuan¹ hsüeh² hsiao⁴** ~軍軍官學校 *n.* Air Force Academy*

~**chün¹ hsüeh² sheng¹** ~軍學生 *n.* aviation cadet

~**chün¹ t'ung¹ hsin⁴ hsüeh² hsiao⁴** ~軍通信學校 *n.* Air Force Signal School*

~**chün¹ tsung³ ssu¹ ling⁴ pu⁴** ~軍總司令部 *n.* Air Force Headquarters*

~**chün¹ wu³ kuan¹** ~軍武官 *n.* air attache

~**chün¹ yü⁴ pei⁴ hsüeh² hsiao⁴** ~軍豫備學校 *n.* Air Force Preparatory School*

~**ch'i⁴** ~氣 *n.* air

~**hsi²** ~襲 *n.* air raid

~**hsi² ching³ pao⁴** ~襲警報 *n.* air raid alarm

~**pao¹** ~包 *n.* blank ammunition

~**yün⁴** ~運 *n.* airborne

~**yün⁴ pu⁴ tui⁴** ~運部隊 *n.* airborne troops

K'UNG³ 恐 *conj.* lest

~**ho⁴** ~嚇 *v.* intimidate; *n.* intimidation

~**huang¹** ~慌 *n.* panic

~**pu⁴** ~怖 *a.* terrible, dreadful; *n.* terror

K'UNG³ 孔 *n.* hole, opening

~**chiao⁴** ~教 *n.* Confucianism

~**ch'iao³** ~雀 *n.* peacock

113

~**fu¹ tzu³** 夫子 *n.* Confucius

~**tzu³ te¹** 子的 *n.* Confucian

K'UO⁴ 擴 *v.* stretch, expand

~**chang¹** 張 *v.* expand

~**ch'ung¹** 充 *v.* expand, extend

~**ta⁴** ～大 *v.* magnify

~**ta⁴ ch'i⁴** ～大器 *n.* loudspeaker

L

LA¹ 拉 *v.* drag, pull, draw

~**ch'e³** ～扯 *v.* pull and drag

~**fa¹** ～發 *n.* detonation by pulling

LA¹ 啦 [a final particle]

LA⁴ 辣 *a.* acrid, pungent, biting

~**chiao¹** ～椒 *n.* pepper

~**shou³** ～手 *a.* cruel, difficult

~**wei⁴** ～味 *a.* pungent

LAI² 來 *v.* come, arrive

~**fu⁴ ch'iang¹** ～復鎗 *n.* rifle

~**fu⁴ hsien⁴** ～復線 *n.* rifling

~**hui² p'iao⁴** ～回票 *n.* round trip ticket

~**jen²** ～人 *n.* comer

~**yüan²** ～源 *n.* source, origin

LAN² 籃 *n.* basket

~**ch'iu²** ～球 *n.* basketball

LAN² 藍 *n.* blue, indigo

~**se⁴** ～色 *n. & a.* blue

~**t'ien¹** ～天 *n.* blue sky

LAN³ 懶 *n.* idleness; *a.* lazy, remiss

~**fu⁴** ～婦 *n.* slut

~**jen²** ～人 *n.* idler

~**to⁴** ～惰 *a.* lazy

LAN⁴ 爛 *a.* rotten, ruined, overcooked

~**chih³** ～紙 *n.* waste paper

~**man⁴** ～縵 *a.* splendid, brilliant

~**pu⁴** ～布 *n.* rag

LANG⁴ 浪 *n.* wave, billow

~**fei⁴** ～費 *v.* squander, waste

~**hua¹** ～花 *n.* spray

~man⁴ ~漫 *a.* romantic ; *n.* romance
~man⁴ chu³ i⁴ ~漫主義 *n.* romanticism
~tang⁴ ~蕩 *a.* dissipated
~tzu³ ~子 *n.* spendthrift

LAO² 勞 *n.* labor ; *v.* toil. ~4 *v.* reward
~hsin¹ ~心 *n.* labor
~kung¹ pu⁴ ~工部 *n.* Department of Labor (*U.S.*)
~kung¹ tui⁴ ~工隊 *n.* labor troops
~k'u³ ~苦 *a.* toilsome, laborious ; *n.* hardship
~li⁴ ~力 *n.* labor
~mo² ~模 *n.* Labor Model**
~tung⁴ ~動 *n.* labor
~tung⁴ chieh¹ chi² ~動階級 *n.* labor class
~tung⁴ chieh² ~動節 *n.* Labor Day
~tung⁴ mo² fan⁴ ~動模範 *n.* Labor Model**
~tung⁴ pao³ hsien³ t'iao² li⁴ ~動保險條例 *n.* Labor Insurance Regulations**
~tung⁴ ying¹ hsiung² ~動英雄 *n.* Labor Hero**
~⁴ chün¹ yün⁴ tung⁴ ~軍運動 *n.* A Comfort-the-Soldiers Movement

LAO³ 老 *a.* old, aged
~chu³ ku⁴ ~主顧 *n.* patron, regular customer
~hu³ ~虎 *n.* tiger
~jo⁴ ~弱 *a.* old and weak
~nien² ~年 *n.* old age
~pao³ ~鴇 *n.* procuress
~p'o² ~婆 *n.* wife
~shu³ ~鼠 *n.* mouse, rat
~ta⁴ ko¹ ~大哥 *n.* Big Brother (Russia)**
~tzu³ ~子 *n.* Lao-tse (Chinese philosopher)
~yu³ ~友 *n.* old friend

LAO⁴ 落 *v.* fall, drop
~ch'eng² ~成 *n.* completion (building)
~hsüan³ ~選 *v.* fail in election
~lei⁴ ~淚 *v.* weep
~wu³ ~伍 *a.* retrogressive
~yeh⁴ ~葉 *n.* fall of the leaf
~yü³ ~雨 *v.* rain
~tui⁴ ~隊 *n.* band, orchestra, ensemble

LE⁴ 樂 *a.* happy, joyful, pleasant ; *n.* pleasure, joy.

YÜEH⁴ 樂 *n.* music. YAO⁴ *v.* rejoice
~i⁴ ~意 *adv.* willingly
~kuan¹ ~觀 *a.* optimistic; *n.* optimism
~t'ien¹ p'ai⁴ ~天派 *n.* optimist
yüeh⁴ ch'i⁴ ~器 *n.* musical instruments
~p'u³ ~譜 *n.* score (music)
LEI² 雷 *n.* thunder
~ming² ~鳴 *n.* thunderclap
~tien⁴ ~電 *n.* thunderbolt
~yü³ ~雨 *n.* thunderstorm
~yün² ~雲 *n.* thundercloud
LEI³ 累 *adv.* often, repeatedly. ~⁴ *v.* involve, tire
~chi¹ ~積 *v.* accumulate
LEI⁴ 淚 *n.* tear
LEI⁴ 類 *n.* species, kind, class
~pieh² ~別 *v.* classify; *n.* classification
~ssu⁴ ~似 *a.* similar
LENG³ 冷 *a.* cold, chilly
~chan⁴ ~戰 *n.* cold war
~ching⁴ ~靜 *a.* quiet
~hsiao⁴ ~笑 *v.* sneer
~hsüeh⁴ ~血 *a.* cold-blooded
~shui³ yü⁴ ~水浴 *n.* cold bath
~tan⁴ ~淡 *a.* indifferent, cold
LI² 離 *n.* distance; *v.* leave, separate
~ch'i² ~奇 *a.* eccentric
~ch'i⁴ ~棄 *v.* desert
~ho² ~合 *n.* parting or meeting
~hun¹ ~婚 *n.* & *v.* divorce
~pieh² ~別 *v.* depart, leave; *n.* departure
LI² 犁 *n.* plow
~tao¹ ~刀 *n.* scythe
~t'ien² ~田 *v.* plow
LI³ 理 *n.* reason, law; *v.* arrange, manage
~chieh³ ~解 *n.* understanding
~fa³ ~髮 *n.* haircut
~fa³ chiang⁴ ~髮匠 *n.* barber
~fa³ tien⁴ ~髮店 *n.* barbershop
~hua⁴ ~化 *n.* physics and chemistry
~hui⁴ ~會 *v.* apprehend
~hsiang³ ~想 *n.* idea; *a.* ideal

116

~hsiang³ chia¹ ~想家 *n.* idealist

~hsing⁴ ~性 *n.* reason

~hsüeh² yüan⁴ ~學院 *n.* college of science

~k'o¹ ~科 *n.* natural science

~lun⁴ ~論 *n.* theory ; *a.* theoretical, theoretic

~yu² ~由 *n.* reason

LI³ 裡 *n.* inside, lining ; *a.* inner

LI³ 李 *n.* plum

LI³ 禮 *n.* etiquette, ceremony, gift, worship, present

~chieh² ~節 *n.* formality

~fu² ~服 *n.* full dress

~mao⁴ ~貌 *n.* manners

~pai⁴ ~拜 *n. & v.* worship

~pai⁴ erh⁴ ~拜二 *n.* Tuesday

~pai⁴ i¹ ~拜一 *n.* Monday

~pai⁴ jih⁴ ~拜日 *n.* Sunday

~pai⁴ liu⁴ ~拜六 *n.* Saturday

~pai⁴ san¹ ~拜三 *n.* Wednesday

~pai⁴ ssu⁴ ~拜四 *n.* Thursday

~pai⁴ t'ang² ~拜堂 *n.* church

~pai⁴ wu³ ~拜五 *n.* Friday

~wu⁴ ~物 *n.* present, gift

LI³ 里 *n.* Chinese measure for old standard of length, about one third mile

LI⁴ 力 *n.* strength, power, force, energy, vigor

~ch'i⁴ ~氣 *n.* vigor, strength

~ch'iang² ~強 *a.* strong

~liang⁴ ~量 *n.* power, force, strength

~ta⁴ ~大 *a.* powerful

LI⁴ 利 *v.* benefit ; *n.* profit

~chi³ ~己 *a.* selfish

~chi³ chu³ i⁴ ~己主義 *n.* egoism, selfishness

~hai⁴ ~害 *a.* severe, strict

~hsi² ~息 *a.* interest (money)

~i⁴ ~益 *n.* advantage, benefit, profit

~t'o¹ chu³ i⁴ ~他主義 *n.* altruism

~yung⁴ ~用 *v.* utilize

LI⁴ 立 *v.* stand, erect, set up, establish ; *a.* erect, upright

~an⁴ ~案 *v.* register

117

~fa³ ~法 *a.* lawmaking, legislative; *n.* legislation

~fa³ yüan⁴ ~法院 *n.* Legislative Yuan*

~fang¹ ken¹ ~方根 *n.* cubic root

~hsien⁴ ~憲 *v.* establish a constitution

~k'o⁴ ~刻 *a.* immediate; *adv.* immediately

~t'i³ ~體 *n.* cubic, solid

LI⁴ 例 *n.* precedent, example, regulation

~hsing² kung¹ shih⁴ ~行公事 *n.* routine matters (*off.*)

~ju² ~如 *adv.* for instance, for example

~wai⁴ ~外 *n.* exception

LI⁴ 粒 *n.* grain, kernel

LI⁴ 歷 *a.* successive; *v.* experience

~ch'ao² ~朝 *n.* successive dynasties

~shih³ ~史 *n.* history, chronicle

~shih³ chia¹ ~史家 *n.* historian

~tai⁴ ~代 *n.* successive generations

LI⁴ 麗 *a.* elegant, graceful, beautiful

~jen² ~人 *n.* feminine beauty

LI⁴ 隸 *n.* underling, subordinate; *v.* be attached to

~shu³ ~屬 *v.* be attached to (*mil.*)

LIANG² 糧 *n.* food, ration, grain, provisions, fodder, forage

~shih² ~食 *n.* food, provisions

~shih² pu⁴ ~食部 *n.* Ministry of Food**

~ts'ao³ ~草 *n.* fodder, forage

LIANG² 量 *v.* measure, consider. **~⁴** *n.* quantity

LIANG² 良 *a.* good, virtuous

~chih¹ ~知 *n.* intuition

~hsin¹ ~心 *n.* conscience

~jen² ~人 *n.* good man, husband

~shan⁴ ~善 *a.* good, fine, nice

~yao⁴ ~藥 *n.* good medicine

~yen² ~言 *n.* good advice

~yu³ ~友 *n.* good friend

LIANG² 涼 *a.* cool

~shuang³ ~爽 *a.* cool

LIANG² 梁 *n.* sorghum, bridge, beam

LIANG³ 兩 *a.* two, both; *n.* tael (Chinese weight for 37.8 grams)

118

~chiao³ kuei¹ ～脚規 *n.* compass

~tz'u⁴ ～次 *adv.* twice

LIANG⁴ 亮 *a.* bright, clear, brilliant

~kuang¹ ～光 *n.* light

LIAO³ 了 *a.* finished, ended, completed, done

~chieh² ～結 *a.* finished, ended, concluded; *v.* settle, conclude

~chieh³ ～解 *n.* understanding; *v.* understand

~pu⁴ ch'i³ ～不起 *a.* extraordinary; *adv.* extraordinarily

LIAO⁴ 料 *n.* material; *v.* imagine

~hsiang³ ～想 *v.* guess, imagine

~li³ ～理 *v.* arrange

LIEH⁴ 列 *v.* arrange, put in the proper order; *n.* row, file

~c'he¹ ～車 *n.* train

~ch'iang² ～強 *n.* world powers

~hsi² ～席 *v.* attend

~ping¹ ～兵 *n.* private (army)

LIEH⁴ 烈 *a.* fierce, violent

~hsing⁴ ～性 *a.* vicious horse

~shih⁴ ～士 *n.* patriot, hero

LIEH⁴ 劣 *a.* vile, bad, low, mean, poor, inferior; *n.* inferiority

~huo⁴ ～貨 *n.* low-grade goods

~hsing² ～行 *n.* bad behavior, misconduct

~shen¹ ～紳 *n.* deprived gentry

LIEN² 聯 *v.* connect, assemble, unite, combine

~chün¹ ～軍 *n.* allied armies

~ho² ～合 *v.* join, unite; *a.* joint

~ho² cheng⁴ fu³ ～合政府 *n.* coalition government

~ho² ch'in² wu⁴ tsung³ ssu¹ ling⁴ pu⁴ ～合勤務總司令部 *n.* Combined Service Forces Headquarters

~ho² kuo² ～合國 *n.* United Nations

~lei⁴ ～累 *v.* implicate, involve (in difficulty)

~lo⁴ ～絡 *n.* liaison, contact; *v.* maintain contact

~lo⁴ kuan¹ ～絡官 *n.* liaison officer

LIEN² 連 *n.* company (army); *v.* connect, continue

119

~chang³ ~長 *n.* company commander, battery commander

~chieh¹ ~接 *v.* connect; *n.* coupling, join

~ho² ~合 *v.* combine; *a.* joint

~hsi⁴ ~繫 *v.* contact

~hsü⁴ ~續 *v.* continue

~ho² tso⁴ chan⁴ ~合作戰 *n.* combined operations, joint operations

~hsiang³ ~想 *v.* associate (in thought)

~lo⁴ ~絡 *v.* affiliate

~meng² ~盟 *n.* alliance

~pang¹ ~邦 *n.* federation

~pang¹ cheng⁴ fu³ ~邦政府 *n.* federal government

~pang¹ chu³ i⁴ ~邦主義 *n.* federalism

LIEN² 憐 *v.* pity

~ai⁴ ~愛 *v.* love, regard

~hsi² ~惜 *v.* sympathize

~min³ ~憫 *v.* pity

LIEN² 鐮 *n.* sickle

~tao¹ ~刀 *n.* scythe, sickle

LIEN³ 臉 *n.* face, honor

~hou⁴ ~厚 *a.* shameless

~mien⁴ ~面 *n.* reputation

~p'en² ~盆 *n.* washbowl, washbasin

LIEN⁴ 練 *v.* practise, train, drill

~hsi² ~習 *v.* practice, train; *n.* exercise

~hsi² pu⁴ ~習簿 *n.* exercise book

~ping¹ ~兵 *v.* train troops

LIEN⁴ 煉 *v.* refine, purify, smelt

~chih⁴ ch'ang³ ~製廠 *n.* refinery

~ju³ ~乳 *n.* condensed milk

~tan¹ shu⁴ ~丹術 *n.* alchemy

~t'ang² ~糖 *n.* refined sugar

LIN² 林 *n.* forest, wood

~hsüeh² ~學 *n.* foresty

~yeh⁴ pu⁴ ~業部 *n.* Ministry of Foresty**

LIN² 臨 *v.* attend

~pieh² ~別 *a.* farewell

~p'en² ~盆 *n.* confinement (birth)

~shih² ~時 *a.* temporary; *adv.* temporarily

~**shih² hui⁴ i⁴** ~時會議 *n.* temporary meeting

LIN² 鄰 *a.* neighboring

~**chin⁴** ~近 *a.* neighboring

~**chü¹** ~居 *n.* neighbor

~**kuo²** ~國 *n.* neighboring countries

LING² 鈴 *n.* bell

LING² 靈 *n.* soul, spiritual

~**ch'iao³** ~巧 *a.* ingenious

~**hun²** ~魂 *n.* soul

~**yen⁴** ~驗 *a.* efficacious

LING² 零 *n.* zero, naught

~**chien⁴** ~件 *n.* accessories, spare part

~**lo⁴** ~落 *a.* scattered

~**shou⁴** ~售 *n. & v.* retail

~**shou⁴ shang¹** ~售商 *n.* retailer

~**tu⁴** ~度 *n.* zero degree

~**t'ou²** ~頭 *n.* change (money)

~**yung⁴ ch'ien²** ~用錢 *n.* pocket money

LING³ 領 *n.* collar; *v.* receive, accept, lead

~**chang¹** ~章 *n.* collar insignia

~**ch'ing²** ~情 *v.* receive kindness

~**hai³** ~海 *n.* marginal sea

~**hua¹** ~花 *n.* collar pin (ornament)

~**hsiu⁴** ~袖 *n.* leader, chief, head

~**kang³** ~港 *n.* ship pilot

~**shih⁴** ~事 *n.* consul

~**shih⁴ kuan³** ~事館 *n.* consulate

~**shih⁴ ts'ai² p'an⁴ ch'üan²** ~事裁判權 *n.* consular jurisdiction

~**shou⁴** ~受 *v.* accept, receive

~**tai⁴** ~帶 *n.* necktie

~**tao³** ~導 *v.* direct, lead

~**t'u³** ~土 *n.* territory, dominion

~**t'u³ wan² cheng³** ~土完整 *n.* territorial integrity

~**tzu¹** ~子 *n.* collar

LING⁴ 令 *n.* order, command. *v.* direct, make

~**ming²** ~名 *n.* reputation

LING⁴ 另 *a.* another, extra, more

~**chia¹** ~加 *a.* additional

~**wai⁴** ~外 *n.* extra

LIU² 留 *v.* remain, stay

~**hsin¹** ~心 *v.* pay attention

~**sheng¹ chi¹** ~聲機 *n.* phonograph

LIU² 流 *v.* flow, pass

~**chih²** ~質 *n.* liquid, fluid

~**ch'ang⁴** ~暢 *a.* fluent

~**han⁴** ~汗 *v.* perspire

~**hsien⁴ hsing²** ~線型 *n.* streamline

~**hsing¹** ~星 *n.* meteor, shooting star

~**hsing²** ~行 *v.* prevail, circulate; *a.* popular, prevalent

~**hsing² kan³ mao⁴** ~行感冒 *n.* influenza

~**hsüeh⁴** ~血 *n.* bloodshed

~**lei⁴** ~淚 *v.* shed tears

~**lo⁴** ~落 *v.* wander

~**mang²** ~氓 *n.* rascal

~**pi⁴** ~弊 *n.* evil practice

~**shui³** ~水 *n.* running water

~**shui³ chang⁴** ~水帳 *n.* cashbook

~**tan⁴** ~彈 *n.* stray bullet

~**t'ung¹** ~通 *v.* circulate; *n.* circulation

~**wang²** ~亡 *a.* fugitive

~**yen²** ~言 *n.* rumor

~**yü⁴** ~域 *n.* river basin

LIU⁴ 六 *n. & a.* six

~**chiao³ hsing²** ~角形 *n.* hexagon

~**yüeh⁴** ~月 *n.* June

LOU² 樓 *n.* upper-story, tower

~**hsia⁴** ~下 *adv.* downstairs

~**shang⁴** ~上 *adv.* upstairs

~**t'i¹** ~梯 *n.* staircase, stairway, stairs

LU² 爐 *n.* stove

LU⁴ 陸 *n.* dry land, continent

~**chün¹** ~軍 *n.* army

~**chün¹ chih³ hui¹ ts'an¹ mou² hsüeh² hsiao⁴** ~軍指揮參謀學校 *n.* Army Command and Staff College*

~**chün¹ chuang¹ chia³ ping¹ hsüeh² hsiao⁴** ~軍裝甲兵學校 *n.* Armored Force School*

~**chün¹ chün¹ kuan¹ hsüeh² hsiao⁴** ~軍軍官學校 *n.* Army Academy*

122

~**chün¹ li³ chieh²** ~軍禮節 *n.* military courtesy

~**chün¹ pu⁴** ~軍部 *n.* War Department (*U.S.*)

~**chün¹ pu⁴ chang³** ~軍部長 *n.* Secretary of the Army

~**chün¹ pu⁴ ping¹ hsüeh² hsiao⁴** ~軍步兵學校 *n.* Infantry School*

~**chün¹ p'ao⁴ ping¹ hsüeh² hsiao⁴** ~軍砲兵學 校 *n.* Artillery School*

~**chün¹ tsung³ ssu¹ ling⁴** ~軍總司令 *n.* Commander in Chief (*mil.*)

~**chün¹ tsung³ ssu¹ ling⁴ pu⁴** ~軍總司令部 *n.* Ground Forces Headquarters*

~**chün¹ wu³ kuan¹** ~軍武官 *n.* military attache

~**hsü⁴** ~續 *a.* continuous; *adv.* continuously

~**k'ung¹ t'ung¹ hsin¹** ~空通信 *n.* air-ground communication

~**ti⁴** ~地 *n.* land

~**yün⁴** ~運 *n.* land transportation

LU⁴ 露 *n.* dew

~**shui³** ~水 *n.* dewdrop

~**t'ai²** ~臺 *n.* balcony

~**t'ien¹** ~天 *n.* open air

~**yen²** ~岩 *n.* exposed rock

~**ying²** ~營 *n. & v.* bivouac

~**ying² ti⁴** ~營地 *n.* bivouac area

LU⁴ 路 *n.* road, path

~**ch'eng²** ~程 *n.* journey

LUAN⁴ 亂 *n.* trouble, disorder, rebellion

~**chiao⁴** ~叫 *v.* shout

~**lun²** ~倫 *n.* incest

~**min²** ~民 *n.* lawless mob, rebel

~**shih⁴** ~世 *n.* chaotic period

LUN² 輪 *n.* wheel, circle, turn, disk; *v.* turn, revolve

~**ch'uan²** ~船 *n.* steamer, steamboat, steamship

~**liu²** ~流 *v.* reverse, rotate; *n.* rotation

~**tu⁴** ~渡 *n.* steam ferry

~**t'ai²** ~胎 *n.* tire

LUN⁴ 論 *v.* discuss, debate, criticize

~**li³ hsüeh²** ~理學 *n.* logic

~**li³ hsüeh² chia¹** ~理學家 *n.* logician

123

~**wen²** ~文 *n.* essay, thesis

LÜ² 驢 *n.* ass, donkey

LÜ³ 旅 *n.* troop, brigade

~**fei⁴** ~費 *n.* traveling expenses

~**hsing²** ~行 *n. & v.* travel

~**kuan³** ~館 *n.* hotel, inn

~**k'o⁴** ~客 *n.* traveler, passenger

LÜ⁴ 律 *n.* law, rule, regulation, code

~**chieh⁴** ~誡 *n.* commandment

~**li⁴** ~例 *n.* law

~**shih¹** ~師 *n.* lawyer, attorney

~**tien³** ~典 *n.* code

LÜ⁴ 綠 *a. & n.* green

~**ch'a²** ~茶 *n.* green tea

~**lin²** ~林 *n.* greenwood

~**se⁴** ~色 *a.* green

~**teng¹** ~燈 *n.* green traffic light

~**tou⁴** ~豆 *n.* green beans

~**yü⁴** ~玉 *n.* emerald

LÜ⁴ 率 *see* **SHUAI⁴**

LÜEH⁴ 略 *a.* simple; *adv.* briefly, simply; *v.* abbreviate

~**t'ung²** ~同 *a.* alike, similar

M

MA¹ 麼 [an interrogative particle]

MA¹ 嗎 [an interrogative form]

MA¹ 媽 *n.* mother, mamma

MA² 麻 *n.* hemp

~**ch'üeh⁴** ~雀 *n.* sparrow. ~**chiang⁴** 雀＝將 *n.* mahjong

~**mu⁴** ~木 *a.* torpid

~**pi⁴** ~痺 *n.* palsy

~**pu⁴** ~布 *n.* linen

~**sheng²** ~繩 *n.* marline

~**tzu³** ~子 *n.* pockmark

~**yao⁴** ~藥 *n.* narcotics

MA³ 馬 *n.* horse

~**an¹** ~鞍 *n.* saddle

~**chang³** ~掌 *n.* horseshoe
~**chiu⁴** ~厩 *n.* stable
~**ch'e¹** ~車 *n.* carriage
~**ch'e¹ fu¹** ~車夫 *n.* coachman
~**fu¹** ~夫 *n.* groom
~**hsi⁴** ~戲 *n.* circus
~**hsüeh¹** ~靴 *n.* field boots, riding boots
~**kan¹** ~乾 *n.* forage, fodder
~**k'o⁴ ssu¹** 克斯 *n.* Marx
~**li⁴** ~力 *n.* horsepower
~**lieh⁴ chu³ i⁴** ~列主義 *n.* Marxism-Leninism**
~**lu⁴** ~路 *n.* road
~**pei⁴** ~背 *n.* horseback
~**pien¹** ~鞭 *n.* horse whip
~**shu⁴** ~術 *n.* horsemanship
~**teng⁴** ~蹬 *n.* stirrup
~**tui⁴** ~隊 *n.* cavalry
~**t'ung³** ~桶 *n.* toilet stool
~**ts'ao²** ~槽 *n.* manger
~**tz'u⁴** ~刺 *n.* spurs
~**ying²** ~蠅 *n.* horsefly
MA⁴ 罵 *v.* curse, scold
MAI² 埋 *v.* bury
~**fu²** ~伏 *n.* ambush
~**tsang⁴** ~葬 *v.* bury
MAI³ 買 *v.* buy, purchase
~**chia⁴** ~價 *n.* cost price
~**huo⁴** ~貨 *v.* purchase goods
~**mai⁴** ~賣 *n.* trade, business
~**pan⁴** ~辦 *n.* compradore
MAI⁴ 賣 *v.* sell; *n.* sale
~**chia⁴** ~價 *n.* selling price
~**chu³** ~主 *n.* seller
~**kuo²** ~國 *n.* treason
~**kuo² tsei²** ~國賊 *n.* traitor
~**nung⁴** ~弄 *v.* show off
~**p'iao⁴ ch'u⁴** ~票處 *n.* booking office
~**yin²** ~淫 *n.* prostitution
MAI⁴ 麥 *n.* wheat, barley
~**chiu³** ~酒 *n.* ale
~**fen³** ~粉 *n.* flour

125

~p'ien⁴ ~片 *n.* white oats

MAN³ 滿 *a.* full, complete; *n.* Manchu

~chou¹ ~洲 *n.* Manchuria

~chou¹ jen² ~洲人 *n.* Manchu, Manchurian

~chou¹ kuo² ~洲國 *n.* Manchukuo

~ch'i¹ ~期 *n.* expiration

~fen¹ ~分 *n.* full mark

~tsu² ~足 *v.* satisfy

~yüeh⁴ ~月 *n.* full moon

MAN⁴ 慢 *a.* slow, remiss, neglectful

~kun³ ~滾 *n.* slow roll (aviation)

~pu⁴ ~步 *v.* walk slowly

~tai⁴ ~待 *v.* treat impolitely

MANG² 忙 *v.* keep busy; *a.* busy

~luan⁴ ~亂 *a.* excited, anxious

~su² ~速 *adv.* quickly, hurriedly

MAO¹ 貓 *n.* cat, kitten, puss

~t'ou² ying¹ ~頭鷹 *n.* owl

MAO² 毛 *n.* feather, hair, dime; *a.* coarse, rough

~chin¹ ~巾 *n.* towel

~pi³ ~筆 *n.* brush-pen

~ping⁴ ~病 *n.* disease, defect, fault, shortcoming

MAO⁴ 冒 *v.* risk, pretend, counterfeit

~ch'ung¹ ~充 *v.* pretend

~fan⁴ ~犯 *v.* offend

~hsien³ ~險 *v.* risk, adventure

~hsien³ chia¹ ~險家 *n.* adventurer

~hsien³ hsing⁴ ~險性 *n.* adventurism**

~shih¹ ~失 *a.* rude

~shih¹ kuei³ ~失鬼 *n.* blunderer

MAO⁴ 帽 *n.* cap, hat, headgear

~chang¹ ~章 *n.* hat insignia

~tien⁴ ~店 *n.* haberdasher

~yen² ~簷 *n.* visor

MEI² 沒 *adv.* not. **MO⁴** *v.* die, varnish, sink; *a.* dead, gone

~yung⁴ ~用 *a.* useless

mo⁴ shou¹ ~收 *v.* confiscate; *n.* confiscation

MEI² 煤 *n.* coal

~ch'i⁴ ~氣 *n.* carbon monoxide

~k'uang⁴ ~礦 *n.* coal mine

~k'uang⁴ kung¹ ssu¹ ～礦公司 *n.* coal mining company

~yu² ～油 *n.* kerosene

MEI² 眉 *n.* eyebrow

~mao² ～毛 *n.* eyebrow

MEI³ 每 *a.* every, each; *prep.* per

~chi⁴ ～季 *a.* quarterly, one fourth of a year

~chou¹ ～週 *a. & adv.* weekly

~hsiao³ shih² ～小時 *prep.* per hour

~jih⁴ ～日 *a. & adv.* daily

~ko⁴ ～個 *a.* each

~mei³ ～每 *adv.* often, always

~nien² ～年 *a. & adv.* yearly

~yüeh⁴ ～月 *a. & adv.* monthly

MEI³ 美 *a.* beautiful, pretty, lovely; *n.* beauty

~ching³ ～景 *a.* beautiful scenery

~chiu³ ～酒 *n.* good wine

~hsüeh² ～學 *n.* aesthetics

~jen² ～人 *n.* a feminine beauty

~kuo² hai³ chün¹ ～國海軍 *n.* Navy (*U.S.*)

~kuo² k'ung¹ chün¹ ～國空軍 *n.* Air Force (*U.S.*)

~kuo² lu⁴ chün¹ ～國陸軍 *n.* Army (*U.S.*)

~kuo² lu⁴ chün¹ chün¹ kuan¹ hsüeh² hsiao⁴ ～國陸軍軍官學校 *n.* Military Academy (*U.S.*)

~li⁴ ～麗 *a.* beautiful, pretty; *n.* beauty

~miao⁴ ～妙 *a.* excellent

~shu⁴ ～術 *n.* fine arts

~shu⁴ chia¹ ～術家 *n.* artist

~shu⁴ kuan³ ～術館 *n.* art museum

~shu⁴ p'in³ ～術品 *n.* work of art

~te² ～德 *n.* virtue

~wei⁴ ～味 *n.* delicious

~yü⁴ ～譽 *n.* good reputation, good name

MEI⁴ 妹 *n.* younger sister

~fu¹ ～夫 *n.* younger sister's husband (brother-in-law)

MEN² 門 *n.* door, gate

~hu⁴ ～戶 *n.* door

~k'ou³ ～口 *n.* doorway, entrance

~p'ai² ～牌 *n.* door number

~shuan¹ ～閂 *n.* gate bar

~t'u² ~徒 *n.* disciple, follower

MEN² 們 [word used to signify plural number of the pronoun I, you, he, she, and it]

MEN⁴ 悶 *a.* depressed

~ssu³ ~死 *v.* suffocate

MENG³ 猛 *a.* violent, fierce, brave, savage

~kung¹ 攻 *v.* make a heavy attack

~lieh⁴ ~烈 *a.* fierce blaze, intense fire

~shou⁴ ~獸 *n.* wild beast

MENG⁴ 夢 *n. & v.* dream

~hsiang³ ~想 *v.* dream of, fancy

~i² ~遺 *n.* seminal emission

~mo² ~魔 *n.* nightmare

~yu² ~遊 *n.* sleepwalking

MI² 迷 *a.* intoxicated

~huo⁴ ~惑 *a.* puzzled

~hsin⁴ ~信 *n.* superstition

~lu⁴ ~路 *a. & adv.* astray; *v.* lose one's way

~luan⁴ ~亂 *n.* perplexity

~t'u² ~途 *v.* stray

MI³ 米 *n.* rice

~fan⁴ ~飯 *n.* cooked rice

~t'ang¹ ~湯 *n.* rice water

~t'u⁴ ~突 *n.* meter

MI⁴ 密 *a.* dense, thick, confidential, secret, private, close, intimate

~ch'ieh⁴ ~切 *a.* close association

~ma³ ~碼 *n.* secret cipher, secret code

~shih³ ~使 *n.* emissary

~wei⁴ ~位 *n.* mil

MIAO² 苗 *n.* sprout, descendant, Southwestern Chinese tribe

~t'iao² ~條 *a.* graceful

MIAO⁴ 廟 *n.* temple, fair

MIEH⁴ 滅 *v.* extinguish, destroy, exterminate

~huo³ ch'i⁴ ~火器 *n.* fire extinguisher

~shih¹ ~虱 *v.* delouse

~ting³ ~頂 *v.* be drowned

~wang² ~亡 *v.* destroy

MIEN² 棉 *n.* cotton

~hua¹ ~花 *n.* raw cotton

~**hsü⁴** ~絮 *n.* cotton rags

~**pu⁴** ~布 *n.* calico, cotton cloth

~**sha¹** ~紗 *n.* cotton yarn

~**yao⁴** ~藥 *n.* nitrocellulose

MIEN³ 免 *v.* take off, avoid, dismiss

~**chih²** ~職 *v.* dismiss from service

~**ch'u²** ~除 *v.* relieve from duty, avoid

~**shui⁴** ~稅 *a.* tax-exempt

~**tsui⁴** ~罪 *v.* acquit; *n.* acquittal

MIEN⁴ 面 *n.* face, surface

~**chi¹** ~積 *n.* area

~**chin¹** ~巾 *n.* towel

~**ch'ih⁴** ~赤 *v.* flush

~**mao⁴** ~貌 *n.* appearance

~**se⁴** ~色 *n.* complexion

~**shih⁴** ~試 *n.* oral examination

MIEN⁴ 麵 *n.* noodle

~**fen³** ~粉 *n.* flour

MIN² 民 *n.* people, citizen

~**cheng¹** ~政 *n.* civil administration

~**chu³** ~主 *n.* democracy

~**chu³ chien⁴ kuo² hui⁴** ~主建國會 *n.* China Democratic National Construction Association**

~**chu³ tang³** ~主黨 *n.* Democratic Party

~**chung⁴ yün⁴ tung⁴** ~眾運動 *n.* popular movement

~**ch'üan²** ~權 *n.* people's rights

~**ch'üan² chu³ i⁴** ~權主義 *n.* principle of democracy*

~**fa³** ~法 *n.* civil law

~**i⁴** ~意 *n.* public opinion

~**sheng¹** ~生 *n.* livelihood

~**sheng¹ chu³ i⁴** ~生主義 *n.* principle of people's livelihood*

~**tsu²** ~族 *n.* nation, race; *a.* national

~**tsu² chu³ i⁴** ~族主義 *n.* nationalism*

~**tsu² shih⁴ wu⁴ wei³ yüan² hui⁴** ~族事務委員會 Commission of Nationalities Affairs**

~**tsu² tzu¹ ch'an³ chieh¹ chi²** ~族資產階級 *n.* national bourgeoisie**

MING² 名 *n.* name, title; *a.* famous, noted

~**ch'eng¹** ~稱 *n.* title

~**jen²** ~人 *n.* celebrity

~**kuei⁴** ~貴 *a.* valuable

~**p'ien⁴** ~片 *n.* calling card

~**tzu⁴** ~字 *n.* name

~**tz'u²** ~詞 *n.* noun

~**wang⁴** ~望 *n.* reputation, fame

~**yü⁴** ~譽 *n.* fame, reputation

MING² 明 *a.* bright, apparent, plain

~**ch'üeh⁴** ~確 *a.* evident

~**hsin¹ p'ien⁴** ~信片 *n.* post card

~**hsing¹** ~星 *n.* movie star

~**jih⁴** ~日 *n.* & *adv.* tomorrow

~**liang⁴** ~亮 *a.* bright, brilliant

~**pai²** ~白 *v.* understand; *a.* clear

MING⁴ 命 *n.* fate, lot, destiny, life, decree, order; *v.* order, command

~**an⁴** ~案 *n.* murder

~**chung⁴ kung¹ suan⁴** ~中公算 *n.* vulnerability factor

~**chung⁴ shu⁴** ~中數 *n.* number of hits

~**chung⁴ tan⁴** ~中彈 *n.* sensing a direct hit

~**ling⁴** ~令 *n.* & *v.* command; *v.* order

~**ling⁴ chu³ i⁴** ~令主義 *n.* frequent issue of orders**

~**yün⁴** ~運 *n.* fate, destiny

MO¹ 摸 *v.* touch, feel

~**so³** ~索 *v.* seek for, feel out

MO² 磨 ~⁴ *n.* mill; *v.* rub, polish, grind

~**² li⁴** ~礪 *n.* discipline

~**nan⁴** ~難 *n.* misfortune

~**sun³** ~損 *v.* wear (deteriorate)

~**tao¹ shih²** ~刀石 *n.* grindstone

~**tien⁴ chi¹** ~電機 *n.* generator, dynamo

~**ts'a¹** ~擦 *n.* friction (physical or personal)

~**fang¹** ~坊 *n.* mill

MO² 模 *see* **MU²**

MO⁴ 末 *a.* final, last

~**chan⁴** ~站 *n.* railroad terminal, terminus

~**liao³** ~了 *n.* end

~**tuan¹** ~端 *a.* terminal; *n.* extremity

~**tso⁴** ~座 *n.* lowest seat

MO⁴ 莫 *v. aux.* don't; *adv.* not; *a.* great

MO⁴ 墨 *n.* Chinese ink

~**shui³** ~水 *n.* ink

~**shui³ chia⁴** ~水架 *n.* inkstand

MO⁴ 没 *see* **MEI²**

MOU² 謀 *n.* strategy; *v.* plot, scheme

~**p'an⁴** ~叛 *v.* rebel; *n.* rebellion

~**sha¹** ~殺 *v.* assassinate, murder

~**sheng¹** ~生 *v.* earn a living

~**shih⁴** ~事 *v.* look for a job

~**shih⁴** ~士 *n.* adviser

MOU³ 某 *n.* certain person, someone

MU² 模 *n.* pattern, fashion, mold. **MO²** *n.* model (after someone)

~**yang⁴** ~樣 *n.* pattern, model, fashion

mo² fan⁴ ~範 *n.* model

~**fan⁴ kung¹ jen²** ~範工人 *n.* model workers**

~**fang³** ~倣 *v.* imitate; *n.* imitation

~**hu²** ~糊 *a.* vague

~**hsing²** ~型 *n.* mold

~**t'e⁴ erh¹** ~特兒 *n.* artists model

MU³ 母 *n.* mother, mamma

~**chiu⁴** ~舅 *n.* mother's brother (uncle)

~**ch'in¹** ~親 *n.* mother

~**hsiao⁴** ~校 *n.* mother school

~**i²** ~姨 *n.* mother's sister (aunt)

~**nü³** ~女 *n.* mother and daughter

~**tzu³** ~子 *n.* mother and son

~**yin¹** ~音 *n.* vowel

MU³ 畝 *n.* Chinese measure for 0. 1666 acre

MU⁴ 木 *n.* wood, timber; *a.* wooden

~**chiang⁴** ~匠 *n.* carpenter

~**hsing¹** ~星 *n.* Jupiter

~**liao⁴** ~料 *n.* lumber, timber

~**mien²** ~棉 *n.* cotton

~**nai³ i¹** ~乃伊 *n.* mummy

~**ou³** ~偶 *n.* idol

~**pan³** ~板 *n.* board, plank

~**t'an⁴** ~炭 *n.* charcoal

MU⁴ 目 *n.* eye
 ~hsia⁴ ~下 *adv.* at present, for the time being
 ~li⁴ ~力 *n.* eyesight
 ~lu⁴ ~錄 *n.* catalog, contents
 ~piao¹ ~標 *n.* goal
 ~ti⁴ ~的 *n.* aim, purpose, objective

N

NA² 拿 *v.* take, seize, arrest
 ~huo⁴ ~獲 *v.* arrest, seize
 ~lai² ~來 *v.* bring here
 ~tsou³ ~走 *v.* take away
NA⁴ 那 *pron.* that; *adv.* there. Also read **NAI³** and **NEI⁴**. [All read 3rd tond when interrogatives]
NAI³ 奶 *n.* milk, nipple
 ~chao⁴ ~罩 *n.* bra, brassiere
 ~mu³ ~母 *n.* baby nurse
 ~t'ou² ~頭 *n.* nipple
 ~t'ou² tun⁴ ~頭盾 *n.* nipple shield
 ~yu² ~油 *n.* butter
NAI⁴ 耐 *v.* suffer, endure
 ~chiu³ te¹ ~久的 *a.* durable
 ~hsing⁴ ~性 *n.* patience; *a.* patient
NAI⁴ 那 *see* **NA⁴**
NAN² 難 *a.* difficult, hard; *n.* difficulty. **~⁴** *n.* calamity
 ~⁴ min² ~民 *n.* refugee
NAN² 南 *a.* & *n.* south; *a.* southern
 ~chi² ~極 *n.* South Pole
 ~fang¹ ~方 *n.* south; *a.* southern
 ~kua¹ ~瓜 *n.* pumpkin
NAN² 男 *n.* man
 ~chüeh² ~爵 *n.* baron
 ~hsing⁴ ~性 *n.* male; *a.* masculine
 ~nü³ t'ung² hsüeh² ~女同學 *n.* co-education
 ~tzu¹ ~子 *n.* man
NAO³ 腦 *n.* brain
 ~ch'ung¹ hsüeh² ~充血 *n.* brain congestion
 ~li⁴ ~力 *n.* brains

~**mo⁴ yen²** ~膜炎 *n.* meningitis

NAO⁴ 鬧 *a.* noisy

~**chung¹** ~鐘 *n.* alarm clock

~**shih⁴** ~市 *n.* busy street

~**shih⁴** ~事 *v.* make disturbance

NEI⁴ 內 *a.* inner, inside; *prep.* within

~**chan⁴** ~戰 *n.* civil war

~**cheng⁴ pu⁴** ~政部 *n.* Ministry of the Interior*, Department of the Interior (*U.S.*)

~**chu⁴** ~助 *n.* wife

~**jung²** ~容 *n.* contents

~**k'o¹** ~科 *n.* medical science

~**luan⁴** ~亂 *n.* civil war

~**meng³ ku³ tzu⁴ chih⁴ ch'ü¹** ~蒙古自治區 *n.* Inner Mongolian Autonomous Region**

~**pu⁴** ~部 *n.* interior, inside, inner part

~**wu⁴** ~務 *n.* home affairs

~**wu⁴ pu⁴** ~務部 *n.* Ministry of the Interior**

NEI⁴ 那 *see* **NA⁴**

NENG² 能 *v. aux.* can; *n.* capacity, ability; *a.* capable, able

~**kan⁴** ~幹 *a.* able

~**li⁴** ~力 *n.* ability, capacity

NI² 呢 *n.* wool. [Also a final particle]

~**jung²** ~絨 *n.* woolens

NI² 泥 *n.* mud, clay

~**shui³ chiang⁴** ~水匠 *n.* mason

~**t'an¹** ~灘 *n.* muddy beach

~**t'u³** ~土 *n.* mud, clay, soil, earth

NI³ 你 *pron.* you

~**men²** ~們 *pron.* you

~**men² te¹** ~們的 *pron.* your, yours

~**men² tzu⁴ chi³** ~們自己 *pron.* yourselves

~**te¹** ~的 *pron.* your, yours

~**tzu⁴ chi³** ~自己 *pron.* yourself

NIANG² 娘 *n.* miss, woman, mother, wife

NIAO³ 鳥 *n.* bird

~**ch'ao²** ~巢 *n.* nest

~**lei⁴ hsüeh²** ~類學 *n.* ornithology

NIAO⁴ 尿 *n.* urine; *v.* urinate; *a.* urinary

NIEN² 年 *n.* year; *a.* annual, yearly

~**chi⁴** ~紀 *n.* age

~**chia⁴** ~假 *n.* vacation, annual leave

~**chien⁴** ~鑑 *n.* yearbook

~**chin¹** ~金 *n.* annuity

~**ch'ing¹** ~青 *a.* young

~**lao³** ~老 *a.* old

~**sui⁴** ~歲 *n.* age

~**tai⁴** ~代 *n.* generation, dynasty, period, age

NIEN² 粘 *see* **CHAN¹**

NIEN⁴ 念 *v.* think, remember

~**ching¹** ~經 *v.* chant psalms or prayers

~**fo² chu¹** ~佛珠 *n.* rosary

~**shu¹** ~書 *v.* read, study

NING² 寧 *n.* peace, repose, rest; *v.* prefer

~**ching⁴** ~靜 *a.* quiet, peaceful

~**k'o³** ~可 *adv.* rather

NIU² 牛 *n.* cattle, cow, bull, ox

~**jou⁴** ~肉 *n.* beef

~**nai³** ~奶 *n.* milk

~**p'ai³** ~排 *n.* beefsteak

~**tou⁴** ~痘 *n.* cowpox

~**yu²** ~油 *n.* butter

NU² 奴 *n.* slave, servant

~**i⁴** ~役 *n.* slavery

~**li⁴** ~隸 *n.* slave

NU³ 努 *v.* endeavor

~**li⁴** ~力 *v.* endeavor

NU⁴ 怒 *a.* angry; *n.* anger

~**ch'i⁴** ~氣 *n.* anger

NUAN³ 暖 *a.* mild, warm

~**ch'i⁴** ~氣 *n.* steam

~**ho²** ~和 *a.* warm climate

~**hua¹ fang²** ~花房 *n.* greenhouse, hothouse

NUNG² 農 *n.* agriculture, farmer; *v.* cultivate

~**fu¹** ~夫 *n.* farmer, peasant

~**min² chieh¹ chi²** ~民階級 *n.* peasant class**

~**ts'un¹** ~村 *a.* rural

~**yeh⁴** ~業 *n.* agriculture

~**yeh⁴ chia¹** ~業家 *n.* agriculturalist

~**yeh⁴ pu⁴** ~業部 *n.* Department of Agriculture (*U.S.*)

134

NUNG⁴ 弄 *v.* play, handle
NU³ ～女 *n.* female, girl, woman, maid, maiden
～**ch'üan²** ～權 *n.* woman's rights
～**erh²** ～兒 *n.* daughter
～**hai² tzu¹** ～孩子 *n.* girl
～**hsing⁴** ～性 *n.* female, womanhood
～**hsü⁴** ～婿 *n.* son-in-law
～**hsüeh² hsiao⁴** ～學校 *n.* girl's school
～**hsüeh² sheng¹** ～學生 *n.* schoolgirl
～**jen²** ～人 *n.* woman
～**ling²** ～伶 *n.* actress
～**p'eng² yu³** ～朋友 *n.* girl friend
～**p'u²** ～僕 *n.* maidservant
～**shen²** ～神 *n.* goddess
～**shih⁴** ～士 *n.* Miss, lady
～**wang²** ～王 *n.* Queen
～**wu¹** ～巫 *n.* witch, sorceress

O

OU³ 偶 *n.* idol, image; *v.* mate; *adv.* unexpectedly
～**hsiang⁴** ～像 *n.* idol
～**jan²** ～然 *adv.* accidentally

P

PA¹ 八 *n.* & *a.* eight
～**che²** ～折 *n.* twenty percent discount
～**ku³ tiao⁴** ～股調 *n.* ancient Chinese examination system ("eight-legged essay")
～**yüeh⁴** ～月 *n.* August
PA¹ 巴 *n.* an ancient State
～**chieh²** ～結 *v.* flatter
PA¹ 吧 *a.* dumb. [Also a final particle]
PA² 拔 *n.* uproot
～**ch'u²** ～除 *v.* uproot, extirpate
～**ho²** ～河 *n.* tug-of-war
～**ken¹** ～根 *v.* uproot

135

~**ts'ao³** ～草 *v.* pull up weeds

~**ya²** ～牙 *v.* extract teeth

~**ya² ch'ien²** ～牙鉗 *n.* forceps (*med.*)

PA³ 把 *v.* hold. ~⁴ *n.* handle

~**ping³** ～柄 *n.* handle, evidence

~**wo⁴** ～握 *n.* security

PA⁴ 爸 *n.* papa, daddy, pop, father

PA⁴ 罷 *v.* stop, cease

~**kung¹** ～工 *n.* work strike; *v.* strike

~**k'o⁴** ～課 *n.* student's strike

~**mien³ ch'üan²** ～免權 *n.* power of recall

PA⁴ 霸 *n.* tyrant; *v.* govern, encroach

~**chan⁴** ～佔 *v.* occupy by force

PAI² 白 *n. & a.* white

~**chin¹** ～金 *n.* platinum, white gold

~**cho²** ～濁 *n.* gonorrhea

~**chou⁴** ～晝 *n.* daytime

~**chung³** ～種 *n.* white race

~**ch'i²** ～旗 *n.* white flag

~**e⁴** ～俄 *n.* White Russian

~**fan²** ～礬 *n.* alum

~**hou²** ～喉 *n.* diphtheria

~**je⁴** ～熱 *n.* white heat

~**kung¹** ～宮 *n.* White House (*U.S.*)

~**lan² ti⁴ chiu³** ～蘭地酒 *n.* brandy

~**se⁴** ～色 *n.* white

~**tai⁴** ～帶 *n.* leucorrhea

~**t'ien¹** ～天 *n.* daytime

~**ts'ai⁴** ～菜 *n.* cabbage

PAI³ 百 *n. & a.* hundred

~**ho²** ～合 *n.* lily flower

~**huo⁴ shang¹ tien⁴** ～貨商店 *n.* department store

~**hsing⁴** ～姓 *n.* people, population

~**k'o¹ ch'üan² shu¹** ～科全書 *n.* encyclopedia

~**ling² niao³** ～靈鳥 *n.* lark

~**wan⁴** ～萬 *n.* million

~**yeh⁴ ch'uang¹** ～葉窗 *n.* venetian blind

PAI³ 擺 *n.* pendulum, ferry; *v.* unfold, expand, expose

~**pu⁴** ～佈 *v.* arrange

~**tu⁴** ~渡 *v.* ferry
~**t'o¹** ~脫 *v.* get rid of
PAI⁴ 拜 *v.* worship
  ~**chin¹ chu³ i⁴** ~金主義 *n.* mammonism
  ~**fang³** ~訪 *v.* visit
  ~**ling³** ~領 *v.* accept
  ~**nien²** ~年 *v.* make a New Year's call
  ~**t'o¹** ~託 *v.* request
PAI⁴ 敗 *n.* defeat; *v.* defeat, ruin, destroy
  ~**chang⁴** ~仗 *n.* defeat
  ~**huai⁴** ~壞 *v.* ruin, destroy
  ~**ping¹** ~兵 *n.* defeated troops
PAN¹ 搬 *v.* remove
  ~**chia¹** ~家 *n.* change living quarters
  ~**ch'ü⁴** ~去 *v.* move away
  ~**nung⁴** ~弄 *v.* carry tales
  ~**yün⁴** ~運 *n.* transportation
PAN¹ 般 *n.* sort, kind, class
PAN¹ 班 *n.* class, squad
  ~**chang³** ~長 *n.* squad leader, class leader
PAN¹ 板 *n.* plank, board, block, metal plate
  ~**teng⁴** ~凳 *n.* bench
PAN⁴ 半 *n.* half; *v.* halve
  ~**ching⁴** ~徑 *n.* radius
  ~**jih⁴** ~日 *n.* half-day
  ~**kuan¹ fang¹** ~官方 *a.* semi-official
  ~**nien²** ~年 *n.* half-year
  ~**tao³** ~島 *n.* peninsula
  ~**tien³ chung¹** ~點鐘 *n.* half-hour
  ~**yeh⁴** ~夜 *n.* midnight
  ~**yüan²** ~圓 *n.* semicircle, half dollar
  ~**yüeh⁴** ~月 *n.* half-month
PAN⁴ 辦 *v.* manage, act, execute
  ~**fa³** ~法 *n.* method, plan
  ~**kung¹ ch'u⁴** ~公處 *n.* office
  ~**kung¹ shih⁴** ~公室 *n.* office
  ~**kung¹ t'ing¹** ~公廳 *n.* office
  ~**li³** ~理 *v.* manage, do
PANG¹ 幫 *n.* clique; *v.* help
  ~**chu⁴** ~助 *v.* help, assist
  ~**hsiung¹** ~兇 *n.* accomplice

~shou³ ~手 *n.* helper, assistant

PAO¹ 包 *v.* wrap; *n.* pack, bundle

~feng¹ ~封 *n.* enclosure

~han² ~含 *v.* contain

~hsiang¹ ~箱 *n.* theater box

~hsiang¹ hsi² ~箱席 *n.* box seat

~kuan³ ~管 *v.* guarantee

~kung¹ ~工 *n.* contract work

~kuo³ ~裹 *n.* parcel, package

~k'uo⁴ ~括 *v.* include

~lan³ ~攬 *v.* monopolize

~pan⁴ ~辦 *n.* contract

~wei² ~圍 *v.* encircle, surround

PAO³ 飽 *v.* eat enough, satiate; *n.* satiety

~ho² ~和 *v.* saturate

~ho² tien³ ~和點 *n.* saturation point

PAO³ 寶 *n.* jewel, gem; *a.* precious, valuable

~chien⁴ ~劍 *n.* sacred sword

~ching⁴ ~鏡 *n.* sacred mirror

~hsi³ ~璽 *n.* privy seal

~kuei⁴ ~貴 *a.* precious

~k'u⁴ ~庫 *n.* treasury

~shih² ~石 *n.* precious stone, gem

~tien⁴ ~殿 *n.* shrine

~t'a³ ~塔 *n.* pagoda

~tso⁴ ~座 *n.* jeweled seat, throne

~wu⁴ ~物 *n.* treasure

PAO³ 保 *n.* guardian, protector, guarantee; *v.* recommend, protect, guarantee

~chang⁴ ~障 *v.* guarantee

~cheng⁴ ~證 *n.* & *v.* guarantee

~cheng⁴ chin¹ ~證金 *n.* monetary security

~cheng⁴ jen² ~證人 *n.* guarantor

~cheng⁴ shu¹ ~證書 *n.* letter of guarantee

~chü³ ~舉 *v.* recommend

~ch'ih² chung¹ li⁴ ~持中立 *v.* be neutral

~ch'üan² ~全 *v.* keep safe, preserve

~hu⁴ ~護 *v.* protect; *n.* protection

~hu⁴ jen² ~護人 *n.* guardian

~hsien³ ~險 *v.* insure; *n.* insurance

~hsien³ fei⁴ ~險費 *n.* insurance premium

138

~**hsien³ hsiang¹** 險箱 *n.* safe

~**hsien³ kung¹ ssu¹** 險公司 *n.* insurance company

~**hsien³ ssu¹** 險絲 *n.* fuse (*elec.*)

~**hsien³ tai⁴** ~險帶 *n.* safety belt

~**hsien³ tan⁴** ~險單 insurance policy

~**kuan³ jen²** 管人 *n.* custodian

~**liu²** ~留 *v.* reserve

~**mu³** ~姆 *n.* baby nurse

~**piao¹** ~標 *v.* escort

~**shou³** ~守 *v.* keep; *a.* conservative

~**shou³ tang³** ~守党 *n.* conservative party

~**ts'un²** ~存 *v.* keep, conserve

~**wei⁴** ~衞 *v.* defend

~**yang³** ~養 *v.* nourish; *n.* maintenance

PAO⁴ 報 *n.* journal, newspaper; *v.* report, recompense

~**chih³** ~紙 *n.* newspaper

~**ch'ou²** ~仇 *v.* revenge

~**ch'ou²** ~酬 *n.* remuneration

~**kao⁴** ~告 *v.* report

~**ming²** ~名 *v.* register

~**ta²** ~答 *v.* recompense

~**ying⁴** ~應 *n.* retribution

PAO⁴ 抱 *v.* embrace, hold

~**ch'ien⁴** ~歉 *v.* feel sorry, apologize

~**fu⁴** ~負 *n.* aspiration

~**k'uei⁴** ~愧 *v,* feel shame

~**ping⁴** ~病 *v.* get sick

~**pu⁴ p'ing²** ~不平 *v.* bear a grudge

~**yüan⁴** ~怨 *v.* grudge

PAO⁴ 暴 *a.* violent; *v.* ill-treat, abuse. **P'U⁴** *v.* expose

~**chün¹** ~君 *n.* tyrant

~**feng¹** ~風 *n.* gale

~**feng¹ yü³** ~風雨 *n.* storm

~**p'o⁴** ~破 *v.* demolish

~**tung⁴** ~動 *n.* riot, uprising, revolt

~**t'u²** ~徒 *n.* rebel

~**tsao⁴** ~躁 *a.* hot-tempered

p'u⁴ lou⁴ ~露 *v.* expose

PEI¹ 悲 *n.* grief, sadness

~**ai¹** ~哀 *a.* melancholy

~**chü⁴** ~劇 *a.* tragic; *n.* tragedy

~**ko¹** ~歌 *n.* monody

~**kuan¹** ~観 *a.* pessimistic

~**kuan¹ che³** ~観者 *n.* pessimist

~**kuan¹ chu³ i⁴** ~観主義 *n.* pessimism

~**shang¹** ~傷 *a.* sad

~**t'ung⁴** ~痛 *a.* grievous

PEI³ 北 *a. & n.* north; *a.* northern

~**chi²** ~極 *n.* North Pole

~**chi² hsing¹** ~極星 *n.* North Star

~**fang¹** ~方 *a. & n.* north; *a.* northern

~**wei⁴ san¹ shih² pa¹ tu⁴** ~緯三十八度 *n.* 38th Parallel

~**yang² chün¹ fa²** ~洋軍閥 *n.* northern warlords

PEI⁴ 被 *v.* cover; *n.* bedcover, quilt; *prep.* by (action)

~**ju⁴** ~褥 *n.* bedclothes, bedding

~**kao⁴** ~告 *n.* defendant

~**p'ien⁴** ~騙 *v.* be deceived

~**sha¹** ~殺 *n.* be killed

~**tan¹** ~單 *n.* sheet, bedspread

~**tan¹ mien⁴** ~單面 *n.* beaten zone

~**tung⁴** ~動 *a.* passive

PEI⁴ 背 *n.* back, opposite

~**chi³** ~脊 *n.* backbone

~**ching³** ~景 *n.* background

~**mien⁴** ~面 *n.* opposite

~**p'an⁴** ~叛 *v.* rebel

~**sung⁴** ~誦 *v.* recite

~**t'ung⁴** ~痛 *n.* backache

~**yüeh¹** ~約 *v.* break the contract

PEI⁴ 倍 *a.* double

~**shu⁴** ~數 *n.* multiple

PEI⁴ 備 *v.* prepare

~**chien⁴** ~件 *n.* spare parts

~**wang⁴ lu⁴** ~忘錄 *n.* memorandum

PEI⁴ 輩 *n.* generation

PEN³ 本 *n.* capital, copy, volume, root, origin, beginning; *a.* original, natural

~**chou**¹ ~週 *n.* this week
~**ch'ien²** ~錢 *n.* monetary capital, principal
~**jen²** ~人 *adv.* in person
~**jih⁴** ~日 *n.* today, this day
~**kuo²** ~國 *n.* native country
~**kuo² yü³** ~國語 *n.* mother tongue
~**li⁴** ~利 *n.* monetary principal and interest
~**neng²** ~能 *n.* instinct
~**nien²** ~年 *n.* this year
~**p'iao⁴** ~票 *n.* bank note
~**ti⁴** ~地 *n.* native
~**wei⁴** ~位 *n.* standard
~**wei⁴ chu³ i⁴** ~位主義 *n.* group egoism**
~**yüeh⁴** ~月 *n.* this month

PI¹ 逼 *v.* press, compel
~**p'o⁴** ~迫 *v.* force

PI² 鼻 *n.* nose
~**ch'u¹ hsüeh⁴** ~出血 *n.* nosebleed
~**k'ung³** ~孔 *n.* nostrils
~**liang²** ~梁 *n.* bridge of nose
~**t'i⁴** ~涕 *n.* snivel
~**tsu³** ~祖 *n.* founder, first ancestor
~**yen¹** ~煙 *n.* snuff

PI³ 筆 *n.* pen, pencil, brush
~**chi⁴** ~記 *n.* note
~**chi⁴** ~跡 *n.* handwriting
~**chi⁴ pu⁴** ~記簿 *n.* notebook
~**hua⁴** ~畫 *n.* stroke (writing)
~**ming²** ~名 *n.* pen name

PI³ 比 *n.* comparison; *v.* compare
~**chiao⁴** ~較 *v.* compare
~**fang¹** ~方 *n. & prep.* for instance
~**li⁴** ~例 *n.* proportion
~**lü⁴** ~率 *n.* rate
~**sai⁴** ~賽 *n.* contest, competition, match
~**yü⁴** ~喻 *n.* metaphor, simile, analogy

PI⁴ 閉 *v.* close, shut
~**hui⁴** ~會 *v.* adjourn a meeting
~**mu⁴** ~幕 *v.* drop the curtain

PI⁴ 避 *v.* flee from, avoid, retire
~**chen⁴ ch'i⁴** ~震器 *n.* absorber

141

　~**hsien²** ~嫌 *v.* avoid suspicion
　~**lei² chen¹** ~雷針 *n.* lightning rod
　~**mien³** ~免 *v.* avoid, prevent
　~**nan⁴** ~難 *v.* flee for refuge
　~**shu³** ~暑 *v.* pass the summer
　~**tsui⁴** ~罪 *v.* avoid punishment
PI⁴ 必 *v. aux.* must, will, ought; *adv.* certainly, surely, necessarily
　~**hsü¹** ~需 *v.* require
　~**ting⁴** ~定 *adv.* certainly
PI⁴ 壁 *n.* wall
　~**hu³** ~虎 *n.* small lizard
PI⁴ 幣 *n.* money, coin, wealth, presents
　~**chih⁴** ~制 *n.* currency
PI⁴ 畢 *v.* finish
　~**ching⁴** ~竟 *adv.* after all, at last
　~**yeh⁴** ~業 *v.* graduate; *n.* graduation
　~**yeh⁴ k'ao³ shih⁴** ~業考試 *n.* graduation examination
　~**yeh⁴ sheng¹** ~業生 *n.* graduate
　~**yeh⁴ tien³ li³** ~業典禮 *n.* commencement ceremonies
　~**yeh⁴ wen² p'ing²** ~業文憑 *n.* diploma
PIAO¹ 標 *n.* signal, flag, warrant
　~**chi⁴** ~記 *n.* mark, sign
　~**chun³** ~準 *n.* standard
　~**ch'iang¹** ~鎗 *n.* javelin
　~**pen³** ~本 *n.* specimen, sample
PIAO³ 表 *v.* display, show; *n.* time table, list, manifest, instrument gage
　~**chüeh²** ~決 *v.* vote
　~**ch'ih³** ~尺 *n.* rear gun sight
　~**hsien⁴** ~現 *n.* demonstration, performance
　~**ko²** ~格 *n.* blank form
　~**mien⁴** ~面 *n.* surface
　~**shuai⁴** ~率 *n.* leadership examples
　~**ts'e⁴** ~册 *n.* reference book
PIEH² 別 *v.* separate, part
　~**chen¹** ~針 *n.* pin
　~**ch'u⁴** ~處 *adv.* elsewhere
　~**hao⁴** ~號 *n.* nickname

~**jen²** ~人 *pron.* other
~**ko⁴** ~個 *a.* else, other
~**li²** ~離 *v.* depart; *n.* departure
~**shu⁴** ~墅 *n.* villa

PIEN¹ 邊 *n.* edge, side, margin, bank, frontier, boundary
~**chiang¹** ~疆 *n.* frontier region
~**ch'ü¹** ~區 *n.* frontier
~**fang²** ~防 *n.* frontier defense
~**hsien⁴** ~線 *n.* boundary line

PIEH¹ 編 *v.* arrange, compose
~**chi²** ~輯 *v.* edit; *n.* editor
~**chih¹** ~織 *v.* knit
~**i⁴** ~譯 *v.* edit and translate
~**p'ai²** ~排 *v.* arrange
~**ting⁴** ~訂 *v.* revise

PIEN⁴ 辨 *v.* distinguish, separate
~**jen⁴** ~認 *v.* recognize, identify
~**pieh²** ~別 *v.* distinguish; *n.* distinction

PIEN⁴ 變 *v.* transform, change, reform; *n.* change, alternation; *a.* changeable
~**ch'ien¹** ~遷 *n.* vicissitude
~**hua⁴** ~化 *n.* change; *v.* transform
~**hsi⁴ fa³** ~戲法 *n.* juggle
~**hsing²** ~形 *n.* metamorphosis
~**hsing² ch'ung²** ~形蟲 *n.* amoeba
~**keng⁴** ~更 *v.* change, alter
~**ku⁴** ~故 *n.* misfortune
~**luan⁴** ~亂 *n.* rebellion
~**t'ai⁴** ~態 *a.* abnormal

PIEN⁴ 遍 *n.* time, frequency. **P'IEN⁴** *adv.* everywhere

PIEN⁴ 便 *n.* convenience
~**cho²** ~酌 *n.* informal dinner
~**i¹** ~衣 *n.* ordinary dress
~**i¹ tui⁴** ~衣隊 *n.* plainclothes men
~**li⁴** ~利 *a.* convenient; *n.* convenience; *v.* facilitate
~**pi⁴** ~祕 *n.* constipation
p'ien² i² ~宜 *a.* cheap

PING¹ 兵 *n.* soldier, enlisted men

143

~**chien⁴** ~艦 *n.* battleship, warship

~**ch'i⁴** ~器 *n.* arms, weapons

~**fa³** ~法 *n.* strategy

~**hsiang³** ~餉 *n.* soldiers' pay

~**kung¹** ~工 *n.* Ordnance (*mil.*)

~**kung¹ ch'ang³** ~工廠 *n.* arsenal

~**k'o¹** ~科 *n.* arm, branch (*mil.*)

~**li⁴** ~力 *n.* unit strength (*mil.*)

~**li⁴ p'ei⁴ pei⁴** ~力配備 *n.* distribution of troops

~**pien⁴** ~變 *n.* mutiny

~**ying²** ~營 *n.* barracks

PING¹ 冰 *n.* ice

~**chu⁴** ~柱 *n.* icicle

~**ch'i⁴ lin²** ~淇淋 *n.* ice cream

~**ch'uan¹** ~川 *n.* glacier

~**hsiang¹** ~箱 *n.* icebox, refrigerator

~**hsieh²** ~鞋 *n.* iceskates

~**pao²** ~雹 *n.* hail (frozen rain)

~**shan¹** ~山 *n.* iceberg

~**tao³** ~島 *n.* iceberg

~**tung⁴** ~凍 *a.* frozen

PING³ 餅 *n.* cake, pastry

~**kan¹** ~乾 *n.* biscuit

PING⁴ 並 *adv.* also, equally; *conj.* and

~**chien¹** ~肩 *adv. & a.* abreast

~**ch'ieh³** ~且 *adv.* also, moreover

~**fei¹** ~非 *adv.* not

~**hsing²** ~行 *a.* parallel

PING⁴ 併 *v.* annex, unite

~**lieh⁴** ~列 *adv. & a.* abreast

~**t'un¹** ~吞 *v.* annex

PING⁴ 病 *n.* disease, illness, sickness

~**cheng¹** ~徵 *n.* sign of disease

~**chuang⁴** ~狀 *n.* symptom

~**chung⁴** ~重 *a.* very sick

~**jen²** ~人 *n.* patient

~**yü⁴** ~愈 *n.* health recovery

~**yüan⁴** ~院 *n.* hospital

PO¹ 波 *n.* wave, ripple

~**chi²** ~及 *v.* get involved

~**ch'ang²** ~長 *n.* wave length

~**lang⁴** ～浪 *n.* wave, ripple

~**lo² mi⁴** ～羅蜜 *n.* pineapple

~**wen²** ～紋 *n.* wave, ripple (shape)

PO¹ 剝 *v.* flay, peel

~**hsüeh¹ chieh¹ chi²** ～削階級 *n.* exploiting class**

~**to²** ～奪 *v.* deprive

PO² 伯 *n.* uncle

~**chüeh¹** ～爵 *n.* Earl, Count

~**fu⁴** ～父 *n.* father's older brother (uncle)

~**mu³** ～母 *n.* wife of father's older brother (aunt)

PO² 薄 ～⁴ *n.* peppermint; *a.* thin, shabby, slight

~² **ch'ing²** ～情 *a.* cold (feeling)

~**jo⁴** ～弱 *n.* week, feeble

~**ming⁴** ～命 *n.* unfortunate life

~**mu⁴** ～暮 *n.* evening

~⁴ **ho²** ～荷 *n.* peppermint

PO⁴ 播 *v.* sow, spread abroad. ～³ *v.* winnow

~³ **ku³** ～穀 *v.* winnow grain

~⁴ **chung³** ～種 *v.* sow seeds

~**nung⁴** ～弄 *v.* instigate

~**sung⁴** ～送 *v.* broadcast

PU³ 捕 *v.* seize, arrest

~**huo⁴** ～獲 *n.* & *v.* capture

PU³ 補 *v.* patch, mend

~**chi³** ～給 *n.* supplies

~**chiu⁴** ～救 *v.* rectify

~**chu⁴** ～助 *a.* auxiliary

~**ch'ung¹** ～充 *v.* refill, replenish

~**ch'ung¹ tui⁴** ～充隊 *n.* troop replacement

PU⁴ 步 *n.* step, pace, infantry

~**ch'iang¹** ～槍 *n.* rifle

~**ch'iang¹ pa³ ch'ang³** ～槍靶場 *n.* rifle range

~**ch'iang¹ pan¹** ～槍班 *n.* rifle squad

~**hsing²** ～行 *v.* go on foot

~**ping¹** ～兵 *n.* infantry

~**ping¹ p'ao⁴** ～兵砲 *n.* rifle

~**shao⁴** ～哨 *n.* outguard

PU⁴ 部 *n.* bureau, department, ministry, headquarters, section, class, genus, category

~**chang³** ～長 *n.* minister, head of a department

~**fen¹** ~分 *n.* part
~**hsia⁴** ~下 *n.* subordinate
~**lao⁴** ~落 *n.* tribe

PU⁴ 不 *adv.* no, not, never
~**an¹** ~安 *a.* uneasy
~**cheng⁴ ch'ang²** ~正常 *a.* abnormal, unusual
~**chi²** ~吉 *a.* unlucky
~**chi² ko²** ~及格 *a.* unqualified
~**chiu³** ~久 *adv.* before long
~**chung⁴ yao⁴** ~重要 *a.* unimportant
~**chüan⁴** ~倦 *a.* untiring
~**ch'in¹ fan⁴ t'iao² yüeh¹** ~侵犯條約 *n.* non aggression treaty
~**ch'ü¹** ~屈 *a.* persistent
~**fa³** ~法 *a.* unlawful, illegal
~**ho² tso⁴** ~合作 *n.* noncooperation
~**hsing⁴** ~幸 *a.* unlucky
~**i⁴** ~意 *a.* unexpected, accidental
~**kou⁴** ~够 *a.* insufficient
~**kuan¹ hsin¹** ~關心 *a.* unconcerned, indifferent
~**kuan⁴** ~慣 *a.* unaccustomed
~**nai⁴ fan²** ~耐煩 *n.* impatience; *a.* impatient
~**pi⁴** ~必 *a.* unnecessary, needless
~**pien⁴** ~變 *a.* unchangeable
~**p'ing² teng³** ~平等 *a.* unequal
~**p'ing² teng³ t'iao² yüeh¹** ~平等條約 *n.* unequal treaty
~**tang¹** ~當 *a.* improper, unsuitable, unfit
~**tung⁴ ch'an³** ~動產 *n.* real estate, real property
~**t'o³** ~妥 *a.* unsafe
~**wen³** ~穩 *a.* unsafe, unstable
~**yao⁴ chin³** ~要緊 *a.* unimportant, insignificant, trifling

PU⁴ 布 *n.* cloth; *v.* display, announce
~**chih⁴** ~置 *v.* arrange; *n.* arrangement
~**kao⁴** ~告 *v.* announce; *n.* announcement
~**shih¹** ~施 *n.* charity; *v.* relieve

PU⁴ 佈 *v.* declare, spread
~**chih⁴** ~置 *v.* arrange; *n.* arrangement
~**ching³** ~景 *n.* scenery
~**kao⁴** ~告 *v.* announce

P'

P'A² 爬 *v.* creep, crawl, climb
~**kao¹** ~高 *v.* climb (aviation)
~**shang⁴** ~上 *v.* climb up
P'A⁴ 怕 *v.* feel fear; *n.* fear, dread; *a.* fearful, dreadful
P'AI² 排 *v.* arrange, dispose, expel; *n.* row (line), platoon
~**chang³** ~長 *n.* platoon commander
~**chieh³** ~解 *v.* mediate, compromise
~**ch'ih⁴** ~斥 *v.* exclude, reject
~**ch'iu²** ~球 *n.* volleyball
~**hsieh⁴** ~泄 *v.* excrete; *n.* excretion
~**hsieh⁴ wu⁴** ~泄物 *n.* excrement, excretion
~**ku³** ~骨 *n.* sparerib
~**lieh⁴** ~列 *v.* arrange
~**shui³ kou¹** ~水溝 *n.* drain
~**tzu⁴ chi¹** ~字機 *n.* linotype
~**wai⁴** ~外 *n.* exclusion
P'AI⁴ 牌 *n.* card, medal, shield
P'AI⁴ 派 *v.* sent, assign; *n.* party
~**ch'ien³** ~遣 *v.* dispatch
~**pieh²** ~別 *n.* branch, sect
~**ssu¹** ~司 *n.* pass
P'AN² 盤 *n.* dish, plate, expense; *v.* examine
~**ch'uan¹** ~川 *n.* traveling expense
~**suan⁴** ~算 *v.* calculate
~**tieh³** ~碟 n. dish
P'AN⁴ 判 *v.* judge
~**chüeh²** ~決 *n.* sentence, decision (law)
~**kuan¹** ~官 *n.* judge
~**tuan⁴** 斷 *v.* judge; *n.* judgement
~**tz'u²** ~詞 *n.* law sentence
P'ANG² 旁 *prep.* by, near, beside; *n.* side
~**jen²** ~人 *pron.* others
~**kuan¹ che³** ~觀者 *n.* bystander
~**pien¹** ~邊 *n.* side
P'AO³ 跑 *v.* run

147

~**ma³** ~馬 *n.* races

~**ma³ ch'ang³** ~馬場 *n.* horse racing co'urse

~**pu⁴** ~步 *v.* run, exercise

~**tao⁴** ~道 *n.* airdrome runway

P'AO⁴ 砲 *n.* gun, cannon, artillery piece

~**chi¹** ~擊 *v.* bombard (artillery)

~**chien⁴** ~艦 *n.* gunboat

~**hui¹** ~灰 *n.* cannon fodder

~**huo³** ~火 *n.* artillery fire, gunfire

~**ping¹** ~兵 *n.* artillery units

~**tan⁴** ~彈 *n.* shell

~**t'ai²** ~臺 *n.* fort

P'EI⁴ 配 *v.* match

~**chi³** ~給 *v.* ration

~**chien⁴** ~件 *n.* spare parts

~**ou³** ~偶 *n.* match (husband or wife)

P'EN² 盆 *n.* basin, tub

~**ching³** ~景 *n.* flowerpot

P'ENG² 朋 *n.* friend, party, group

~**tang³** ~黨 *n.* party, clique

~**yu³** ~友 *n.* friend

P'ENG⁴ 碰 *v.* bump, crash

~**chien⁴** ~見 *v.* meet

~**p'o⁴** ~破 *v.* damage by collision

P'I¹ 匹 *n.* pair, mate

~³**fu¹** ~夫 *n.* common people

~**ti²** ~敵 *v.* get a match for

P'I¹ 批 *v.* criticize, comment

~**fa¹** ~發 *n.* wholesale

~**p'ing²** ~評 *n.* criticism

P'I² 皮 *n.* skin, bark, fur

~**huo⁴** ~貨 *n.* fur

~**ko²** ~革 *n.* leather

~**pao¹** ~包 *n.* woman's handbag

~**p'ao²** ~袍 *n.* fur gown

~**tai⁴** ~帶 *n.* waistband

~**t'iao²** ~條 *n.* strap

P'I² 疲 *a.* tired, exhausted, fatigued

~**chüan²** ~倦 *a.* tired, fatigued; *n.* fatigue

P'IAO⁴ 票 *n.* ticket, banknote, warrant, bill

~**fang²** ~房 *n.* ticket office

~**hui⁴** ~匯 *v.* remit by draft
~**mien⁴ e³** ~面額 *n.* face value
P'IEN¹ 偏 *a.* inclined, partial ; *n.* leaning
~**chien⁴** ~見 *n.* prejudice
~**ch'a¹** ~差 *n.* deviation, bias
P'IEN⁴ 篇 *n.* leaf, essay, chapter, page
~**fu²** ~幅 *n.* pages
P'IEN⁴ 片 *n.* piece, slice, strip, visiting card
~**k'o⁴** ~刻 *n.* moment, instant
~**mien⁴** ~面 *a.* one-sided ; *n.* prejudice
~**mien⁴ hsing⁴** ~面性 *n.* one-sidedness**
~**yen²** ~言 *n.* a few words
P'IEN⁴ 騙 *v.* cheat, deceive, dupe, swindle, defraud
~**jen²** ~人 *v.* defraud
~**tzu¹** ~子 *n.* swindler
P'IEN⁴ 遍 *see* **PIEN⁴**
P'IN² 貧 *a.* poor
~**hsüeh⁴ cheng⁴** ~血症 *n.* anemia
~**jen²** ~人 *n.* poor people
~**k'u³** ~苦 *a.* poor
P'IN³ 品 *n.* behavior, conduct, goods, class
~**chi²** ~級 *n.* class, grade
~**chih²** ~質 *n.* brand, quality
~**hsing²** ~行 *n.* behavior, conduct
~**ko²** ~格 *n.* character
~**mao⁴** ~貌 *n.* conduct and appearance
~**p'ing²** ~評 *v.* criticize
P'ING² ~平 *n.* flat, level ; *a.* smooth, flat, level, plain
~**ching⁴** ~靜 *a.* quiet
~**chün¹** ~均 *n.* average
~**ch'ang²** ~常 *a.* ordinary, common, usual
~**fang¹** ~方 *n.* square (*math.*)
~**hsing²** ~行 *a.* parallel
~**mien⁴** ~面 *n.* plane
~**min²** ~民 *n.* commons, commoner
~**teng³** ~等 *n.* equality ; *a.* equal
~**yüan²** ~原 *n.* plain
P'ING² 評 *v.* discuss, settle, criticize
~**lun⁴** ~論 *v.* criticize

149

~**p'an⁴** 判 v. judge

~**p'an⁴ yüan²** ~判員 n. umpire, referee

P'ING² 瓶 n. bottle

P'ING² 憑 n. proof, evidence; v. lean upon, trust to; adv. according to

~**chü⁴** ~據 n. evidence, proof

~**hsin⁴** ~信 v. believe

~**tan¹** ~單 n. certificate

P'O¹ 坡 n. slope

~**tu⁴** ~度 n. slope, gradient

P'O² 婆 n. grandmother, grandma, dame, husband's mother (mother-in-law)

~**chia¹** ~家 n. husband's family

P'O⁴ 迫 v. compel, urge, force, press

~**chin⁴** ~近 a. imminent

~**ch'ieh⁴** ~切 a. urgent

~**hsieh²** ~脅 v. coerce

P'O⁴ 破 v. break, destroy

~**ch'an³** ~產 n. bankruptcy

~**fei⁴** ~費 v. spend

~**huai⁴** ~壞 v. destroy

~**lieh⁴** ~裂 v. crack

~**sui⁴** ~碎 v. smash

~**sun³** ~損 n. damage

P'U¹ 鋪 ~⁴ n. [same as 舖] shop, bed; v. spread out

~**¹ chang¹** ~張 v. overdo

~**kai⁴** ~蓋 n. quilt

~**⁴ tzu¹** ~子 n. shop

P'U¹ 撲 v. strike, quench, whip

~**k'o⁴ p'ai⁴** ~克牌 n. poker (card game)

~**mieh⁴** ~滅 v. quench

P'U³ 普 a. all, general, universal; adv. everywhere

~**chi² te¹** ~及的 a. universal

~**pien⁴** ~遍 a. universal

~**t'ung¹** ~通 a. common, general

P'U⁴ 暴 see **PAO⁴**

S

SA³ 灑 *v.* sprinkle
  ~shui³ ～水 *v.* sprinkle with water
SAI¹ 塞 *v.* stop up, obstruct; *n.* cork, plug, stopper. ~⁴ *n.* frontier
  ~ k'ou³ ～口 *n.* line jack
  ~tse² ～責 *v.* avoid responsibility
  ~tzu¹ ～子 *n.* stopper, cork, plug
  ~⁴ wai⁴ ～外 *n.* beyond the frontier
SAI⁴ 賽 *v.* contest, compete; *n.* rivalry, match
  ~ch'uan² ～船 *n.* boat race
  ~kuo⁴ ～過 *v.* surpass
  ~ma³ ～馬 *n.* horse race
  ~ma³ ch'ang³ ～馬場 *n.* race course
  ~p'ao³ ～跑 *n. & v.* race
SAN¹ 三 *n. & a.* three
  ~chiao³ ～角 *n.* trigonometry
  ~chiao³ chia⁴ ～脚架 *n.* tripod
  ~chiao³ hsing² ～角形 *n.* triangle
  ~chiao³ lien⁴ ai⁴ ～角戀愛 *n.* triangular love
  ~chiao³ pan³ ～角板 *n.* set square
  ~ch'i¹ wu³ chien³ tsu¹ ～七五減租 *n.* 37.5% rent reduction*
  ~fan³ yün⁴ tung⁴ ～反運動 *n.* three anti-movements**
  ~ho² t'u³ ～合土 *n.* concrete
  ~kuo² yen³ i⁴ ～國演義 *n.* Romance of the Three Kingdoms
  ~meng³ chan⁴ shu⁴ ～猛戰術 *n.* "three fierce movements" tactics**
  ~min² chu³ i⁴ ～民主義 *n.* Three Principles of the People*
  ~min² chu³ i⁴ ch'ing¹ nien² t'uan² ～民主義青年團 *n.* Three Principles Youth Corps*
  ~ming² chih⁴ ～明治 *n.* sandwich
  ~pa¹ hsien⁴ ～八線 *n.* 38th Parallel
  ~ta⁴ chi⁴ lü⁴ pa¹ hsiang⁴ chu⁴ i⁴ ～大紀律八項注意 *n.* Three Rules and Eight Remarks**

~**tang⁴** ~檔 n. high gear

~**tien³ lao⁴ ti⁴** ~點落地 n. three-point landing

~**tzu⁴ ching¹** ~字經 n. Trimetrical Classic

~**yüeh¹** ~月 n. March

SAN⁴ 散 v. scatter, disperse. ~³ v. break up; n. powder

~³ **chi⁴** ~劑 n. powder (*med.*)

~**fei¹** ~飛 n. gunnery dispersion

~**po⁴** ~播 v. spread

~**pu⁴** ~步 n. walk

~**wen²** ~文 n. prose

~⁴ **hui⁴** ~會 a. adjourned

~**ping¹ tung⁴** ~兵洞 n. foxhole

~**pu⁴** ~布 v. scatter

SANG¹ 桑 n. mulberry

~**shu⁴** ~樹 n. mulberry tree

~**tzu³** ~子 n. mulberry seed

~**tzu³** ~梓 n. one's native place

SANG¹ 喪 n. funeral; v. die, mourn. ~⁴ v. lose, ruin, destroy

~¹ **li³** ~禮 n. funeral rites

~**shih⁴** ~事 n. funeral

~⁴ **shih¹** ~失 v. lose

~**tan³** ~膽 a. discouraged

SAO³ 掃 v. sweep, brush

~**ch'u²** ~除 v. sweep

~**ch'u² wen² mang² kung¹ tso⁴ wei³ yüan² hui⁴** ~除文盲工作委員會 n. Commission for Eliminating Illiteracy**

~**ch'u⁴** ~帚 n. broom

~**ch'u⁴ hsing¹** ~帚星 n. comet

~**mu⁴** ~墓 v. visit the grave

~**tang⁴** ~蕩 v. mop up

~**ti⁴** ~地 v. clean a floor

SAO³ 嫂 n. wife of one's older brother (sister-in-law)

SE⁴ 色 n. color, tint

~**ch'ing²** ~情 a. obscene, erotic

~**yü⁴** ~慾 n. lust (sex)

SEN¹ 森 n. forest, abundance; a. somber, thick

~**lin²** ~林 n. forest

~lin² hsüeh² ~林學 *n.* forestry

SO¹ 縮 *v.* shorten, abbreviate, draw back
 ~hsiao³ ~小 *v.* reduce (lose weight)
 ~hsieh³ ~寫 *n.* abbreviation
 ~shao³ ~少 *v.* decrease, reduce
 ~tuan³ ~短 *v.* shorten

SO³ 所 *n.* place. [suffix] station, department
 ~i³ ~以 *adv.* therefore, so
 ~te² shui⁴ ~得税 *n.* income tax
 ~yu³ ~有 *n.* possession
 ~yu³ ch'üan² ~有權 *n.* ownership

SO³ 索 *n.* rope, cord; *v.* demand, search
 ~cha⁴ ~詐 *v.* blackmail
 ~ch'iao² ~橋 *n.* cable bridge
 ~ch'ü³ ~取 *v.* demand
 ~p'ei² ~賠 *v.* claim damages
 ~yin³ ~引| *n.* index

SO³ 鎖 *n.* lock, chain; *v.* lock
 ~lien⁴ ~鏈 *n.* shackles, bonds, chains

SU¹ 蘇 *v.* revive
 ~hsing³ ~醒 *v.* awake

SU² 俗 *a.* common; *n.* custom
 ~hsi² ~習 *n.* custom
 ~t'ao⁴ te¹ ~套的 *a.* customary, conventional
 ~yü³ ~語 *n.* proverb

SU⁴ 速 *v.* invite, urge on; *a.* quick, speedy, swift; *adv.* speedily, quickly
 ~chan⁴ su⁴ chüeh² ~戰速決 *n.* a quick war and a quick decision
 ~chi⁴ ~記 *n.* shorthand
 ~she⁴ ~射 *n.* rapid fire
 ~she⁴ p'ao⁴ ~射砲 *n.* rapid-fire gun
 ~tu⁴ ~度 *n.* speed
 ~tu⁴ piao³ ~度表 *n.* speedometer

SU⁴ 素 *a.* plain, pure, simple
 ~chiao¹ ~交 *n.* old acquaintance
 ~hsing⁴ ~性 *n.* habit
 ~lai² ~來 *adv.* usually
 ~ts'ai⁴ ~菜 *n.* vegetable
 ~yüan⁴ ~願 *n.* original desire

SU⁴ 宿 *v.* lodge

153

~**she⁴** ~舍 *n.* dormitory
~**ying²** ~營 *v.* encamp
~**ying² ti⁴** ~營地 *n.* encampment
~**yüan⁴** ~怨 *n.* grudge
SU⁴ 訴 *v.* tell, complain
~**k'u³** ~苦 *v.* complain
~**sung⁴** ~訟 *v.* accuse, charge
SUAN¹ 酸 *n.* acid ; *a.* sour
~**su⁴** ~素 *n.* acid
~**t'ung⁴** ~痛 *a.* sore
SUAN⁴ 算 *v.* count, calculate, plan ; *n* calculation
~**hsüeh²** ~學 *n.* mathematics
~**ming⁴ che³** ~命者 *n.* fortune teller
~**p'an²** ~盤 *n.* abacus
~**shu⁴** ~術 *n.* arithmetic
SUI¹ 雖 *conj.* although, but
~**jan²** ~然 *adv.* however
SUI² 隨 *v.* follow, accompany, imitate
~**hou⁴** ~後 *adv.* afterward
~**i⁴** ~意 *adv.* optionally, freely
~**shih²** ~時 *adv.* whenever
~**ti⁴** ~地 *adv.* anywhere
~**yüan²** ~員 *n.* attache, aid-de-camp
SUI⁴ 歲 *n.* year, age ; *a.* yearly, annual
~**ch'u¹** ~出 *n.* year expenditure
~**ch'u¹** ~初 *n.* beginning of the year
~**mu⁴** ~暮 *n.* end of the year
~**shou¹** ~收 *n.* annual income
~**shu⁴** ~數 *n.* age
SUI⁴ 碎 *a.* broken ; *n.* fragment
~**p'ien⁴** ~片 *n.* fragment
~**te¹** ~的 *a.* broken
SUN¹ 孫 *n.* grandson
~**erh² nü³** ~兒女 *n.* child of one's son (grand-child)
SUN³ 損 *a.* injurious, damaged ; *v.* injure
~**hai⁴** ~害 *v.* injure, damage ; *n.* harm
~**shang¹** ~傷 *n.* injury
~**shih¹** ~失 *n.* loss
SUNG¹ 鬆 *v.* untie, loosen, unfasten ; *a.* loose, lax
SUNG⁴ 送 *v.* give, send

154

~**li³** ～禮 *v.* present
~**pieh²** ～別 *v.* see off

SH

SHA¹ 沙 *n.* sand
~**mo⁴** ～漠 *n.* desert
~**ting¹ yü²** ～丁魚 *n.* sardine
~**t'an¹** ～灘 *n.* beach
SHA¹ 紗 *n.* yarn, gauze
~**ch'uang¹** ～窗 *n.* window screen
~**pu⁴** ～布 *n.* gauze
SHA¹ 殺 *v.* kill, slay; *n.* slaughter
SHAI⁴ 曬 *v.* dry
~**kan¹** ～乾 *v.* make dry
SHAN¹ 山 *n.* mountain, hill
~**feng¹** ～峰 *n.* peak
~**hai³ ching¹** ～海經 *n.* Books of Mountains and Seas
~**ku³** ～谷 *n.* valley, glen
~**mo⁴** ～脈 *n.* mountain range
~**shui³** ～水 *n.* landscape
~**ting³** ～頂 *n.* hilltop
~**tung⁴** ～洞 *n.* cave
~**yang²** ～羊 *n.* goat
SHAN³ 閃 *v.* shun, avoid; *n.* flash
~**kuang¹** ～光 *n.* glare
~**shuo⁴** ～爍 *v.* twinkle
~**tien⁴** ～電 *n.* lightning
~**tien⁴ chan⁴** ～電站 *n.* blitzkrieg
SHAN⁴ 善 *a.* good, honest, virtuous; *v.* approve
SHAN⁴ 扇 *n.* fan. ～¹ *v.* fan
SHANG¹ 商 *n.* trade, merchant; *v.* deliberate, consult
~**chieh⁴** ～界 *n.* business circle
~**ch'uan²** ～船 *n.* merchantman
~**fu⁴** ～埠 *n.* commercial port
~**hao⁴** ～號 *n.* firm
~**hui⁴** ～會 *n.* Chamber of Commerce
~**hsüeh² yuan⁴** ～學院 *n.* college commerce

~i⁴ ~議 *v.* consult, discuss; *n.* consultation

~jen² ~人 *n.* merchant

~piao¹ ~標 *n.* trademark

~p'in³ ~品 *n.* commodity

~tien⁴ ~店 *n.* shop, store, firm

~wu⁴ ~務 *n.* commerce; *a.* commercial

~yeh⁴ ching⁴ cheng¹ ~業競争 *n.* commercial competition

~yeh⁴ hua⁴ ~業化 *v.* commercialize

~yeh⁴ hsün² huan² ~業循環 *n.* business cycle

~yeh⁴ pu⁴ ~業部 *n.* Ministry of Commerce**

SHANG¹ 傷 *n.* & *v.* wound; *n.* injury, harm; *v.* injure

~feng¹ ~風 *v.* catch cold

~hai⁴ ~害 *v.* injure, hurt

~han² cheng⁴ ~寒症 *n.* typhoid fever

~hen² ~痕 *n.* scar

~hsin¹ ~心 *n.* heartbreak

~wang² ~亡 *n.* casualties, dead and wounded

SHANG³ 賞 *v.* bestow, reward

~shih⁴ ~識 *v.* appreciate

~tz'u⁴ ~賜 *v.* bestow

SHANG⁴ 上 *adv.* above, up; *prep.* above, on; *a.* high, superior, excellent

~an⁴ ~岸 *v.* land, disembark

~chi² ~級 *n.* superior, superior grades, superior classes

~chiang⁴ ~将 *n.* general, admiral (*mil.*)

~chieh¹ ~街 *v.* go on the street

~ch'ien² ~前 *adv.* forward

~ch'uan² ~船 *v.* embark; *adv.* aboard

~hsia⁴ ~下 *adv.* up and down

~hsiao⁴ ~校 *n.* colonel, captain (*mil.*)

~hsüeh² ~學 *v.* go to school

~k'o⁴ ~課 *v.* attend a class

~lou² ~樓 *v.* go upstairs

~pan¹ ~班 *v.* go on duty

~su⁴ ~訴 *v.* appeal (law)

~suan⁴ ~算 *a.* profitable

~shen¹ ~身 *n.* upper part of the body

~shih⁴ ~士 *n.* master sergeant (army)

~**ssu¹** ~司 *n.* superior
~**tang⁴** ~當 *a.* cheated
~**teng³** ~等 *a.* &. *adv.* first-class
~**teng³ ping¹** ~等兵 *n.* coporal (army)
~**ti⁴** ~帝 *n.* God
~**ts'eng² she⁴ hui⁴** ~層社會 *n.* upper-class
~**tz'u⁴** ~次 *n.* last time
~**wei⁴** ~尉 *n.* captain, lieutenant (*mil.*)
~**wu³** ~午 *n.* forenoon
~**yu²** ~游 *adv.* & *a.* upstream
~**yüeh¹** ~月 *n.* last month
SHANG⁴ 尚 *adv.* yet, notwithstanding
~**wei⁴** ~未 *adv.* not yet
~**wu³ ching¹ shen²** ~武精神 *n.* militarism
SHAO¹ 稍 *a.* little; *adv.* gradually
SHAO¹ 燒 *a.* feverish; *v.* burn, roast
SHAO³ 少 *a.* few, little, rare, scarce; *adv.* rarely, seldom
~**³ shu⁴** ~數 *n.* minority
~**⁴ fu⁴** ~婦 *n.* young lady
~**nien²** ~年 *n.* youngster, youth
~**nien² erh² t'ung² tui¹** ~年兒童隊 *n.* Young Pioneers**
~**nien² hsien¹ feng¹ tui¹** ~年先鋒隊 *n.* Young Vanguard**
~**nü³** ~女 *n.* lass, girl
SHAO⁴ 紹 *v.* connect, continue
SHE² 舌 *n.* tongue
~**chan⁴** ~戰 *v.* argue; *n.* argument
SHE² 蛇 *n.* snake, serpent
~**hsing²** ~行 *v.* crawl
SHE⁴ 設 *v.* establish, set up
~**chi⁴** ~計 *n.* design
~**hsiang³** ~想 *v.* imagine
~**li⁴** ~立 *v.* establish, found
~**pei⁴** ~備 *n.* equipment
SHE⁴ 射 *v.* shoot, fire
~**chi¹** ~擊 *v.* fire, firearms
~**chi¹ chih³ hui¹** ~擊指揮 *n.* fire control
~**chi¹ shu⁴** ~擊術 *n.* gunnery
~**chiao³** ~角 *n.* quadrant angle of elevation

157

~**chieh⁴** ~界 *n.* field of fire

~**chien⁴** ~箭 *v.* shoot arrows

~**ching¹ kuan³** ~精管 *n.* body ejaculation

~**chung⁴** ~中 *v.* shoot and hit

~**ch'eng²** ~程 *n.* range of target

~**hsiang⁴** ~向 *n.* line of fire

~**hsien⁴** ~線 *n.* line of elevation

~**k'ou³** ~口 *n.* jet

~**lieh⁴** ~獵 *n.* shooting and hunting

~**mien⁴** ~面 *n.* plane of fire

SHE⁴ 社 *n.* society, association

~**chiao¹** ~交 *n.* social

~**hui⁴** ~會 *n.* society

~**hui⁴ hsüeh²** ~會學 *n.* sociology

~**hui⁴ ko² ming⁴** ~會革命 *n.* social revolution

~**hui⁴ k'o¹ hsüeh²** ~會科學 *n.* social science

~**hui⁴ tang³** ~會黨 *n.* Socialist Party

~**hui⁴ te¹** ~會的 *n.* social

~**lun⁴** ~論 *n.* editorial

SHE⁴ 涉 *v.* interfere

SHEN¹ 身 *n.* body, tree trunk, ship hull; *pron.* I, me, myself

~**fen⁴** ~份 *n.* social or professional status

~**hsien¹ shih⁴ tsu²** ~先士卒 *v.* be at the head of one's men

~**t'i³** ~體 *n.* body

~**ts'ai²** ~材 *n.* human figure

SHEN¹ 深 *a.* deep, profound

~**ao⁴** ~奧 *a.* profound

~**chiao¹** ~交 *a.* intimate

~**ch'ieh⁴** ~切 *adv.* intensely

~**ch'ing²** ~情 *n.* deep affection

~**hai³** ~海 *n.* deep sea

~**hu¹ hsi¹** ~呼吸 *n.* deep breath

~**hsin⁴** ~信 *v.* believe firmly

~**ju⁴** ~入 *v.* penetrate

~**miao⁴** ~妙 *a.* profound

~**shui⁴** ~睡 *n.* sound sleep

~**ssu¹** ~思 *n.* deep thinking

~**yüan¹** ~淵 *n.* abyss

SHEN¹ 伸 *v.* stretch, draw out, extend, express

~**chih²** ~直 *v.* straighten

~**hsieh⁴** ~謝 *v.* thank

~**yüan¹** ~冤 *v.* redress an imagined wrong

SHEN² 神 *n.* god, goddess, deity

~**ching¹** ~經 *n.* nerve

~**ching¹ kuo⁴ min³** ~經過敏 *n.* nervousness

~**ching¹ shuai¹ jo⁴** ~經衰弱 *n.* neurasthenia

~**hua⁴** ~話 *n.* myth, mythology; *a.* mythical

~**hsien¹** ~仙 *n.* fairy

SHEN² 什 *see* **SHIH²**

SHEN⁴ 甚 *a.* excessive, too much; *adv.* very

~**hao³** 好 *a.* very well

~**to¹** ~多 *a.* very much

SHENG¹ 生 *n.* student, pupil life, livelihood; *v.* produce, give birth to; *a.* raw, unfamiliar

~**chang³** ~長 *v.* grow up; *n.* growth

~**chi** ~計 *n.* livelihood

~**chiang¹** ~薑 *n.* ginger

~**chih²** ~殖 *n.* reproduction (biology)

~**ch'i¹** ~氣 *v.* become angry

~**huo²** ~活 *n.* livelihood, living

~**huo² ch'eng² tu⁴** ~活程度 *n.* standard of living

~**jih⁴** ~日 *n.* birthday

~**k'o⁴** ~客 *n.* stranger

~**li³ hsüeh²** ~理學 *n.* psysiology

~**ming⁴** ~命 *n.* life

~**ping⁴** ~病 *v.* fall sick

~**shou³** ~手 *n.* green-hand

~**tung⁴** ~動 *a.* lively, spirited

~**ts'ai⁴** ~菜 *n.* lettuce

~**ts'un²** ~存 *n.* living

~**wu⁴ hsüeh²** ~物學 *n.* biology

~**yü⁴** ~育 *v.* give birth to; *n.* birth

SHENG¹ 聲 *n.* voice, sound, noise

~**ch'eng¹** ~稱 *v.* declare

~**lang⁴** ~浪 *n.* sound wave

~**ming²** ~明 *v.* declare

~**shih⁴** ~勢 *n.* power, influence

~**tai⁴** ~帶 *n.* vocal cords

~**tiao⁴** ~調 *n.* tone

~**tung¹ chi¹ hsi¹** ~東擊西 *v.* feint and strike

~ts'e⁴ ~測 *n*. sound ranging

~wang⁴ ~望 *n*. reputation

~yin¹ ~音 *n*. voice, sound

~yü⁴ ~譽 *n*. reputation

~yüeh⁴ ~樂 *n*. vocal music

~yüeh⁴ chia¹ ~樂家 *n*. vocalist

SHENG¹ 牲 *n*. livestock, cattle

~k'ou³ ~口 *n*. livestock

SHENG¹ 勝 *v*. sustain. ~⁴ *v*. conquer

~¹ jen⁴ ~任 *a*. competent

~⁴ chang⁴ ~仗 *n*. victory

~kuo⁴ ~過 *v*. outdo

~li⁴ ~利 *n*. victory

~li⁴ kung¹ chai⁴ yün⁴ tung⁴ ~利公債運動 *n*. Victory Bond Campaign**

SHENG¹ 升 *n*. Chinese measure for 1.09 liquid quarts or 1.035 liters; *v*. ascend, promote

~chiang⁴ chi¹ ~降機 *n*. elevator

~cho² ~擢 *n*. promotion

~shang⁴ ~上 *v*. rise

SHENG² 繩 *n*. cord, string, rope; *v*. tie, restrain, correct

~so³ ~索 *n*. rope

~tzu³ ~子 *n*. rope, cord, string

SHENG³ 省 *a*. frugal; *n*. province; *v*. save. HSING³ *v*. visit, perceive

~cheng⁴ fu³ ~政府 *n*. provincial government

~chien³ ~儉 *a*. frugal

~chien³ ~減 *v*. reduce

~chu³ hsi² ~主席 *n*. provincial governor

~ch'üeh⁴ ~却 *v*. spare

~fen¹ ~分 *n*. province

~lüeh⁴ ~略 *n*. abbreviate

~shih² ~時 *v*. save time

SHENG⁴ 盛 *a*. abundant, prosperous; *n*. abundance. CH'ENG² *v*. contain, hold

~hsing² ~行 *n*. prevalence

~ming² ~名 *a*. well-known, noted

SHENG⁴ 剩 *n*. surplus, leavings

~yü² ~餘 *n*. surplus, remainder

~yü² chia⁴ chih² ~餘價值 *n*. surplus profit**

SHIH¹ 失 *n.* loss, fault, mistake; *v.* lose, miss
~**ch'ang²** ~常 *a.* abnormal
~**huo³** ~火 *v.* catch fire
~**li³** ~禮 *n.* disrespect; *a.* disrespectful
~**pai⁴** ~敗 *v.* defeat, fail; *n.* failure
~**shen²** ~神 *a.* abstracted, absent-minded
~**tang⁴** ~當 *n.* improper
~**wang⁴** ~望 *v.* disappoint; *n.* disappointment
~**yeh⁴** ~業 *a.* unemployed; *n.* unemployment
~**yüeh¹** ~約 *v.* break one's promise

SHIH¹ 師 *n.* teacher, army division
~**chang³** ~長 *n.* division commander, teacher
~**fan⁴ hsüeh² hsiao⁴** ~範學校 *n.* normal school

SHIH¹ 湿 *a.* wet, moist, damp
~**ch'i⁴** ~氣 *n.* moisture
~**ti⁴** ~地 *n.* marsh
~**tu⁴** ~度 *n.* humidity

SHIH¹ 詩 *n.* poem, poetry
~**i⁴** ~意 *a.* poetic
~**jen²** ~人 *n.* poet
~**yün⁴** ~韻 *n.* rhyme

SHIH² 十 *n. & a.* ten
~**tzu⁴ chia⁴** ~字架 *n.* religious cross
~**tzu⁴ chieh¹** ~字街 *n.* crossroad
~**tzu⁴ chün¹** ~字軍 *n.* religious crusade
~**yüeh⁴** ~月 *n.* October

SHIH² 拾 *v.* pick up; *a.* ten
~**ch'ü³** ~取 *v.* pick up

SHIH² 什 *a.* miscellaneous
 SHEN² **mo¹** ~麼 *pron.* what

SHIH² 石 *n.* stone, rock
~**hui¹** ~灰 *n.* lime
~**kao¹** ~膏 *n.* gypsum
~**kung¹** ~工 *n.* stonemason
~**liu²** ~榴 *n.* pomegranate
~**mien²** ~綿 *n.* asbestos
~**pan³** ~版 *n.* slate
~**t'ou²** ~頭 *n.* stone, rock
~**yin⁴** ~印 *n. & v.* lithograph
~**ying¹** ~英 *n.* quartz
~**yu²** ~油 *n.* petroleum

161

SHIH² 實 *a.* real, actual; *n.* fact
~**chi⁴** ~際 *a.* actual
~**chien⁴** ~踐 *v.* practice
~**chien⁴ lun⁴** ~踐論 *n.* "On Practice" **
~**hsien⁴** ~現 *v.* realize; *n.* realization
~**hsing²** ~行 *v.* carry out
~**li⁴** ~力 *n.* strength
~**shih¹** ~施 *v.* carry out
~**tan⁴ she⁴ chi¹** ~彈射擊 *n.* firing live ammunition
~**tsai⁴** ~在 *a.* real, true
~**yeh⁴** ~業 *n.* industry
~**yen⁴** ~驗 *n.* experiment
~**yen⁴ shih⁴** ~驗室 *n.* laboratory
~**yung⁴** ~用 *a.* practical
SHIH² 時 *n.* time, season, hour
~**cheng⁴** ~症 *n.* epidemic
~**chi¹** ~機 *n.* opportunity
~**chien¹** ~間 *n.* time, period, duration
~**chien¹ piao³** ~間表 *n.* timetable
~**chung¹** ~鐘 *n.* clock
~**chü²** ~局 *n.* situation (condition)
~**ch'ang²** ~常 *adv.* often
~**k'o⁴** ~刻 *n.* time (hour)
~**mao²** ~髦 *a.* modern, fashionable, stylish
~**tai⁴** ~代 *n.* age (period)
SHIH² 食 *v.* eat
~**chih³** ~指 *n.* forefinger
~**liang⁴** ~量 *n.* appetite
~**liao⁴** ~料 *n.* foodstuff
~**p'in³** ~品 *n.* food
~**wu⁴** ~物 *n.* food, provisions
~**yen²** ~鹽 *n.* salt
~**yü⁴** ~慾 *n.* appetite
SHIH³ 使 ~⁴ *n.* messenger, envoy; *v.* cause, use
~**che³** ~者 *n.* messenger
~**kuan³** ~館 *n.* legation, embassy
~**ming⁴** ~命 *n.* mission
~**nü³** ~女 *n.* maid, maidservant
~**t'u²** ~徒 *n.* apostle
~**yung⁴** ~用 *v.* use, employ, spend

SHIH³ 始 *n.* beginning; *v.* begin; *a.* first
　~**chung¹** ~終 *adv.* from beginning to end, from first to last
SHIH³ 史 *n.* history
　~**ch'ien²** ~前 *a.* prehistoric, prehistorical
SHIH⁴ 是 *v.* be; *adv.* yes
SHIH⁴ 市 *n.* municipality, city, town
　~**chang³** ~長 *n.* mayor
　~**cheng⁴** ~政 *n.* municipal administration
　~**chia⁴** ~價 *n.* market price, value
　~**min²** ~民 *n.* citizen
SHIH⁴ 式 *n.* form, style, fashion, model
　~**yang⁴** ~樣 *n.* style, fashion, model
SHIH⁴ 世 *n.* generation, age, world
　~**chi** ~紀 *n.* century
　~**chieh⁴** ~界 *n.* world, earth
　~**chieh⁴ yü³** ~界語 *n.* Esperanto
　~**su²** ~俗 *a.* secular, worldly
　~**tai⁴** ~代 *n.* generation
SHIH⁴ 勢 *n.* power, authority, influence
　~**li⁴** ~力 *n.* influence (personal or political)
SHIH⁴ 試 *v.* try, examine; *n.* test
　~**fei¹** ~飛 *n.* test flight
　~**yen⁴** ~驗 *n.* test
　~**yen⁴ ch'ang³** ~驗場 *n.* proving ground
　~**yen⁴ shih⁴** ~驗室 *n.* laboratory
　~**yung⁴** ~用 *n.* probation
SHIH⁴ 士 *n.* scholar
　~**ch'i⁴** ~氣 *n.* morale
　~**ping¹** ~兵 *n.* soldier
SHIH⁴ 室 *n.* room, chamber, apartment
　~**nei⁴** ~內 *a.* indoor; *adv.* indoors
　~**wai⁴** ~外 *a.* outdoor; *adv.* outdoors
SHIH⁴ 示 *v.* proclaim, show
　~**wei¹ yün⁴ tung⁴** ~威運動 *n.* demonstration parade
SHIH⁴ 識 *n.* experience; *v.* know, recognize
　~**p'o⁴** ~破 *v.* discover, detect
　~**t'ou⁴** ~透 *v.* see through
SHIH⁴ 適 *n.* pleasure, comfort; *v.* go to, reach, make fit; *a.* pleasant, comfortable; *adv.* sud-

denly, just

~feng² ~逢 *v.* happen

~ho² ~合 *v.* fit; *a.* suitable, fit

~i² ~宜 *a.* suitable

~k'ou³ ~口 *a.* palatable

~tu⁴ ~度 *adv.* moderately

~ying⁴ ~應 *n.* adaptation

~yung⁴ ~用 *a.* useful

SHIH⁴ 事 *n.* affair, matter

~ch'ing² ~情 *n.* affair, matter, business

~pien⁴ ~變 *n.* accident, emergency

~shih² ~實 *n.* fact

~wu⁴ ~務 *n.* affair

~wu⁴ chu³ i⁴ chia¹ ~務主義家 *n.* plodder**

~wu⁴ so³ ~務所 *n.* office

~yeh⁴ ~業 *n.* business, occupation

SHOU¹ 收 *v.* receive, collect, close

~chang⁴ ~帳 *v.* collect debts

~chi² ~集 *v.* collect; *n.* collection

~chü⁴ ~據 *n.* receipt

~huo⁴ ~獲 *n.* & *v.* harvest

~ju⁴ ~入 *n.* income

~liu² ~留 *v.* give shelter

~tao⁴ ~到 *v.* receive

~yin¹ chi¹ ~音機 *n.* radio

SHOU² 熟 *a.* ripe, mature, cooked

~hsi² ~悉 *a.* familiar, acquainted

~jen² ~人 *n.* acquaintance

~lien⁴ ~練 *a.* skillful

~shui⁴ ~睡 *n.* sound sleep

~t'ieh³ ~鐵 *n.* wrought iron

SHOU³ 手 *n.* hand

~chang³ ~掌 *n.* palm

~chih³ ~指 *n.* finger

~chin¹ ~巾 *n.* handkerchief

~ch'iang¹ ~鎗 *n.* pistol

~kung¹ ~工 *n.* handiwork, handcraft

~k'ao³ ~銬 *n.* handcuffs

~piao³ ~錶 *n.* watch device

~shih⁴ ~勢 *n.* gesture

~shu⁴ ~術 *n.* operation (*med.*)

~tuan⁴ ~段 *n.* tact, method
~t'ao⁴ ~套 *n.* glove
~ts'e⁴ ~册 *n.* manual
~wan⁴ ~腕 *n.* wrist
~yin² ~淫 *n.* masturbation, self-abuse
SHOU³ 守 *v.* watch, guard, hold, keep for defense
　~chiu⁴ ~舊 *a.* conservative
　~chiu⁴ p'ai⁴ ~舊派 *n.* old school
　~chung¹ li⁴ ~中立 *v.* be neutral
　~ping¹ ~兵 *n.* defending troops
　~shih⁴ ~勢 *n.* strategic defense
　~ts'ai² nu² ~財奴 *n.* miser
　~wei⁴ ~衛 *v.* guard
　~yeh⁴ ~夜 *v.* keep watch at night
　~yüeh¹ ~約 *v.* keep a promise
SHOU³ 首 *n.* head, chief, boss; *a.* first
　~hsiang⁴ ~相 *n.* premier, prime minister
　~hsien¹ ~先 *adv.* first
　~ling³ ~領 *n.* chief, head, leader, boss
　~shih⁴ ~飾 *n.* ornaments
　~tu¹ ~都 *n.* national capital
　~wei³ ~尾 *n.* head and tail
SHOU⁴ 受 *v.* receive, accept
　~hai⁴ ~害 *v.* damage
　~hsi³ ~洗 *v.* be baptized
　~k'u³ ~苦 *v.* suffer
SHOU⁴ 獸 *n.* wild animal, beast
　~p'i² ~皮 *n.* animal skin
SHU¹ 書 *n.* book, handwriting
　~chi⁴ ~記 *n.* clerk
　~chia⁴ ~架 *n.* bookcase, bookstand
　~cho¹ ~桌 *n.* desk
　~fa³ ~法 *n.* handwriting
　~shang¹ ~商 *n.* bookseller
　~tai¹ tzu¹ ~獃子 *n.* bookworm (person)
　~tien⁴ ~店 *n.* bookstore
SHU¹ 梳 *n. & v.* comb
SHU¹ 輸 *v.* lose, pay, transport
　~ch'ien² ~錢 *v.* lose money
　~ch'u¹ ~出 *v.* export
　~ch'u¹ p'in³ ~出品 *n.* export goods

165

~ju⁴ ~入 *v.* import

~ju⁴ p'in³ ~入品 *n.* import goods

~sung⁴ ~送 *v.* transport; *n.* transportation

SHU² 叔 *n.* father's younger brother (uncle)

SHU³ 暑 *n.* summer heat

~chia⁴ ~假 *n.* summer vacation

SHU³ 署 *n.* public court, tribunal; *v.* write

~chang³ ~長 *n.* director

SHU³ 數 *v.* to count. ~⁴ *n.* number; *a.* several

~⁴ hsüeh² ~學 *n.* mathematics

~hsüeh² chia¹ ~學家 *n.* mathematician

~liang⁴ ~量 *n.* quantity

~mu⁴ ~目 *n.* number, amount, sum

SHU³ 鼠 *n.* rat, mouse

~i⁴ ~疫 *n.* plague, pest

SHU³ 属 *n.* sort, kind, class; *v.* belong to

~ti⁴ ~地 *n.* dependency

~yü² ~於 *v.* belong to

SHU⁴ 樹 *n.* tree; *v.* plant, establish

~chiao¹ ~膠 *n.* gum

~chih¹ ~枝 *n.* tree branch

~kan⁴ ~幹 *n.* tree trunk

~ken¹ ~根 *n.* root

~lin² ~林 *n.* forest, woods

~yeh⁴ ~葉 *n.* leaf

SHU⁴ 術 *n.* path, art, plan

~yü³ ~語 *n.* terminology

SHUA 刷 *n.* & *v.* brush

~hsi³ ~洗 *v.* scrub

~pai² ~白 *v.* whitewash

~tzu¹ ~子 *n.* brush

SHUA³ 要 *v.* play

SHUAI⁴ 率 *v.* lead, follow, obey. **LÜ⁴** *n.* rule, rate, ratio

~ling³ ~領 *v.* lead

SHUAN¹ 拴 *n.* pin

SHUANG¹ 雙 *a.* double, two, both; *n.* pair, couple, mate

~ch'in¹ ~親 *n.* parents

~fang¹ ~方 *a.* both

~kuan¹ yü³ ~關語 *n.* pun

~**sheng¹ tzu³** ~生子 *n.* twin

~**t‘ai¹** ~胎 *n.* twins

SHUANG¹ 霜 *n.* frozen dew, hoar frost ; *a.* crystallized

~**hsüeh³** ~雪 *n.* frost and snow

SHUANG³ 爽 *a.* sunny, alert ; *v.* fail

~**k‘uai⁴** ~快 *a.* pleasant

~**yüeh¹** ~約 *v.* break a promise

SHUI² 誰 *pron.* who, whom, whose

SHUI³ 水 *n.* water, liquid, flood

~**cha²** ~閘 *n.* floodgate, dam

~**ching¹** ~晶 *n.* crystal

~**ch‘an³** ~産 *n.* marine products

~**ch‘ih²** ~池 *n.* pool

~**ch‘iu²** ~球 *n.* water polo

~**hu³ chuan⁴** ~滸傳 *n.* Water Margin (Chinese novel)

~**hsien³** ~險 *n.* marine insurance

~**hsing¹** ~星 *n.* Mercury (planet)

~**kang¹** ~缸 *n.* cistern

~**kou¹** ~溝 *n.* ditch

~**kuo³** ~果 *n.* fruit

~**lei²** ~雷 n. torpedo

~**li⁴** ~力 *n.* water power

~**li⁴ pu⁴** ~利部 *n.* Ministry of Water Conservancy**

~**lung²** ~龍 *n.* fire engine

~**men² t‘ing¹** ~門汀 *n.* cement

~**niu²** ~牛 *n.* buffalo

~**ping¹** ~兵 *n.* sailor, seaman (navy)

~**p‘ing²** ~平 *n.* level

~**shou³** ~手 *n.* sailor

~**tao⁴** ~道 *n.* waterway

~**t‘u³** ~土 *n.* climate

~**tsu² kuan³** ~族館 *n.* aquarium

~**ts‘ai³ hua⁴** ~彩畫 *n.* water color

~**yin²** ~銀 *n.* mercury

SHUI⁴ 睡 *v.* sleep

~**chiao⁴** ~覺 *v.* sleep

~**ch‘e¹** ~車 *n.* sleeping car

~**hsing³** ~醒 *v.* awaken, wake up

~i¹ ~衣 *n.* nightgown, nightdress, pajamas

SHUI⁴ 税 *n.* tax, taxation, duty

~kuan¹ ~關 *n.* custom house

~lü⁴ ~率 *n.* rate of tax

SHUN⁴ 順 *a.* obedient; *v.* obey, follow

~feng¹ ~風 *n.* tail wind

~hsü⁴ ~序 *n.* order

~li⁴ ~利 *n.* & *a.* prosperous

~shih² chen¹ fang¹ hsiang⁴ ~時針方向 *adv.* & *a.* clockwise

~ts'ung² ~從 *v.* obey

SHUO¹ 説 *v.* say, speak

~fu² ~服 *v.* persuade

~huang³ ~謊 *v.* tell lies

~hsiao⁴ hua⁴ ~笑話 *v.* make a joke

~ming² ~明 *v.* explain; explanation

SS

SSU¹ 思 *v.* think, consider

~hsiang³ ~想 *n.* thought

~hsiang³ kai³ tsao⁴ ~想改造 *n.* thought reform**, ideological reform**

~hsiang³ tzu⁴ yu² ~想自由 *n.* freedom of thought

~hsiang³ wen⁴ t'i² ~想問題 *n.* question of thought**

~k'ao³ ~考 *v.* think

~lü⁴ ~慮 *v.* consider

SSU¹ 私 *a.* private, personal, secret

~fa³ ~法 *n.* private law

~hsin¹ ~心 *n.* selfishness

~hsing² ~刑 *n.* illegal punishment

~jen² te¹ ~人的 *a.* personal

~li⁴ hsüeh hsiao⁴ ~立學校 *n.* private school

~pen¹ ~奔 *n.* elopement

~sheng¹ tzu³ ~生子 *n.* bastard, illegitimate child

~t'ao² ~逃 *v.* escape

~t'ung¹ ~通 *n.* adultery

~**yü³** ~語 *v.* whisper

~**yün⁴** ~運 *v.* smuggle

SSU¹ 司 *v.* manage; *n.* departments under the ministry

~**fa³** ~法 *a.* judicial

~**fa³ hsing² cheng⁴ pu⁴** ~法行政部 *n.* Ministry of Judicial Administration*

~**fa³ pu⁴** ~法部 *n.* Ministry of Justice**, Department of Justice (*U.S.*)

~**fa³ yüan⁴** ~法院 *n.* Judicial Yuan*

~**ling⁴** ~令 *n.* commander

~**ling⁴ pu⁴** ~令部 *n.* large unit headquarters

SSU¹ 糸 *n.* silk, thread

~**chih¹ p'in³** ~織品 *n.* silk goods

~**wa⁴** ~襪 *n.* silk stockings

SSU¹ 斯 *n.* final particle; *pron.* this, he, they; *adv.* then

SSU³ 死 *v.* die; *a.* dead; *n.* death

~**hsing²** ~刑 *v.* be executed

~**jen²** ~人 *n.* dead person

~**te¹** ~的 *a.* dead

~**tsui⁴** ~罪 *n.* the penalty of death

~**wang² lü⁴** ~亡率 *n.* death rate

~**wang² piao³** ~亡表 *n.* obituary notice

SSU⁴ 四 *n.* & *a.* four

~**chi⁴** ~季 *n.* four seasons

~**fang¹ te¹** ~方的 *a.* square

~**yüeh⁴** ~月 *n.* April

SSU⁴ 似 *a.* alike, similar, like

~**hu¹** ~乎 *v.* seem, appear; *adv.* likely

~**shih⁴** ~是 *adv.* plausibly

SSU⁴ 厠 *n.* privy

~**so³** ~所 *n.* toilet, water closet

T

TA² 答 *v.* answer, reply

~¹ **ying⁴** ~應 *v.* promise

~² **an⁴** ~案 *n.* answer (solution)

~**fu⁴** ~復 *v.* answer

169

~hsieh⁴ ~謝 *v.* return thanks

~pien⁴ ~辯 *v.* rebut

~tui⁴ ~對 *v.* reply

TA² 達 *v.* inform, reach

~mu³ tan⁴ ~姆彈 *n.* dumdum bullet

~tao⁴ ~到 *v.* attain

TA³ 打 *v.* beat, strike, thrash. **~²** *n.* dozen

~chang⁴ ~仗 *v.* fight

~chia⁴ ~架 *v.* fight

~pai⁴ ~敗 *v.* defeat

~p'ai² ~牌 *v.* play mah-jong

~tun³ ~盹 *v.* take a nap

~t'ing¹ ~聽 *v.* detect

~tzu⁴ ~字 *v.* typewrite

~tzu⁴ chi¹ ~字機 *n.* typewriter

~tzu⁴ yüan² ~字員 *n.* typist

TA⁴ 大 *a.* big, large, great, huge, enormous; *adv.* largely, greatly, highly, extremely

~feng¹ ~風 *n.* typhoon

~hsiao³ ~小 *n.* size

~hsing² cheng⁴ ch'ü¹ ~行政區 *n.* Great Administrative Areas**

~hsüeh² ~學 *n.* university

~i¹ ~衣 *n.* overcoat

~i⁴ ~意 *n.* general idea

~kai⁴ ~概 *adv.* generally, in general

~kang¹ ~綱 *n.* outline

~li³ shih² ~理石 *n.* marble

~liang⁴ ~量 *n.* large quantity, mass; *a.* generous

~lu⁴ ~路 *n.* highroad, highway

~lu⁴ ~陸 n. continent, mainland

~lu⁴ kung¹ tso⁴ ch'u⁴ ~陸工作處 *n.* Mainland Operations Department*

~mai⁴ ~麥 *n.* barley

~men² ~門 *n.* front door

~pan⁴ ~半 *adv.* largely, chiefly

~pien⁴ ~便 *n.* excrement, stool

~p'ao⁴ ~砲 *n.* cannon, artillery

~she⁴ ~赦 *n.* amnesty

~shih⁴ ~使 *n.* ambassador

~tan³ ~膽 *a.* bold, daring, courageous

~t'ing¹ ~廳 *n.* hall

~to¹ shu⁴ ~多數 *n.* majority

~tsung³ t'ung³ ~總統 *n.* President, Executive (*U.S.*)

~t'ui³ hsi⁴ ~腿戲 *n.* burlesque

~yüeh¹ ~約 *adv.* about, probably, approximately, generally

TAI⁴ 待 *v.* wait, treat

~yü⁴ ~遇 *n.* treatment

TAI⁴ 帶 *n.* ribbon, belt, zone, bandage, region; *v.* lead, bring

~lai² ~來 *v.* bring

~lei⁴ ~累 *v.* involve (someone)

~ling³ ~領 *v.* lead

~tzu¹ ~子 *n.* belt

TAI⁴ 代 *n.* dynasty, generation; *v.* represent, replace; *prep.* instead of, in place of

~chia⁴ ~價 *n.* price

~li³ ~理 *v.* act for another

~li³ ch'u⁴ ~理處 *n.* agent

~piao³ ~表 *n.* representative; *v.* represent

~shu⁴ hsüeh² ~數學 *n.* algebra

~t'i⁴ ~替 *n.* substitution; *v.* substitute

TAI⁴ 袋 *n.* bag, pocket, purse

~shu³ ~鼠 *n.* kangaroo

TAI⁴ 貸 *v.* lend, borrow

~chin¹ ~金 *n.* loan

~ch'u¹ ~出 *v.* lend

~ju⁴ ~入 *v.* borrow

TAN¹ 單 *a.* single, alone

~fa¹ ~發 *n.* single shot

~fei¹ ~飛 *n.* solo flight

~jen² ch'uang² ~人床 *n.* single bed

~tu² ~獨 *a.* alone

~wei⁴ ~位 *n.* unit

TAN¹ 擔 *v.* carry, sustain, bear

~hsin¹ ~心 *v.* worry

~jen⁴ ~任 *v.* undertake, take part

~ko¹ ~擱 *v.* delay

~kun⁴ ~棍 *n.* crowbar

~pao³ ~保 *n. & v.* guarantee

171

~**pao³ jen²** ~保人 *n.* guarantor

~**yu¹** ~憂 *v.* worry

TAN³ 膽 *n.* gall, bile, courage

~**chih¹** ~汁 *n.* gall, bile

~**hsiao³** ~小 *a.* cowardly

~**kan³** ~敢 *v.* dare

~**liang⁴** ~量 *n.* courage, bravery

~**nang²** ~囊 *n.* gall bladder

~**shih²** ~石 *n.* gall stone

~**ta⁴** ~大 *a.* courageous, brave

TAN⁴ 蛋 *n.* egg

~**huang²** ~黃 *n.* yolk

~**k'o²** ~殼 *n.* eggshell

~**pai²** ~白 *n.* albumen

~**pai² chih²** ~白質 *n.* albumen

TAN⁴ 彈 *n.* bullet, shot, shell. **T'AN²** *v.* rebound, shoot

~**chao² tien³** ~着點 *n.* point of impact

~**hen²** ~痕 *n.* crater, shell hole

~**tao⁴** ~道 *n.* trajectory

~**tao⁴ hsüeh²** ~道學 *n.* ballistics

~**tzu³ fang²** ~子房 *n.* billiard room

~**tzu¹ hsi⁴** ~子戲 *n.* billiards

~**yao⁴** ~藥 *n.* ammunition

t'an² ch'ang⁴ ~唱 *v.* play and sing

~**ch'in²** ~琴 *v.* play an instrument

~**ho²** ~劾 *v.* impeach (accuse)

~**hsing⁴** ~性 *n.* elasticity

~**ya¹** ~壓 *v.* repress (put down)

TAN⁴ 但 *conj.* but, yet

~**shih⁴** ~是 *conj.* but

TAN⁴ 淡 *a.* insipid, tasteless, weak

~**ch'i⁴** ~氣 *n.* nitrogen

~**po²** ~薄 *a.* dilute, thin

~**te¹** ~的 *a.* fresh (food)

TANG¹ 當 *v.* act, bear; *conj.* when, while; *prep.* during. ~⁴ *a.* suitable; *v.* pawn

~¹ **chen¹** ~眞 *adv.* really

~**chü²** ~局 *n.* authority

~**hsüan³** ~選 *v.* be elected

~**jan²** ~然 *adv.* certainly, surely, naturally

172

~**shih²** ～時 *prep.* during
~**⁴ p'u⁴** ～舖 *n.* pawnshop
~**shui⁴** ～税 *n.* pawnshop tax

TANG³ 黨 *n.* party, cabal
~**kuo² yao⁴ jen⁴** ～國要人 *n.* important figures in the party and government
~**p'ai⁴** ～派 *n.* political party
~**shou³** ～首 *n.* party leader
~**yüan²** ～員 *n.* party member

TAO¹ 刀 *n.* knife, sword
~**ch'iao⁴** ～鞘 *n.* scabbard, sheath
~**feng¹** ～鋒 *n.* point of a knife
~**pei⁴** ～背 *n.* back of a knife
~**p'ien⁴** ～片 *n.* blade

TAO³ 島 *n.* island, isle
~**min²** ～民 *n.* islander
~**yü³** ～嶼 *n.* isle, islet

TAO³ 導 *v.* lead, guide
~**huo³ hsien⁴** ～火線 *n.* explosive's fuse
~**kuan³** ～管 *n.* pipe, fuel conductor
~**piao¹** ～標 guidepost
~**yen²** ～言 *n.* introduction, preface
~**yen³** ～演 *n. & v.* director

TAO⁴ 道 *v.* speak, tell; *n.* road
~**ho⁴** ～賀 *v.* congratulate
~**hsieh⁴** ～謝 *v.* express thanks
~**li³** ～理 *n.* reason
~**lu⁴** ～路 *n.* road
~**shih⁴** ～士 *n.* taoist
~**te²** ～德 *n.* virtue

TAO⁴ 到 *v.* arrive, reach
~**ch'i¹** ～期 *a.* due (promised to come)
~**ch'u⁴** ～處 *adv.* everywhere
~**jen⁴** ～任 *v.* take the post
~**ta²** ～達 *v.* arrive at; *n.* arrival
~**ti³** ～底 *adv.* at last

TAO⁴ 倒 *a.* inverted, upset, upside-down. ～³ *v.* fall down
~**³ ch'u¹** ～出 *v.* pour out
~**hsia⁴** ～下 *v.* fall down
~**mei²** ～霉 *a.* unlucky

173

~**pi⁴** ~閉 *v.* bankrupt
~**yün⁴** ~運 *a.* unlucky
~**⁴ t'ui⁴** ~退 *v.* withdraw

TAO⁴ 盜 *n.* robber; *v.* rob
~**an⁴** ~案 *n.* a case of robbery
~**ch'ieh⁴** ~竊 *v.* steal
~**k'ou⁴** ~寇 *n.* robber

TAO⁴ 稻 *n.* rice-plant
~**ts'ao³** ~草 *n.* straw

TE¹ 的 *see* **TI⁴**

TE² 德 *n.* virtue, quality, goodness
~**hsing²** ~行 *n.* virtue, morality
~**hsing⁴** ~性 *n.* morality
~**yü⁴** ~育 *n.* moral education

TE² 得 *v.* get. **TEI³** *v. aux.* must, ought
~**i⁴** ~意 *a.* elated
~**li⁴** ~力 *a.* helpful
~**ping⁴** ~病 *v.* get sick
~**sheng⁴** ~勝 *n.* victory
~**tsui⁴** ~罪 *v.* offend

TEI³ 得 *see* **TE²**

TENG¹ 燈 *n.* light
~**hsin¹** ~心 *n.* wick
~**kuang¹** ~光 *n.* light (lamp)
~**lung²** ~籠 *n.* lantern
~**t'a³** ~塔 *n.* lighthouse

TENG¹ 登 *v.* ascend, record
~**an⁴** ~岸 *v.* disembark
~**chi⁴** ~記 *v.* register; *n.* registration
~**lu⁴** ~陸 *v.* land (come ashore)
~**lu⁴ ch'uan² chih¹** ~陸船隻 *n.* landing craft

TENG³ 等 *v.* wait; *n.* rank, grade, degree
~**chi²** ~級 *n.* grade
~**kao¹ hsien⁴** ~高線 *n.* contour
~**tai⁴** ~待 *v.* wait for
~**teng³** ~等 *conj.* and so forth, etcetera

TI¹ 低 *a.* low, mean, base
~**chia⁴** ~價 *a.* cheap
~**chien⁴** ~賤 *a.* mean, humble
~**k'ung¹ fei¹ hsing²** ~空飛行 *n.* low-flying
~**neng²** ~能 *a.* feeble-minded

~**shen¹ tan⁴ tao⁴**~伸彈道 *n.* flat trajectory

~**ti⁴** ~地 *n.* low ground

~**wei¹** ~微 *a.* base, mean

~**wu⁴** ~霧 *n.* low fog

TI² 敵 *n.* enemy, competitor; *v.* oppose

~**chi¹** ~機 *n.* enemy aircraft

~**ch'iao²** ~僑 *n.* enemy alien

~**ch'ing²** ~情 *n.* enemy situation

~**fang¹** ~方 *n.* enemy's side

~**i⁴** ~意 *a.* hostile; *n.* hostility

~**jen²** ~人 *n.* enemy

~**tui⁴** ~對 *a.* hostile

TI³ 底 *n.* base, bottom

~**hsia⁴** ~下 *prep.* under, below

~**kao³** ~稿 *n.* draft copy

~**mien⁴** ~面 *n.* undersurface

TI³ 抵 *v.* arrive, reach, resist

~**chih⁴** ~制 *n. & v.* boycott

~**hsiao¹** ~消 *n.* offset

~**k'ang⁴** ~抗 *v.* resist; *n.* resistance

~**k'ang⁴ hsien⁴** ~抗線 *n.* line of resistance

~**k'ang⁴ li⁴** ~抗力 *n.* powerful resistance

~**ya¹** ~押 *n. & v.* mortgage

TI⁴ 弟 *n.* younger brother

TI⁴ 地 *n.* earth, ground, land

~**chen⁴** ~震 *n.* earthquake

~**chih² hsüeh²** ~質學 *n.* geology

~**chih² pu⁴** ~質部 *n.* Ministry of Geological Survey**

~**chih³** ~址 *n.* mail address

~**chu³ chieh¹ chi²** ~主階級 *n.* landlord class**

~**ch'an³** ~産 *n.* real estate

~**ch'in² jen² yüan²** ~勤人員 *n.* ground crew

~**ch'iu²** ~球 *n.* earth, globe

~**fang¹ cheng⁴ fu³** ~方政府 *n.* local government

~**fang¹ hung² chün¹** ~方紅軍 *n.* local Red Army**

~**hsin¹ hsi¹ li⁴** ~心吸力 *n.* gravitation

~**hsing²** ~形 *n.* terrain

~**lei²** ~雷 *n.* land mine

~**lei² chen¹ ch'a² ch'i⁴** ~雷偵察器 *n.* mine detector

~**mao⁴** ~貌 *n.* terrain feature

~**pan³** ~板 *n.* floor

~**p'ing²** **hsien⁴** ~平線 *n.* horizon

~**tai⁴** ~帶 *n.* zone

~**tien⁴** ~點 *n.* location, locality

~**t'an³** ~毯 *n.* carpet, rug

~**t'u²** ~圖 *n.* map

~**wei³** ~委 *n.* County Group Committee of the Chinese Communist Party**

~**wei⁴** ~位 *n.* position, place, site, rank

~**yü⁴** ~獄 *n.* hell

TI⁴ 第 *n.* class, order, series, mansion

~**erh⁴** **chi¹** **hsieh⁴** **kung¹** **yeh⁴** **pu⁴** ~二機械工業部 *n.* Second Ministry of Machine Industry**

~**erh⁴** **tz'u⁴** **shih⁴** **chieh⁴** **ta⁴** **chan⁴** ~二次世界大戰 *n.* World War II

~**i¹** **chi¹** **hsieh⁴** **kung¹** **yeh⁴** **pu⁴** ~一機械工業部 *n.* First Ministry of Machine Industry**

~**san¹** **kuo²** **chi⁴** ~三國際 *n.* Third International, Communist International

~**san¹** **shih⁴** **li⁴** ~三勢力 *n.* Third Force

~**san¹** **tang³** ~三黨 *n.* Third Party

~**wu³** **tsung¹** **tui⁴** ~五縱隊 *n.* Fifth Column

TI⁴ 的 *n.* target, mark. **TE¹** [a subordinate]

~² **ch'üeh⁴** ~確 *adv.* really

~⁴ **shih⁴** ~士 *n.* taxi

TI⁴ 帝 *n.* emperor

~**hou⁴** ~后 *n.* empress, queen

~**kuo²** ~國 *n.* empire, kingdom

~**kuo²** **chu³** **i⁴** ~國主義 *n.* imperialism

~**kuo²** **te¹** ~國的 *a.* imperial

~**wang²** ~王 *n.* emperor, king, ruler

~**wei⁴** ~位 *n.* throne

TIAO⁴ 掉 *v.* move, fall, change

~**huan⁴** ~換 *v.* exchange

~**lao⁴** ~落 *v.* fall

~**t'ou²** ~頭 *v.* return, fall back

TIAO⁴ 調 *see* **T'IAO²**

TIEH¹ 爹 *n.* father, daddy, papa

TIEN³ 點 *n.* point, spot, speck, dot, stain, little; *v.* nod, light

~chung¹ ~鐘 *n.* o'clock
~hao⁴ ~號 *n.* period
~huo³ ~火 *v.* kindle
~hsin¹ ~心 *n.* refreshments
~ming² ~名 *v.* call the roll; *n.* roll call
~ming² **ts'e⁴** ~名冊 *n.* roll (list of names)
~teng¹ ~燈 *v.* light a lamp
~t'ou² ~頭 *v.* nod
~ts'ai⁴ ~菜 *v.* order the dish
TIEN³ 典 *v.* pawn; *n.* rite, ceremony
~hsing² ~型 *n.* model, pattern, example
~ku⁴ ~故 *n.* allusion
~li³ ~禮 *n.* ceremony
~tang⁴ ~當 *v.* pawn
TIEN⁴ 店 *n.* shop, store
~chu³ ~主 *n.* storekeeper
~huo³ ~夥 *n.* employee, clerk
~p'u⁴ ~舖 *n.* store, shop
TIEN⁴ 電 *n.* electricity, telegraphy, lightning
~ch'e¹ ~車 *n.* streetcar, trolley car
~ch'i⁴ ~氣 *a.* electric
~ch'ih² ~池 *n.* electric battery
~feng¹ shan⁴ ~風扇 *n.* electric fan
~hua⁴ ~話 *n.* telephone
~hua⁴ chü² ~話局 *n.* telephone office
~hsien⁴ ~綫 *n.* electric wires
~hsin⁴ ~信 *n.* telegram
~i³ ~椅 *n.* electric chair
~li⁴ ~力 *n.* electric power
~ling² ~鈴 *n.* electric bell
~liu² ~流 *n.* electric current
~lu² ~爐 *n.* electric stove, electric furnace
~ma³ ~碼 *n.* (telegraph) code
~nao³ ~腦 *n.* electric brain
~pao⁴ ~報 *n.* telegram, telegraph
~pao⁴ chü² ~報局 *n.* telegraph office
~shih⁴ ~視 *n.* television
~shih⁴ fang⁴ sung⁴ ~視放送 *v.* telecast
~teng¹ ~燈 *n.* electric lights
~teng¹ p'ao⁴ ~燈泡 *n.* electric bulb
~tung⁴ chi¹ ~動機 *n.* electromotor

177

~t'i¹ ～梯 *n.* elevator, escalator

~tz'u² ～磁 *n.* electromagnet

~ya¹ chi⁴ ～壓計 *n.* voltmeter

~ying³ ～影 *n.* movie, moving picture

~ying³ ming² hsing¹ ～影明星 *n.* movie star

~ying³ yüan⁴ ～影院 *n.* movie theater

TING¹ 丁 *n.* adult, individual, person

~hsiang¹ ～香 *n.* clove (plant)

~tzu⁴ ch'ih³ ～字尺 *n.* T square

TING³ 頂 *n.* top; *v.* oppose

~tien³ ～點 *n.* apex

TING⁴ 定 *v.* determine, order; *a.* fixed, firm

~chia⁴ ～價 *n.* list price

~ch'i¹ ～期 *a.* periodic

~ch'i¹ ts'un² k'uan³ ～期存款 *n.* savings account

~hun¹ ～婚 *n.* engagement (promise to marry)

~huo⁴ ～貨 *v.* order goods

~i⁴ ～義 *n.* definition

~li³ ～理 *n.* theorem

~lü⁴ ～律 *n.* theorem

~tsui⁴ ～罪 *v.* sentence

TING⁴ 訂 *v.* subscribe, examine, decide

~hun¹ ～婚 *v.* engage (pledge to marry)

~huo⁴ tan¹ ～貨單 *n.* bill of order

~meng² ～盟 *v.* pledge

~yüeh¹ ～約 *v.* conclude a treaty

TIU¹ 丟 *v.* lose

~ch'ou³ ～醜 *n.* disgrace, shame

~ch'i⁴ ～棄 *v.* abandon

~lien³ ～臉 *v.* lose face

TO¹ 多 *a.* many, numerous; *n.* plenty

~hsieh⁴ ～謝 *n.* thanks

~hsin¹ ～心 *a.* suspicious

~liang⁴ ～量 *a.* a great deal

~pien⁴ ～辯 *a.* arguable

~shao³ ～少 *adv.* how many?, how much?

~shu⁴ ～數 *n.* majority

TO² 奪 *v.* snatch, strive, take by force

~ch'ü³ ～取 *v.* take by force

~hui² ～回 *v.* recover

TO³ 朵 *n.* cluster

TOU¹ 都 *see* **TU¹**

TOU³ 斗 Chinese measure for 10.35 liters, bushel, peck
　~**p'eng²** ~篷 *n.* mantle, cape

TOU⁴ 豆 *n.* bean, pea
　~**chia¹** ~荚 *n.* bean pod
　~**fu³** ~腐 *n.* bean curd
　~**ya²** ~芽 *n.* bean sprout
　~**yu²** ~油 *n.* bean oil

TOU⁴ 鬥 *v.* fight
　~**cheng¹** ~争 *n. & v.* struggle
　~**chi¹** ~雞 *n.* cockfight
　~**chi¹ yen³** ~雞眼 *n.* cross-eye
　~**niu²** ~牛 *n.* bullfight

TU¹ 都 *n.* capital, metropolis. **TOU¹** *a.* all
　~**hui⁴** ~會 *n.* metropolis; *a.* metropolitan
　~**shih⁴** ~市 *n.* capital, metropolis

TU² 讀 *v.* read, study
　~**che³** ~者 *n.* reader
　~**pen³** ~本 *n.* textbook
　~**shu¹** ~書 *n. & v.* study

TU² 毒 *n.* poison; *a.* poisonous
　~**ch'i⁴** ~氣 *n.* poison gas
　~**wa³ ssu¹** ~瓦斯 *n.* gas
　~**wu⁴** ~物 *n.* poison

TU² 獨 *a.* solitary, single, only
　~**chan⁴** ~占 *n.* monopoly
　~**li⁴** ~立 *n.* independence; *a.* independent
　~**shen¹** ~身 *n.* single life
　~**shen¹ chu³ i⁴** ~身主義 *n.* bachelorhood
　~**ts'ai²** ~裁 *a.* dictatorial
　~**ts'ai² cheng⁴ chih⁴** ~裁政治 *n.* dictatorship
　~**tzu³** ~子 *n.* only son
　~**tzu⁴** ~自 *pron.* oneself

TU³ 賭 *v.* gamble, bet
　~**po²** ~博 *n.* gambling
　~**t'u²** ~徒 *n.* gambler

TU⁴ 度 *v.* spend, measure; *n.* degree (scale)
　~**liang⁴** ~量 *v.* measure
　~**liang⁴ heng²** ~量衡 *n.* length, capacity and weight

~shu⁴ ~數 *n*. degree (scale)

TU⁴ 肚 *n*. abdomen, belly

~ch'i² ~臍 *n*. navel

~tai⁴ ~帶 *n*. girth, cinch

~t'ung⁴ ~痛 *n*. belly-ache

TUAN³ 短 *a*. short, brief

~ch'u⁴ ~處 *n*. defect

~kung¹ ~工 *n*. piece work

~lu⁴ ~路 *n*. short circuit (*elec.*)

~ming⁴ ~命 *a*. short-lived

~p'ien¹ hsiao³ shuo¹ ~篇小説 *n*. short stories

~shao³ ~少 *v*. lack

TUAN⁴ 斷 *v*. cut apart, stop, settle, judge

~ai² ~崖 *n*. cliff

~chüeh² ~絶 *v*. break off, cut off

~chüeh² ti⁴ ~絶的 *n*. broken terrain

~t'ou² chi¹ ~頭機 *n*. guillotine

TUAN⁴ 段 *n*. portion, section

~lao⁴ ~落 *n*. paragraph, stop

TUI¹ 堆 *n*. heap, pile, mass

~chan⁴ ~棧 *n*. warehouse

~chi¹ ~積 *v*. pile

TUI⁴ 對 *n*. pair, couple; *v*. pair, answer; *a*. opposite

~chao⁴ ~照 *v*. contrast

~cheng⁴ ~證 *n*. witness

~chih⁴ chuang⁴ t'ai⁴ ~峙狀態 *n*. stalemate

~hua⁴ ~話 *n*. dialogue

~huan⁴ ~換 *v*. exchange

~k'ang⁴ ~抗 *n*. antagonism; *v*. oppose

~mien⁴ ~面 *v*. confront; *n*. confrontation

~pi³ ~比 *v*. contrast

~shou³ ~手 *n*. rival

~shu⁴ ~數 *n*. logarithm

~ta² ~答 *v*. answer, reply

~te¹ ~的 *a*. right

~t'ou² ~頭 *n*. opponent

~wai⁴ mao⁴ i⁴ pu⁴ ~外貿易部 *n*. Ministry of Foreign Trade**

TUI⁴ 隊 *n*. team, group, gang, squadron

~chang³ ~長 *n*. captain

~**hsing²** ~形 *n.* formation

~**wu³** ~伍 *n.* troop

TUN⁴ 頓 *v.* bow the head

TUNG¹ 東 *n.* east; *a.* east, eastern

~**fang¹** ~方 *n.* east, the Orient, the East; *a.* Oriental, Eastern

~**fang¹ jen²** ~方人 *n.* Orientals

~**pan⁴ ch'iu²** ~半球 *n.* Eastern Hemisphere

~**tao⁴ chu³** ~道主 *n.* host

~**yang²** ~洋 *n.* Japan

TUNG¹ 冬 *n.* winter

~**chi⁴** ~季 *n. & a.* winter

~**chih⁴** ~至 *n.* winter solstice

~**ch'ing¹ shu⁴** ~青樹 *n.* evergreen

~**mien²** ~眠 *n.* hibernation

TUNG³ 懂 *v.* understand

TUNG⁴ 動 *v.* move, shake, stir, act

~**chi¹** ~機 *n.* motive

~**ch'an³** ~産 *n.* movable property

~**i⁴** ~議 *n.* motion (suggestion)

~**mo⁴** ~脈 *n.* artery

~**tso⁴** ~作 *n.* action, movement (in drill)

~**tz'u²** ~詞 *n.* verb

~**wu⁴** ~物 *n.* animal

~**wu⁴ hsüeh²** ~物學 *n.* zoology

~**wu⁴ hsüeh² chia¹** ~物學家 *n.* zoologist

~**wu⁴ yüan²** ~物園 *n.* zoo

~**yao²** ~搖 *v.* shake

~**yüan²** ~員 *n.* mobilization

~**yüan² chi⁴ hua⁴** ~員計劃 *n.* mobilization plan

~**yüan² ling⁴** ~員令 *n.* mobilization order

TUNG⁴ 凍 *v.* freeze, congeal

~**ch'uang¹** ~瘡 *n.* chilblain

~**jou⁴** ~肉 *n.* cold mcat

~**ssu³** ~死 *v.* be frozen to death

TUNG⁴ 洞 *n.* cave, tunnel, hole

~**hsi²** ~悉 *v.* understand thoroughly

~**hsüeh⁴** ~穴 *n.* cave

T'

T'A¹ 他 *pron.* he
  ~**ch'u⁴** ~處 *adv.* elsewhere
  ~**hsiang⁴** ~項 *n.* other items
  ~**jih⁴** ~日 *n.* another day
  ~**men²** ~們 *pron.* they, them
  ~**men² te¹** ~們的 *pron.* their, theirs
  ~**te¹** ~的 *a.* his
  ~**tzu⁴ chi³** ~自己 *pron.* himself
T'A¹ 它 *pron.* it
T'A¹ 她 *pron.* she
  ~**men²** ~們 *pron.* they, them
  ~**te¹** ~的 *a.* her
  ~**tzu⁴ chi³** ~自己 *pron.* herself
T'AI² 台 *n.* platform, terrace
T'AI² 抬 *v.* lift, carry
  ~**kao¹** ~高 *v.* raise
T'AI⁴ 太 *adv.* very, too, extremely
  ~**chien⁴** ~監 *n.* eunuch, a castrated man
  ~**hsi²** ~息 *v.* sigh
  ~**ku³** ~古 *n.* antiquity, early ages of history
  ~**p'ing²** ~平 *n.* peace
  ~**p'ing² t'ien¹ kuo²** ~平天國 *n.* Taiping Heavenly Kingdom
  ~**yang²** ~陽 *n.* sun
T'AI⁴ 態 *n.* manner, attitude, bearing, mien
  ~**tu⁴** ~度 *n.* behavior, manner, attitude
T'AN¹ 貪 *v.* covet; *a.* greedy
  ~**hsin¹** ~心 *a.* greedy
  ~**se⁴** ~色 *a.* lustful
  ~**ts'ai²** ~財 *a.* greedy of money
  ~**wu¹** ~污 *n.* graft (corruption)
T'AN² 談 *v.* talk, chat
  ~**hua⁴** ~話 *v.* talk; *n.* conversation
  ~**p'an⁴** ~判 *v.* negotiate; *n.* negotiation
T'AN² 痰 *n.* phlegm, sputum
  ~**yü²** ~盂 *n.* cuspidor, spittoon
T'AN² 彈 *see* **TAN⁴**

T'AN⁴ 探 *v.* spy, visit, explore, sound
~**chih¹** ～知 *v.* find out
~**ch'iu²** ～求 *v.* search
~**fang³** ～訪 *v.* visit
~**hsien³** ～險 *v.* explore
~**hsien³ chia¹** ～險家 *n.* explorer, adventurer
~**hsien³ tui⁴** ～險隊 *n.* exploration party
~**so³** ～索 *v.* search out
~**wen⁴** ～問 *v.* ask
T'AN⁴ 炭 *n.* charcoal, carbon
T'AN⁴ 歎 *n.* & *v.* sigh
~**hsi²** ～息 *n.* & *v.* sigh
~**hsi²** ～惜 *v.* pity
~**hsien⁴** ～羨 *v.* admire
T'ANG¹ 湯 *n.* soup, hot water
~**ch'ih²** ～匙 *n.* soup spoon
T'ANG² 堂 *n.* hall, court, church
~**hsiung¹ ti⁴** ～兄弟 *n.* son of one's father's brother (cousin)
~**kuan³** ～館 *n.* waiter
~**t'ang²** ～堂 *a.* stately
~**tzu¹** ～子 *n.* brothel
~**tzu³ mei⁴** ～姊妹 *n.* daughter of one's father's brother (cousin)
T'ANG² 糖 *n.* sugar, candy
~**chiang¹** ～漿 *n.* syrup
~**ching¹** ～精 *n.* saccharin
~**chiu³** ～酒 *n.* rum
~**kuo³** ～果 *n.* candy, sweets
~**kuo³ tien⁴** ～果店 *n.* confectioner
~**niao³ ping⁴** ～尿病 *n.* sugar diabetes
~**shih²** ～食 *n.* sweetmeats
T'AO² 逃 *v.* escape, flee
~**nan⁴** ～難 *v.* take a refuge
~**pi⁴** ～避 *v.* escape
~**ping¹** ～兵 *n.* deserter
~**shih¹** ～失 *a.* lost horse
~**ting¹** ～丁 *n.* draft dodger
~**t'o¹** ～脱 *v.* escape
~**wang²** ～亡 *v.* desert; *n.* desertion
T'AO² 桃 *n.* peach

T'AO³ 討 *v.* punish, demand, beg
~**fa²** ~伐 *n.* punitive expedition
~**fan⁴** ~飯 *n.* beggar
~**hao³** ~好 *v.* please
~**jao²** ~饒 *v.* seek forgiveness
~**lun⁴** ~論 *v.* discuss; *n.* discussion
~**yen⁴** ~厭 *a.* disgusted; *v.* dislike

T'AO⁴ 套 *n.* suit, case, envelope, covering, set
~**hsieh²** ~鞋 *n.* overshoe

T'E⁴ 特 *a.* special, particular; *adv.* specially, particularly
~**ch'uan²** ~權 *n.* priviledge
~**hsing⁴** ~性 *n.* characteristic
~**hsü³** ~許 *n.* patent
~**pieh²** ~別 *a.* special, particular
~**pieh² pan¹** ~別班 *n.* special course
~**pieh² shih⁴** ~別市 *n.* special municipality
~**she⁴** ~赦 *n.* amnesty
~**tien³** ~點 *n.* feature (distinct part), specialty
~**wu⁴** ~務 *n.* secret service
~**yüeh¹** ~約 *n.* special contract

T'ENG² 疼 *n.* pain, ache, pity, love
~**ai⁴** ~愛 *v.* be fond of
~**t'ung⁴** ~痛 *n.* pain

T'ENG² 騰 *v.* ascend, mount
~**k'ung¹** ~空 *v.* soar, fly upward
~**ta²** ~達 *v.* become prosperous

T'I¹ 梯 *n.* ladder, stairs

T'I² 提 *v.* lift, carry, mention
~**ch'ang⁴** ~倡 *v.* promote growth
~**ch'iang¹** ~槍 *v.* trail arms
~**ch'in²** ~琴 *n.* violin
~**fang²** ~防 *v.* guard, watch
~**hsing³** ~醒 *v.* remind
~**i⁴** ~議 *v.* suggest; *n.* suggestion

T'I² 題 *n.* subject, heading; *v.* propose, name
~**mu⁴** ~目 *n.* subject, title, topic
~**tseng⁴** ~贈 *n.* inscription

T'I³ 體 *n.* body, style, form, manner, substance
~**chi¹** ~積 *n.* volume (measure)
~**hui⁴** ~會 *v.* comprehend

184

~**hsü⁴** ~恤 *v.* conserve

~**ko²** ~格 *n.* physique

~**ko² chien³ ch'a²** ~格检查 *n.* physical examination

~**li⁴** ~力 *n.* strength (vigor)

~**mien⁴** ~面 *n.* honor

~**t'ieh¹** ~贴 *v.* sympathize

~**ts'ao¹** ~操 *n.* physical training

~**yü⁴** ~育 *n.* physical culture

~**yü⁴ kuan³** ~育馆 *n.* gymnasium

~**yü⁴ yün⁴ tung⁴ wei³ yüan² hui⁴** ~育运动委员會 *n.* Commission of Physical Culture**

T'I⁴ 替 *v.* substitute, replace; *prep.* for, instead of

~**huan⁴** ~换 *v.* alternate

~**shen¹** ~身 *n.* substitute (person)

T'IAO¹ 挑 *v.* select, lift, carry

~**¹ fu¹** ~夫 *n.* porter

~**hsüan³** ~选 *n.* select

~**³ chan⁴** ~战 *v.* challenge

~**po¹** ~拨 *v.* instigate, stir up

T'IAO² 调 *v.* stir up, mix. **TIAO⁴** *v.* transfer; *n.* tune, rhyme

~**chieh³ jen²** ~解人 *n.* mediator

~**ho²** ~和 *n.* harmony

~**hsi⁴** ~戏 *v.* dally with

~**hsiao⁴** ~笑 *v.* dally with

~**t'ing²** ~停 *v.* mediate, adjust

~**wei⁴** ~味 *v.* season

~**yin¹** ~音 *v.* put in tune

tiao⁴ ch'a² ~查 *v.* investigate

~**ch'a² yüan²** ~查员 *n.* investigator

~**huan⁴** ~换 *v.* exchange

T'IAO² 条 *n.* twig, classifier, bill, article, clause

~**chien⁴** ~件 *n.* conditions, terms (of agreement)

~**k'uan³** ~款 *n.* article, clause

~**li⁴** ~例 *n.* regulation

~**wen²** ~文 *n.* provision

~**yüeh¹** ~约 *n.* treaty

T'IAO⁴ 跳 *v.* jump, leap; *n.* ricochet

~**kao¹** ~高 *n.* high jump

~**lan²** ~栏 *n.* hurdle race, hurdles

~san³ 傘 v. bail out
~san³ t'a³ 傘塔 n. parachute tower
~tsao³ 蚤 n. flea
~wu³ 舞 n. & v. dance
~wu³ hui⁴ ~舞會 n. ball (dance)
~wu³ t'ing¹ ~舞廳 n. dance hall
T'IEH¹ 貼 v. paste up, stick
~pu³ ~補 v. subsidize
T'IEH³ 帖 n. copybook, invitation card
T'IEH³ 鐵 n. iron
~chia³ ~甲 a. armored; n. armor
~chiang⁴ ~匠 n. blacksmith
~ch'ang³ ~廠 n. ironworks
~ch'i⁴ ~器 n. ironware
~lu⁴ ~路 n. railroad, railway
~mu⁴ ~幕 n. iron curtain
~ssu¹ ~糸 n. iron wire
~tao⁴ pu⁴ ~道部 n. Ministry of Railways**
~ting¹ ~釘 n. iron nail
T'IEN¹ 天 n. sky, heaven, day
~ching³ ~井 n. yard
~chu³ chiao⁴ ~主教 n. Catholicism, Catholicity
~chu³ chiao⁴ t'u² ~主教徒 n. Catholic
~ch'eng⁴ ~秤 n. balance
~ch'i⁴ ~気 n. weather
~ch'uang¹ ~窗 n. skylight
~e² jung² ~鵝絨 n. velvet
~hua¹ ~花 n. smallpox
~hua¹ pan³ ~花板 n. ceiling
~hsing⁴ ~性 n. instinct, nature
~k'ung¹ ~空 n. sky
~liang² ~良 n. conscience
~shih³ ~使 n. angel
~ti⁴ ~地 n. heaven and earth
~t'ang² ~堂 n. heaven, paradise
~tsai¹ ~災 n. catastrophe, disaster, calamity
~ts'ai² ~才 n. talent
~tzu¹ ~資 n. endowments
~wen² ~文 n. astronomy
~wen² t'ai² ~文臺 n. observatory
~ai² ~涯 n. horizon

T'IEN¹ 添 *v.* increase, add to
T'IEN² 甜 *a.* sweet
　~mi⁴ ~蜜 *a.* sweet
　~shui⁴ 睡 *n.* sound sleep
　~yen² ~言 *n.* sweet words
T'IEN² 田 *n.* field
　~ch'an³ ~產 *n.* estate, landed property
　~ti⁴ ~地 *n.* field
　~tsu¹ ~租 *n.* rent for the use of fields
T'IEN² 填 *v.* fill up, complete
　~liao⁴ ~料 *n.* gasket
　~shih² ~實 *v.* tamp
　~t'u³ ~土 *v.* fill (*engin.*)
T'ING¹ 聽 *v.* hear, listen. **~⁴** *v.* comply
　~¹ chung⁴ ~衆 *n.* audience (meet)
　~chüeh² ~覺 *n.* sense of hearing
　~ch'ai¹ ~差 *n.* servant
　~shuo¹ ~説 *v.* hear of
　~⁴ hsin⁴ ~信 *v.* believe
　~jen⁴ ~任 *v.* allow
　~ming⁴ ~命 *v.* accept one's fate, obey orders
　~ts'ung² ~從 *v.* obey
T'ING¹ 廳 *n.* hall, parlor, court, tribunal
　~chang³ ~長 *n.* department commissioner
T'ING² 停 *v.* stop, delay, cease; *a.* settled
　~chan⁴ ~戰 *n.* truce, armistice
　~chan⁴ hsieh² ting⁴ ~戰協定 *n.* armistice agreement
　~chih³ ~止 *v.* cease, stop, halt
　~chih³ ying² yeh⁴ ~止營業 *n.* cessation of business
　~hsin¹ ~薪 *n.* stoppage of officers' pay
　~liu² ~留 *v.* stay, remain
　~po² ~泊 *v.* anchor
　~po² teng¹ ~泊燈 *n.* anchor light
　~pu⁴ ~步 *v.* halt
T'ING² 庭 *n.* courtyard
　~yüan⁴ ~院 *n.* courtyard
T'O¹ 脱 *v.* doff, take off, remove, strip, escape
　~chieh² ~節 *n.* dislocation (joint)
　~li² ~離 *v.* disengage, break contact tactics, free

187

~t'ao² ~逃 *v.* escape

T'O¹ 託 *v.* entrust, ask

~erh² so³ ~兒所 *n.* day nursery

~fu⁴ ~付 *v.* entrust

~ku⁴ ~故 *v.* give a pretext

~tz'u² ~辭 *n.* excuse, pretext

T'O¹ 拖 *v.* pull, drag

~ch'ien⁴ ~欠 *v.* be in debt

~ch'uan² ~船 *n.* tug-boat

~hsieh² ~鞋 *n.* slipper

~lei³ ~累 *v.* involve

~yen² ~延 *v.* delay

T'O³ 妥 *a.* safe, secure

~hsieh² ~協 *n.* & *v.* compromise

~tang¹ ~當 *a.* safe, settled

T'OU¹ 偷 *v.* steal; *a.* fraudulent; *n.* theft

~an¹ ~安 *a.* sedentary

~ch'ieh⁴ ~竊 *v.* steal; *n.* theft, larceny

~p'ao³ ~跑 *v.* escape

~shui⁴ ~稅 *n.* tax-evasion

~yün⁴ ~運 *v.* smuggle

T'OU² 頭 *n.* head, top, end, chief; *a.* first

~chin¹ ~巾 *n.* head scarf

~ling³ ~領 *n.* chief

~nao³ ~腦 *n.* brain

~tang⁴ ~檔 *n.* low gear

~teng³ ~等 *n.* first class

~t'ung⁴ ~痛 *n.* headache

~yün¹ ~暈 *n.* dizziness, vertigo

T'OU² 投 *v.* throw, fling, invest

~chi¹ ~機 *v.* speculate (business)

~chün¹ ~軍 *v.* enlist

~hsiang² ~降 *n.* & *v.* surrender

~ju⁴ sheng¹ ch'an³ ~入生産 *v.* commence production**

~kao³ ~稿 *v.* contribute (write)

~piao¹ ~標 *n.* auction bidding

~p'iao⁴ ~票 *v.* vote

~p'iao⁴ ch'üan² ~票權 *n.* suffrage

~tzu¹ ~資 *v.* invest

T'OU⁴ 透 *v.* penetrate

~chih¹ ～支 *v.* overdraw
~ch'e⁴ ～澈 *adv.* thoroughly
~feng¹ ～風 *v.* ventilate
~kuang¹ ～光 *a.* translucent
~ming² ～明 *a.* transparent; *n.* transparency
T'U² 塗 *n.* mud, dirt, mire; *v.* plaster
~kai³ ～改 *v.* alter
~mo³ ～抹 *v.* obliterate
~wu¹ ～污 *v.* daub (stain)
T'U² 途 *n.* road, path, way
~chung¹ ～中 *adv.* on the way, en route
~ch'eng² ～程 *n.* journey
T'U² 徒 *adv.* barely, only
~hsing² ～刑 *n.* penal servitude
~jan² ～然 *adv.* in vain
~pu⁴ ～步 *v.* walk on foot
~she⁴ ～涉 *v.* ford (on foot)
~shou³ ～手 *a.* unarmed
~ti⁴ ～弟 *n.* apprentice, pupil
T'U² 圖 *n.* figure, map, picture; *v.* sketch, try for
~chang¹ ～章 *n.* seal
~chieh³ ～解 *n. & v.* diagram
~hua⁴ ～畫 *n.* drawing, picture
~mou² ～謀 *v.* conspire
~piao³ ～表 *n.* diagram
~shu¹ ～書 *n.* books
~shu¹ kuan³ ～書館 *n.* library
~shu¹ kuan³ yüan² ～書館員 *n.* librarian
~yang⁴ ～樣 *n.* design
T'U² 屠 *v.* kill, butcher, slaughter
~ch'ang³ ～場 *n.* slaughter house
~fu¹ ～夫 *n.* butcher
~sha¹ ～殺 *v.* slaughter
~tsai³ shui⁴ ～宰稅 *n.* butchery tax
T'U³ 土 *n.* earth, ground, soil, land, territory
~ch'an³ ～産 *n.* native product
~fei³ ～匪 *n.* bandit, highwayman, robber
~hao² ～豪 *n.* local bully
~hua⁴ ～話 *n.* dialect
~hsing¹ ～星 *n.* Saturn (astronomy)
~jang³ ～壞 *n.* soil

189

~**jen²** ~人 *n.* native
~**kai³** ~改 *n.* land reform**
~**kun⁴** ~棍 *n.* local bully
~**mu⁴ kung¹ ch'eng²** ~木工程 *n.* civil engineering
~**ti⁴** ~地 *n.* land, territory
~**ti⁴ kai³ ko²** ~地改革 *n.* Agrarian Reform**
~**ti⁴ ko² ming⁴ chan⁴ cheng¹** ~地革命戰争 *n.* Agrarian Revolutionary War**

T'U⁴ 吐 *v.* reveal, spit, vomit
~**hsüeh⁴** ~血 *v.* spit blood
~**lu⁴** ~露 *v.* tell, disclose
~**t'an²** ~痰 *v.* spit phlegm

T'U⁴ 突 *v.* rush; *adv.* suddenly
~**chi¹** ~擊 *n.* assault, shock action
~**ch'i³** ~起 *n.* protuberance
~**ch'u¹** ~出 *v.* protrude
~**jan²** ~然 *adv.* suddenly
~**p'o⁴** ~破 *v.* break through, penetrate
~**p'o⁴ k'ou³** ~破口 *n.* breach
~**wei²** ~圍 *v.* break out (from encirclement)

T'UAN² 團 *n.* regiment, lump, sphere, body
~**chang³** ~長 *n.* regimental commander
~**chieh²** ~結 *n.* solidarity; *v.* unite
~**chieh² ching¹ shen²** ~結精神 *n.* esprit de corps
~**t'i³** ~體 *n.* organization, body
~**t'i³ kuan¹ nien⁴** ~體觀念 *n.* group feeling
~**t'i³ sheng¹ huo²** ~體生活 *n.* group life
~**yüan²** ~圓 *n.* reunion

T'UI¹ 推 *v.* push, expel, decline, ram
~**chin⁴** ~進 *v.* push, advance (on a place)
~**chin⁴ chi¹** ~進機 *n.* pusher airplane
~**chiu¹** ~究 *v.* examine
~**ch'üeh⁴** ~却 *v.* refuse
~**fan¹** ~翻 *v.* overthrow, upset
~**hsüan³** ~選 *v.* elect
~**kan³** ~桿 *n.* plunger
~**kuang³** ~廣 *v.* extend
~**lun⁴** ~論 *v.* deduce, infer; *n.* logical deduction
~**shih⁴** ~事 *n.* judge

190

~**t'o**¹ ～託 *v.* make excuse

~**tse**⁴ ～測 *v.* guess, suppose

T'UI³ 腿 *n.* thigh, leg

T'UI⁴ 退 *v.* withdraw, retire, retreat

~**chih**² ～職 *n.* retirement

~**ch'u**¹ ～出 *v.* quit

~**hou**⁴ ～後 *v.* retreat

~**hua**⁴ ～化 *v.* degenerate ; *n.* degeneration

~**huan**² ～還 *v.* send back, return

~**jang**⁴ ～讓 *v.* give up, yield

~**pi**⁴ ～避 *v.* avert

~**pu**⁴ ～步 *a.* backward (retrogressive)

~**se**⁴ ～色 *v.* fade

~**so**¹ ～縮 *v.* shrink back

~**yin**³ ～隱 *v.* retire

T'UN¹ 吞 *v.* swallow, gulp, engross

~**chan**⁴ ～佔 *v.* usurp

~**k'uan**³ ～款 *v.* squeeze money

~**ping**⁴ ～併 *v.* engross

~**shih**² ～食 *v.* swallow

T'UNG¹ 通 *v.* go through, communicate with, contact

~**chih**¹ ～知 *v.* notify

~**ch'ang**² ～常 *a.* ordinary

~**hsin**⁴ ～信 *v.* correspond ; *n.* correspondence

~**hsin**⁴ **ch'u**¹ ～信处 *n.* mail address

~**hsin**⁴ **yüan**² ～信員 *n.* correspondent

~**hsing**² ～行 *a.* current

~**jung**² ～融 *v.* accommodate (oblige)

~**kao**⁴ ～告 *n.* written notice

~**kuo**⁴ ～過 *v.* pass ; *n.* passage

~**li**⁴ ～例 *n.* custom

~**su**² ～俗 *a.* common (below ordinary)

~**shang**¹ ～商 *v.* trade with foreign countries

T'UNG² 童 *n.* boy

~**chen**¹ ～眞 *n.* virgin

~**hua**⁴ ～話 *n.* fairy tale

~**nien**² ～年 *n.* boyhood

~**tz'u**³ ～子 *n.* boy

~**tzu**³ **chün**¹ ～子軍 *n.* boy scout

T'UNG² 同 *conj.* and, with ; *adv.* together ; *a.*

191

same, alike
~**chih⁴** ~志 *n.* comrade
~**chung³** ~種 *n.* the same race
~**ch'ing²** ~情 *n.* sympathy
~**ch'ou² ti² k'ai⁴** ~仇敵愾 *v.* have a common
enmity and hatred
~**hua⁴** ~化 *n.* amalgamation
~**hsiang¹** ~鄉 *n.* natives of the same province
~**hsüeh²** ~學 *n.* schoolmate
~**i² hsing⁴** ~一性 *n.* unity
~**i⁴** ~意 *v.* agree ; *n.* agreement
~**kan¹ k'u³** ~甘苦 *v.* share the joys and privations
~**meng²** ~盟 *n.* alliance
~**meng² kuo²** ~盟國 *n.* alliance, allies
~**pan¹ t'ung² hsüeh²** ~班同學 *n.* classmate
~**pan⁴** ~伴 *n.* companion
~**pao¹** ~胞 *n.* brothers, countryman, compatriot
~**p'ao²** ~袍 *n.* fellow officer
~**shih²** ~時 *n.* meantime
~**shih⁴** ~事 *n.* colleague, fellow worker
~**teng³** ~等 *n.* equality
~**wen²** ~文 *a.* of the same language
~**yang⁴** ~樣 *a.* same, alike
T'UNG² 銅 *n.* copper, brass
~**chiang⁴** ~匠 *n.* coppersmith
~**k'uang⁴** ~鑛 *n.* copper mine
~**pi⁴** ~幣 *n.* copper coin
T'UNG³ 統 *a.* all, whole, total
~**chi⁴ hsüeh²** ~計學 *n.* statistics
~**chih⁴** ~治 *v.* govern, rule
~**i¹** ~一 *v.* unify ; *n.* unification
~**i² hsing⁴** ~一性 *n.* unity
~**kung⁴** ~共 *a.* total
T'UNG³ 筒 *n.* tube, pipe
T'UNG³ 桶 *n.* bucket, barrel
T'UNG⁴ 痛 *n.* pain, ache, anguish
~**hen⁴** ~恨 *v.* abhor, hate
~**k'u¹** ~哭 *v.* weep bitterly
~**k'u³** ~苦 *n.* pain, ache, grief

192

TS

TSA² 咱 *pron*. I, me
  ~chia¹ ~家 *pron*. I, me
  ~men² ~們 *pron*. we, us
TSA² 雜 *a*. various, mixed, miscellaneous, mingled
  ~chi⁴ pu⁴ ~記簿 *n*. notebook
  ~chih⁴ ~誌 *n*. magazine
  ~chung³ ~種 *n*. mixed race; *a*. illegitimate
  ~fei⁴ ~費 *n*. miscellaneous expenses
  ~huo⁴ ~貨 *n*. sundries
  ~huo⁴ tien⁴ ~貨店 *n*. grocery
  ~luan⁴ ~亂 *a*. disorderly, mix-up
TSAI¹ 栽 *v*. plant, cultivate
  ~chung⁴ ~種 *v*. plant, cultivate
  ~hua¹ ~花 *v*. plant flowers
  ~p'ei² ~培 *v*. educate
TSAI¹ 災 *n*. calamity, misfortune, disaster
  ~hai⁴ ~害 *n*. calamity
  ~huo⁴ ~禍 *n*. disaster
  ~nan² ~難 *n*. disaster
TSAI⁴ 再 *adv*. again, once more
  ~che³ ~者 *n*. postscript
  ~chieh¹ tsai⁴ li⁴ ~接再厲 *v*. work hard against difficulties
  ~fan⁴ ~犯 *n*. recommitment
  ~hui⁴ ~會 *int*. & *n*. good-bye, farewell
  ~hun¹ ~婚 *v*. marry again
  ~pan³ ~版 *v*. reprint
  ~san¹ ~三 *adv*. repeatedly
  ~sheng¹ ch'an³ ~生產 *n*. reproduction (goods)
TSAI⁴ 在 *v*. remain, consist in; *prep*. at, in, on, within; *adv*. present
  ~chih² ~職 *adv*. in office
  ~ch'ang³ ~場 *a*. present
  ~ch'ien² ~前 *prep*. before; *adv*. ahead, in front
  ~hou⁴ ~後 *adv*. behind, in the rear
  ~hsia⁴ ~下 *prep*. below, beneath, down, under
  ~nei⁴ ~內 *prep*. within, in, among

~**shang⁴** 上 *prep.* on, above

~**wai⁴** 外 *adv.* out

TSAN⁴ 贊 *v.* advise, assist

~**chu⁴** ~助 *v.* assist, help

~**ch'eng²** ~成 *v.* second

~**mei³** ~美 *v.* praise

TSANG¹ 髒 *a.* filthy, dirty, foul

TSANG⁴ 藏 *see* TS'ANG²

TSAO³ 早 *adv.* early; *a.* previous; *n.* morning, good morning

~**ch'en²** ~晨 *n.* morning

~**ch'i³** ~起 *v.* get up early

~**hun¹** ~婚 *n.* early marriage

~**shou²** ~熟 *a.* premature; *adv.* prematurely

~**shui⁴** ~睡 *v.* sleep early

~**ts'an¹** ~餐 *n.* breakfast

TSAO⁴ 造 *v.* build, construct, make

~**ch'uan²** ~船 *n.* shipbuilding

~**ch'uan² ch'ang³** ~船廠 *n.* dockyard

~**pi⁴ ch'ang³** ~幣廠 *n.* money mint

~**yao²** ~謠 *v.* rumor

TSE² 責 *v.* reprove, punish, rebuke, require from; *n.* duty

~**fa²** ~罰 *v.* punish

~**jen⁴** ~任 *n.* responsibility

~**ma⁴** ~罵 *v.* reprove, rebuke

TSE² 澤 *n.* marsh, swamp, bog

TSE² 則 *n.* rule, regulation; *conj.* then, so

TSEI² 賊 *n.* thief, bandit, robber

TSEN³ 怎 *adv.* how, why, what

~**yang⁴** ~樣 *adv.* how, why, what

TSENG¹ 增 *v.* increase, add

~**chia¹** ~加 *v.* increase

~**chih²** ~殖 *n.* propagation

~**pu³** ~補 *v.* supplement

~**ta⁴** ~大 *v.* enlarge

~**ting⁴** ~訂 *v.* revise; *n.* revision

~**yüan²** ~援 *v.* reinforce

TSO² 昨 *n.* yesterday; *adv.* formerly

~**jih⁴** ~日 *n.* yesterday

~**yeh⁴** ~夜 *n.* last night

TSO³ 左 *a. & n.* left

~**ch'ing¹** ~傾 *a.* leftist idea

~**ch'ing¹ yu⁴ chih⁴ ping⁴** ~傾幼稚病 *n.* "Left" infantile errors**

~**i⁴ k'ung¹ t'an² chu³ i⁴** ~翼空談主義 *n.* phrase-mongering of the "leftists"**

~**p'ai⁴** ~派 *n.* leftist member

~**shou³** ~手 *a.* left-hand, left-handed

TSO⁴ 作 *v.* make, do

~² **liao⁴** ~料 *n.* stuff, material

~⁴ **chia¹** ~家 *n.* writer, author

~**fei⁴** ~廢 *v.* rescind, cancel

~**kung¹** ~工 *v.* work

~**luan⁴** ~亂 *v.* rebel; *n.* rebellion

~**meng⁴** ~夢 *v.* dream

~**pao³** ~保 *v.* guarantee

~**pi⁴** ~弊 *v.* cheat

~**wen²** ~文 *n.* composition

~**yeh⁴** ~業 *n.* work (field)

~**yeh⁴ pan¹** ~業班 *n.* work party

~**yung⁴** ~用 *n.* function

TSO⁴ 做 *v.* do, act, make

~**kung¹** ~工 *v.* work

~**mei²** ~媒 *n.* matchmaking

TSO⁴ 坐 *v.* sit

~**chien¹** ~監 *v.* imprison

~**hsia⁴** ~下 *v.* sit down

~**tien⁴** ~墊 *n.* cushion

~**wei⁴** ~位 *n.* seat

TSO⁴ 座 *n.* seat, place

~**wei⁴** ~位 *n.* seat

TSOU³ 走 *v.* walk; *n.* walking

~**feng¹** ~風 *v.* leak out the secret

~**kou³** ~狗 *n.* hound (person)

~**lang²** ~廊 *n.* corridor

~**lu⁴** ~路 *v.* walk

~**shou⁴** ~獸 *n.* beast

~**ts'o⁴** ~錯 *n.* go astray

TSU¹ 租 *n.* tax, rent; *v.* rent, lease

~**chia⁴** ~價 *n.* rent

~**chieh⁴** ~界 *n.* concession, settlement

~**chieh⁴ ti⁴** ～借地 *n.* leased territory

~**chin¹** ～金 *n.* rent

~**ch'i⁴** ～契 *n.* lease

~**fang²** ～房 *v.* rent a house

~**hu⁴** ～戶 *n.* tenant

~**lin⁴** ～賃 *v.* rent

~**shui⁴** ～稅 *n.* tax

TSU² 足 *n.* foot; *a.* enough, sufficient

~**chi¹** ～跡 *n.* trace

~**chih³** ～趾 *n.* toe

~**ch'iu²** ～球 *n.* football

~**ch'iu² ch'ang³** ～球場 *n.* football ground

~**ch'iu² sai⁴** ～球賽 *n.* football

~**hsia⁴** ～下 *n.* sir

~**kou⁴** ～夠 *a.* enough

TSU² 族 *n.* family, relatives, tribe, clan; *adv.* together

TSU³ 組 *n.* section, group, part; *v.* organize

~**chih¹** ～織 *v.* organize; *n.* organization

~**chih¹ cheng⁴ fu³** ～織政府 *v.* organize a government

~**ho²** ～合 *n.* combination

TSU³ 祖 *n.* grandfather, ancestor

~**fu⁴** ～父 *n.* father's father (grandfather)

~**hsien¹** ～先 *n.* ancestor

~**mu³** ～母 *n.* father's mother (grandmother)

TSU³ 阻 *v.* stop, prevent, hinder; *n.* prevention

~**ai⁴** ～礙 *v.* hinder, stop, prevent, impede

~**chih³** ～止 *v.* stop, interdict

~**chüeh²** ～絕 *v.* block, barricade

~**li⁴** ～力 *n.* air resistance

~**se⁴** ～塞 *v.* barricade

TSUI³ 嘴 *n.* mouth, bill, peak

~**ch'an²** ～饞 *v.* desire for food

~**ch'un²** ～唇 *n.* lip

TSUI⁴ 最 *adv.* very, most, extremely

~**chia¹** ～佳 *a.* best

~**chin⁴** ～近 *a.* nearest

~**hou⁴** ～後 *a.* last

~**hsiao³** ～小 *a.* smallest

~**kao¹** ～高 *n.* highest

~kao¹ chia⁴ ~高價 *n.* maximum price

~kao¹ jen² min² chien³ ch'a² shu³ ~高人民檢察署 *n.* People's Procurator-General's Office**

~kao¹ jen² min² fa³ yüan⁴ ~高人民法院 *n.* Supreme People's Court**

~lieh⁴ ~劣 *a.* worst

~ta⁴ ~大 *a.* largest, greatest, biggest

~ti¹ ~低 *a.* lowest

~ti¹ chia⁴ ~低價 *n.* minimum price

~yüan³ ~遠 *a.* farthest

TSUI⁴ 醉 *a.* drunk, intoxicated

~han⁴ ~漢 *n.* drunkard

TSUI⁴ 罪 *n.* crime, sin, wrong

~chuang⁴ ~狀 *n.* legal charge

~e⁴ ~惡 *n.* crime, sin, evil

~fan⁴ ~犯 *n.* criminal

TSUN¹ 遵 *v.* follow, conform, obey

~shou³ ~守 *v.* obey regulations

~ts'ung² ~從 *v.* obey

TSUNG¹ 宗 *n.* clan, kind, sort; *a.* ancestral

~chiao⁴ ~教 *n.* religion

~chih³ ~旨 *n.* purpose

~miao⁴ ~廟 *n.* ancestral temple

~p'ai⁴ ~派 *n.* sect

~p'ai⁴ chu³ i⁴ ~派主義 *n.* sectarianism**

~tsu² ~族 *n.* kindred

TSUNG³ 總 *v.* unite, comprise, sum up

~chang⁴ ~帳 *n.* total account

~cheng⁴ chih⁴ pu⁴ ~政治部 *n.* General Political Department*

~chi⁴ ~計 *n.* total, sum

~chieh² sheng¹ ch'an³ kung¹ tso⁴ ~結生産工作 *v.* sum up production work**

~chih¹ ~之 *adv.* in short

~ching¹ li³ ~經理 *n.* general manager

~hou⁴ fang¹ chin² wu⁴ pu⁴ ~後方勤務部 *n.* General Logistics Department**

~kan⁴ pu⁴ kuan³ li³ pu⁴ ~幹部管理部 *n.* General Cadre Control Department**

~kung⁴ ~共 *n.* total, whole, all

~li³ ~理 *n.* premier, prime minister

~**ling³ shih⁴** ~領事 *n.* consul general

~**shang¹ hui⁴** ~商會 *n.* general chamber of commerce

~**shu⁴** ~數 *n.* total, sum

~**ssu¹ ling⁴** ~司令 *n.* commander-in-chief

~**tai⁴ piao³** ~代表 *n.* chief delegate

~**tien⁴** ~店 *n.* head office, general office

~**t'ung³** ~統 *n.* President, Executive (*U.S.*)

~**t'ung³ fu³** ~統府 *n.* Office of the President*

~**ts'ai²** ~裁 *n.* director-general

~**ts'ai² wu⁴ pu⁴** ~財務部 *n.* General Finance Department**

~**ts'an¹ mou² pu⁴** ~参謀部 *n.* General Staff Department**

~**wu⁴ chü²** ~務局 *n.* General Affairs Bureau*

TS'

TS'A¹ 擦 *v.* rub, wipe

~**ch'u⁴** ~去 *v.* wipe out

~**hsieh²** ~鞋 *v.* polish shoes

~**lien³** ~臉 *v.* clean the face

~**yu²** ~油 *v.* varnish, oil

TS'AI¹ 猜 *v.* guess, doubt, suspect

~**chi⁴** ~忌 *a.* jealous; *n.* jealousy

~**hsiang³** ~想 *v.* guess

~**i²** ~疑 *a.* suspicious; *n.* suspicion

TS'AI² 財 *n.* money, wealth

~**cheng⁴** ~政 *n.* finance

~**cheng⁴ chia¹** ~政家 *n.* financier

~**cheng⁴ ching¹ chi⁴** ~政經濟 *n.* finance and economics

~**cheng⁴ ching¹ chi⁴ wei³ yüan² hui⁴** ~政經濟委員會 *n.* Committee of Financial and Economic Affairs**

~**cheng⁴ hsüeh²** ~政學 *n.* finance

~**cheng⁴ pu⁴** ~政部 *n.* Ministry of Finance

~**chu³** ~主 *n.* millionaire, rich man

~**ch'an³** ~產 *n.* property

~**ch'an³ shui⁴** ~産税 *n.* estate duty

~fa² ~閥 *n.* capitalist
~fu⁴ ~富 *n.* wealth
~huo⁴ ~貨 *n.* riches
~li⁴ ~力 *n.* resources (wealth)
~shih⁴ ~勢 *n.* wealth and influence
~t'uan² ~團 *n.* foundation fund
TS'AI² 才 *n.* ability, talent
　~chih⁴ ~智 *n.* intelligence, wisdom
　~hsüeh² ~學 *n.* scholarship, learning, ability
　~kan⁴ ~幹 *n.* talent, ability
　~neng² ~能 *n.* ability, talent
　~tzu³ ~子 *n.* genius, a man of talent
TS'AI² 材 *n.* ability, material
　~liao⁴ ~料 *n.* material
　~mu⁴ ~木 *n.* wood, timber
TS'AI² 裁 *n.* cut, reduce, decide ; *n.* cut
　~feng² ~縫 *n.* tailor
　~p'an⁴ ~判 *v.* judge
TS'AI³ 採 *v.* pick, gather, select
　~ch'a² ~茶 *v.* pick tea
　~hua¹ ~花 *v.* deflower
　~kuang⁴ ~鑛 *n.* mining
　~na⁴ ~納 *v.* agree to accept
　~shih² ch'ang³ ~石場 *n.* quarry
　~tse² ~擇 *v.* choose
　~yung⁴ ~用 *v.* adopt (accept)
TS'AI⁴ 菜 *n.* vegetable
　~ch'ang³ ~場 *n.* market (provisions)
　~tan¹ ~單 *n.* menu, bill of fare
　~tzu³ ~子 *n.* rape (plant)
　~yüan² ~園 *n.* vegetable garden
TS'AN¹ 參 *v.* counsel, advise, consult
　~chia¹ ~加 *v.* join, participate
　~chün¹ yün⁴ tung⁴ ~軍運動 *n.* " Join the Army Movement "**
　~i⁴ yüan² ~議員 *n.* senator
　~i⁴ yüan⁴ ~議院 *n.* Senate (*U.S.*)
　~kuan¹ ~觀 *v.* visit
　~k'ao³ ~考 *n.* reference
　~k'ao³ shu¹ ~考書 *n.* reference book
　~mou² ~謀 *n.* staff officer

199

~**mou² chang³** ～謀長 *n*. chief of staff

~**mou² tsung³ chang³** ～謀總長 *n*. Chief of the General Staff*

~**mou² tz'u¹ chang³** ～謀次長 *n*. Assistant Chief of the General Staff*

~**mou² yeh⁴ wu⁴** ～謀業務 *n*. staff duty

~**shih⁴** ～事 *n*. councilor

~**tsa²** ～雜 *a*. mixed

~**yü³** ～與 *v*. participate

TS'AN² 殘 *a*. maimed, cruel; *v*. injure; *n*. cruelty, leavings

~**fei⁴** ～廢 *a*. maimed

~**hai⁴** ～害 *v*. destroy

~**jen³** ～忍 *a*. cruel

~**k'u⁴** ～酷 *a*. cruel

~**ping¹** ～兵 *n*. disabled soldiers, remnants

~**sha¹** ～殺 *v*. slaughter

~**yü²** ～餘 *n*. leavings

TS'AN² 蠶 *n*. silkworm

~**shih²** ～食 *a*. piecemeal

TS'AN³ 慘 *a*. sad, grievous

~**chuang⁴** ～狀 *a*. wretched

~**lieh⁴** ～烈 *a*. bloodshed (*mil.*)

~**t'ung⁴** ～痛 *a*. grievous

TS'ANG¹ 倉 *n*. barn, bin, storehouse, warehouse

~**k'u⁴** ～庫 *n*. storehouse, warehouse

~**ts'u⁴** ～促 *a*. hurried; *adv*. hurriedly

TS'ANG¹ 蒼 *a*. green, azure

~**huang²** ～黃 *a*. yellow

~**pai²** ～白 *a*. pale

~**t'ien¹** ～天 *n*. sky

~**ts'ui⁴** ～翠 *a*. green

~**ying²** ～蠅 *n*. fly

TS'ANG² 藏 **TSANG⁴** *n*. Tibet; *v*. hide

~**ni⁴** ～匿 *v*. hide

TS'AO¹ 操 *n*. exercise; *v*. practise, drill

~**ch'ang³** ～場 *n*. playground

~**hsin¹** ～心 *a*. anxious

~**lao²** ～勞 *a*. laborious (hard-working)

~**lien⁴** ～練 *v*. drill, train

~**tsung⁴** ～縱 *v*. control

TS'AO³ 草 *n.* grass, herb, plant, hay
~**an⁴** ~案 *n.* draft, proposal
~**hsieh²** ~鞋 *n.* sandals
~**kao³** ~稿 *n.* draft (rough copy)
~**liao⁴** ~料 *n.* forage
~**mei²** ~莓 *n.* strawberry
~**p'eng²** ~棚 *n.* thatched hut
~**p'ing²** ~坪 *n.* lawn
~**ti⁴** ~地 *n.* meadow, grassland
~**yüeh¹** ~約 *n.* protocol
TS'E⁴ 策 *n.* plan, policy
~**hua⁴** ~劃 *v.* plan
~**lüeh⁴** ~略 *n.* stratagem
TS'ENG² 曾 *a.* past, done; *adv.* still, yet
~**ching¹** ~經 *adv.* already
TS'ENG² 層 *n.* layer, story, stratum
~**tieh²** ~疊 *n.* stratification
~**tz'u⁴** ~次 *n.* gradations
TS'O⁴ 錯 *n.* mistake, error; *a.* wrong, incorrect
~**ch'u⁴** ~處 *n.* error, mistake
~**luan⁴** ~亂 *a.* confused
~**tsung⁴** ~綜 *n.* intricacy
~**tzu⁴** ~字 *n.* erratum
~**wu⁴** ~誤 *n.* mistake, error; *a.* wrong
TS'U¹ 粗 *a.* coarse, rude, rough, vulgar
~**ts'ao¹** ~糙 *a.* coarse
~**yü³** ~語 *n.* obscene language
TS'U⁴ 醋 *n.* vinegar
TS'UI¹ 催 *v.* urge, press, importune
~**mien²** ~眠 *v.* hypnotize
~**mien² shu⁴** ~眠術 *n.* hypnotism (science)
~**mien² yao⁴** ~眠藥 *n.* hypnotic drug
~**ts'u⁴** ~促 *v.* urge, press
TS'UN¹ 村 *n.* village
~**chuang¹** ~莊 *n.* village
~**fu¹** ~夫 *n.* villager
TS'UN² 存 *v.* keep, preserve, store, deposit, exist; *a.* alive
~**chan⁴** ~棧 *v.* keep in a warehouse
~**huo⁴** ~貨 *n.* stock
~**ken¹** ~根 *n.* counterpart, copy, duplicate

~**k'uan³** ~款 *n.* & *v.* deposit

~**liu²** ~留 *v.* remain

~**tsai⁴** ~在 *n.* existence, substance, continuance

TS'UN⁴ 寸 *n.* Chinese measure for 1.41 inches

TS'UNG¹ 聰 *a.* clever

~**ming²** ~明 *a.* clever, intelligent

TS'UNG² 從 *v.* follow, pursue, comply with ; *prep.* from, by, since

~**chün¹** ~軍 *v.* join the army

~**ch'ien²** ~前 *adv.* formerly

~**ming⁴** ~命 *v.* obey

~**shih⁴** ~事 *v.* pursue

~**tz'u³** ~此 *prep.* henceforth

~**wei⁴** ~未 *adv.* never

TZ

TZU¹ 資 *n.* wealth, property ; *v.* help

~**chu⁴** ~助 *v.* help

~**ch'an³** ~産 *n.* capital (money)

~**ch'an³ chieh¹ chi²** ~産階級 *n.* bourgeoisie**

~**ko²** ~格 *n.* qualification

~**pen³** ~本 *n.* capital (money)

~**pen³ chia¹** ~本家 *n.* capitalist

~**pen³ chu³ i⁴** ~本主義 *n.* capitalism

~**pen³ chu³ i⁴ kuo² chia¹** ~本主義國家 *n.* capitalistic nation**

~**pen³ chu³ i⁴ she⁴ hui⁴** ~本主義社會 *n.* capitalist society**

~**pen³ lun³** ~本論 *n.* Capital**

~**wang⁴** ~望 *n.* reputation

TZU³ 子 *n.* child, son ; *pron.* you. ~¹ [a suffix]

~**kung¹** ~宮 *n.* womb, uterus

~**nü³** ~女 *n.* child

~**sun¹** ~孫 *n.* descendant

~**tan⁴** ~彈 *n.* bullet

~**wu³ hsien⁴** ~午線 *n.* meridian

~**yin¹** ~音 *n.* consonant

TZU⁴ 自 *n.* self ; *prep.* since, from

~**ai⁴** ~愛 *n.* self-respect

~**chi**³ ～己 *n.* self
~**chih⁴** ～治 *n.* self-control
~**chih⁴** ～制 *n.* self-control
~**chih⁴ ch'ü¹** ～治區 *n.* Autonomous Region**
~**chu⁴** ～助 *n.* self-help
~**chung⁴** ～重 *n.* self-esteem
~**ch'i⁴** ～欺 *a.* self-deceptive
~**ch'ien¹** ～謙 *n.* humble
~**ch'uan²** ～傳 *n.* autobiography
~**fa¹ ch'ü¹ shih⁴** ～發趨勢 *n.* spontaneous tendency toward capitalism**
~**hsin⁴** ～信 *a.* confident; *n.* confidence
~**hsing² ch'e¹** ～行車 *n.* bicycle
~**hsiu¹** ～修 *a.* self-taught
~**jan²** ～然 *adv.* of course, naturally; *a.* natural; *n.* natural, nature
~**k'ua¹** ～誇 *n.* self-conceit
~**lai² shui² ch'ang³** ～來水廠 *n.* waterworks
~**li⁴** ～立 *n.* self-support; *a.* self-supporting
~**sha¹** ～殺 *n.* suicide; *v.* commit suicide
~**ssu¹** ～私 *a.* selfish
~**tung⁴** ～動 *a.* automatic
~**tung⁴ pu⁴ ch'iang¹** ～動步槍 *n.* automatic rifle
~**tung⁴ shou³ ch'iang¹** ～動手槍 *n.* automatic pistol
~**tsai⁴ te¹ chieh¹ chi²** ～在的階級 " class in itself "**
~**tsun¹** ～尊 *n.* self-respect
~**wei² te¹ chieh¹ chi²** ～爲的階級 " class for itself "**
~**wei⁴** ～衛 *n.* self-defense
~**wo³ p'i¹ p'ing²** ～我批評 *n.* self-criticism**
~**yu°** ～由 *n.* liberty, freedom; *a.* free
TZU⁴ 字 *n.* letter, character, word
~**chi⁴** ～跡 *n.* handwriting
~**chih³ lou³** ～紙簍 *n.* wastebasket
~**hua⁴** ～畫 *n.* stroke
~**hui⁴** ～彙 *n.* glossary, terminology, vocabulary
~**i⁴** ～義 *n.* the meaning of a word
~**ma³** ～碼 *n.* figure
~**mu³** ～母 *n.* alphabet

203

~**tien³** ～典 *n.* dictionary
~**t'ieh⁴** ～帖 *n.* copybook

TZ'

TZ'U² 辭 *n.* expression, plea; *v.* decline, resign
~**chih²** ～職 *v.* resign; *n.* resignation
~**pieh²** ～別 *v.* bid farewell
~**tien³** ～典 *n.* n. dictionary
~**t'ui⁴** ～退 *v.* discharge, resign
TZ'U² 磁 *n.* porcelain, magnet; *a.* magnetic
~**chen¹** ～針 *n.* compass
~**chi²** ～極 *n.* magnetic pole
~**ch'ang³** ～場 *n.* magnetic field
~**ch'i⁴** ～器 *n.* porcelain, china
~**hsing⁴** ～性 *n.* magnetism
~**li⁴** ～力 *n.* magnetism
~**shih²** ～石 *n.* magnet
TZ'U³ 此 *pron. & a.* this, these; *art.* the
~**hou⁴** ～後 *adv.* hereafter
~**k'o⁴** ～刻 *n.* this moment
~**shih²** ～時 *adv.* now, at present
~**ti⁴** ～地 *adv.* here
~**wai⁴** ～外 *adv.* besides, moreover, further
TZ'U⁴ 次 *n.* time, occasion; *a.* second, next
~**chang³** ～長 *n.* vice-minister
~**hsü⁴** ～序 *n.* order, series
~**teng³** ～等 *n.* second class
TZ'U⁴ 刺 *v.* stab, sting, assassinate; *n.* thorn
~**chi¹** ～激 *v.* stimulate
~**hsiu⁴** ～繡 *v.* embroider; *n.* embroidery
~**ju⁴** ～入 *v.* bore into
~**k'o⁴** ～客 *n.* assassin, murderer
~**sha¹** ～殺 *v.* stab; *n.* assassination
~**tao¹** ～刀 *n.* bayonet
~**tzu⁴** ～字 *v.* brand (skin)

W

WA¹ 控 *v.* excavate, hollow out, dig out, scoop
~**ch'ien² li⁴** 潛力 *v.* develop hidden strength**
WA³ 瓦 *n.* tile
~**chieh³** ~解 *v.* disintegrate, dismember
~**ssu¹** ~斯 *n.* gas (for heating)
WA⁴ 襪 *n.* sock, stocking
WAI⁴ 外 *adv.* out, outside; *prep.* outside, beyond
~**chiao¹** ~交 *n.* diplomacy; *a.* diplomatic; *adv.* diplomatically
~**chiao¹ cheng⁴ ts'e⁴** ~交政策 *n.* diplomatic policy
~**chiao¹ chia¹** ~交家 *n.* diplomat
~**chiao¹ chieh⁴** 交界 *n.* diplomatic circle
~**chiao¹ pu⁴** ~交部 *n.* Ministry of Foreign Affairs
~**chiao¹ t'uan²** ~交團 *n.* diplomatic corps
~**hang²** ~行 *a.* unskilled
~**hao⁴** ~號 *n.* nickname
~**hui⁴** ~匯 *n.* foreign exchange
~**kuo²** ~國 *n.* foreign country
~**kuo² yü³** ~國語 *n.* foreign language
~**k'o¹** ~科 *n.* surgery
~**k'o¹ i¹ sheng¹** ~科醫生 *n.* surgeon
~**mien⁴** ~面 *n.* outside
~**piao³** ~表 *n.* appearance
~**p'o²** ~婆 *n.* mother's mother (grandmother)
~**sun¹** ~孫 *n.* daughter's son (grandson)
~**sun¹ nü³** ~孫女 *n.* daughter's daughter (granddaughter)
~**sheng¹** ~甥 *n.* son of one's sister (nephew)
~**sheng¹ nü³** ~甥女 *n.* daughter of one's sister (niece)
~**t'ao⁴** ~套 *n.* overcoat
~**tsu³ fu⁴** ~祖父 *n.* mother's father (grandfather)
~**tsu³ mu³** ~祖母 *n.* mother's mother (grandmother)
~**tzu³** ~子 *n.* husband

WAN¹ 灣 *n.* bay, gulf, cove

WAN² 完 *v.* complete; *adv.* entirely; *a.* complete, perfect, entire; *n.* perfection

~**chüan²** ~全 *a.* perfect; *n.* perfection

~**pei⁴** ~備 *a.* well prepared

~**pi⁴** ~畢 *a.* & *v.* complete

WAN² 玩 *v.* play; *n.* amusement

~**chü⁴** ~具 *n.* toy

~**hsiao⁴** ~笑 *v.* joke

~**shang³** ~賞 *v.* enjoy

~**shua³** ~耍 *v.* play

WAN³ 晚 *n.* evening; *a.* late; *adv.* lately

~**an¹** ~安 *n.* good evening, good night

~**fan⁴** ~飯 *n.* supper

~**nien²** ~年 *a.* aged

~**pao⁴** ~報 *n.* evening newspaper

WAN³ 碗 *n.* bowl

WAN⁴ 萬 *n.* ten thousand; *a.* numerous

~**kuo²** ~國 *a.* international

~**kuo² hung² shih² tzu⁴ hui⁴** ~國紅十字會 *n.* International Red Cross Committee

~**li³ chang² ch'eng²** ~里長城 *n.* Great Wall of China

~**neng²** ~能 *a.* almighty

~**sui⁴** ~歲 *a.* long-lived

~**shih⁴** ~事 *pron.* everything

WANG² 亡 *v.* be lost, perish, escape, die

~**ming⁴ chih¹ t'u²** ~命之徒 *n.* desperado, fugitive

WANG² 王 *n.* king, ruler; *a.* royal

~**kung¹** ~宮 *n.* palace

~**kuo²** ~國 *n.* kingdom

~**tzu³** ~子 *n.* prince

WANG³ 往 *v.* go; *a.* past; *adv.* formerly

~**hsi²** ~昔 *adv.* formerly, before

~**lai²** ~來 *adv.* to and fro, intercourse

~**wang³** ~往 *adv.* often, frequently

~**⁴ hou⁴** ~後 *adv.* hereafter

WANG⁴ 望 *v.* look at, hope; *n.* hope

~**pu⁴ chien⁴** ~不見 *v.* be out of sight

~**yüan³ ching⁴** ~遠鏡 *n.* telescope, binoculars

206

WANG⁴ 忘 v. forget
  ~chi⁴ ～記 v. forget
  ~en¹ ～恩 a. ungrateful
WANG⁴ 旺 a. prosperous; n. prosperity
  ~sheng⁴ ～盛 n. prosperity
WEI¹ 威 n. awe
  ~ch'üan² ～權 n. authority
  ~ho⁴ ～嚇 v. intimidate; n. intimidation
  ~ming² ～名 n. prestige
  ~wang⁴ ～望 n. prestige
  ~wu³ ～武 a. majestic
  ~yen² ～嚴 n. dignity
WEI² 爲 v. act, do, make, perform. conj. for, because
  ~⁴ ho² ～何 adv. why, for what reason
WEI² 危 n. danger; a. dangerous
  ~chi¹ ～機 n. crisis
  ~chi² ～急 a. dangerous, perilous
  ~hsien³ ～險 n. danger
  ~nan⁴ ～難 adv. in danger
WEI² 違 v. oppose, disobey
  ~chin⁴ p'in³ ～禁品 n. contraband
  ~fa³ ～法 n. breach of law
  ~yüeh¹ ～約 n. breach of contract
WEI² 維 n. [an initial particle] rule, law; v. tie, connect
  ~ch'ih² ～持 v. maintain
  ~ch'ih² chih⁴ hsü⁴ ～持秩序 v. maintain order
WEI² 圍 v. surround, besiege; n. circumference
  ~chin¹ ～巾 n. scarf, muffler
  ~ch'ün² ～裙 n. apron
  ~jao⁴ ～繞 v. surround
  ~kung¹ ～攻 v. besiege, seige
  ~k'un⁴ ～困 v. surround
WEI³ 委 v. appoint, assign, trust
  ~ch'ü¹ ～曲 n. injustice
  ~jen⁴ ～任 v. commission
  ~jen⁴ chuang⁴ ～任狀 n. commission, warrant (the document)
  ~p'ai⁴ ～派 v. appoint, assign
  ~t'o¹ ～託 v. entrust

~**yüan²** ~員 *n.* committeeman, council member

~**yüan² chang³** ~員長 *n.* committee chairman

~**yüan² chih⁴** ~員制 *n.* committee system

WEI³ 尾 *n.* tail, end; *a.* last

~**pa¹** ~巴 *n.* tail

~**sui²** ~隨 *v.* follow

WEI³ 偉 *n.* hero; *a.* great, brave

~**jen²** ~人 *n.* great man

~**ta⁴** ~大 *a.* great

WEI⁴ 位 *n.* seat, position

~**chih⁴** 置 *n.* position, location

~**chü¹** ~居 *v.* situate

WEI⁴ 味 *n.* taste, flavor

~**chüeh²** ~覺 *n.* sense of taste

~**mei³** ~美 *a.* delicious

~**tao⁴** ~道 *n.* taste

WEI⁴ 喂 *v.* feed animals; *int.* hello

WEI⁴ 胃 *n.* stomach

~**k'ou³** ~口 *n.* appetite

~**k'uei¹ yang²** ~潰瘍 *n.* gastric ulcer

~**ping¹** ~病 *n.* gastropathy

~**t'ung⁴** ~痛 *n.* gastrodynia, gastralgia

~**yen²** ~炎 *n.* gastritis

WEI⁴ 慰 *n.* comfort, console

~**lao²** ~勞 *v.* comfort

~**wen⁴** ~問 *v.* console

~**yen²** ~唁 *v.* condole

WEI⁴ 衛 *n.* escort, guard, protect, defend

~**hsing¹** ~星 *n.* satellite

~**ping¹** ~兵 *n.* guard

~**ping¹ shih⁴** ~兵室 *n.* guardhouse

~**sheng¹** ~生 *n.* hygiene, sanitation; *a.* sanitary

~**sheng¹ chü²** ~生局 *n.* health office

~**shu⁴** ~戍 *v.* garrison

~**shu⁴ ssu¹ ling⁴ pu⁴** ~戍司令部 *n.* garrison
headquarters

WEI⁴ 未 *adv.* not, not yet

~**chih¹ shu⁴** ~知數 *n.* unknown number

~**ch'ang²** ~嘗 *adv.* never, not yet

~**hun¹ ch'i¹** ~婚妻 *n.* fiancee

~**hun¹ fu¹** ~婚夫 *n.* fiance

~**lai²** ~來 *n.* & *a.* future

~**ting⁴** ~定 *a.* uncertain, undecided

WEN¹ 溫 *a.* & *v.* warm

~**ch'üan²** ~泉 *n.* hot spring

~**ho²** ~和 *a.* mild

~**hsi⁴** ~習 *n.* review

~**nuan³** ~暖 *a.* warm

~**shih⁴** ~室 *n.* greenhouse

~**tai⁴** ~帶 *n.* temperate zone

~**tu⁴** ~度 *n.* temperature

~**tu⁴ piao³** ~度表 *n.* heat indicator

WEN² 聞 *v.* hear ; ~⁴ *a.* noted, famous

~² **hsiang¹ chiao⁴ chu³** ~香教主 *n.* Bishop Smell Incense (Chinese religion)

~**hsiang¹ tui⁴** ~香隊 *n.* snooping team**

~⁴ **jen²** ~人 *n.* celebrity

WEN² 文 *n.* essay, literature

~**chang¹** ~章 *n.* essay, composition

~**chien⁴** ~件 *n.* document, papers, script, dispatch

~**chü⁴** ~具 *n.* stationery

~**fa³** ~法 *n.* grammar

~**hua⁴** ~化 *n.* civilization, culture

~**hua⁴ chiao⁴ yü⁴ wei³ yüan² hui⁴** ~化教育委員會 *n.* Committee of Cultural and Educational Affairs**

~**hua⁴ pu⁴** ~化部 *n.* Ministry of Cultural Affairs**

~**hsüeh²** ~學 *n.* literature, letters

~**jen²** ~人 *n.* scholarly, literary people

~**mang²** ~盲 *n.* illiteracy ; *a.* illiterate

~**ming²** ~明 *n.* civilization, civility, *a.* civilized

~**p'ing²** ~憑 *n.* diploma

~**shu¹** ~書 *n.* document, papers

~**ya³** ~雅 *a.* graceful, elegant, refined, gentle

WEN² 蚊 *n.* mosquito

~**chang⁴** ~帳 *n.* mosquito net

~**yen¹** ~烟 *n.* mosquito incense

WEN⁴ 問 *v.* ask, inquire

~**an⁴** ~案 *n.* trial

~**hou⁴** ~候 *v.* greet

~ta² 答 *n.* dialogue

~t'i² 題 *n.* question

WO³ 我 *pron.* I, me

~men² 們 *pron.* we

~men² te¹ 們的 *pron.* our, ours

~men² tzu⁴ chi³ 們自己 *pron.* ourself, ourselves

~te¹ 的 *pron.* my, mine

WO⁴ 握 *v.* grasp, shake, hold

~shou³ ~手 *v.* shake hands

WU¹ 屋 *n.* room, house

~chu³ ~主 *n.* landlord

~ting³ ~頂 *n.* roof

~ting³ hua² yüan² ~頂花園 *n.* roof garden

~ting³ shih⁴ t'ieh³ ssu¹ wang³ ~頂式鐵糸網 *n.* double apron fence

~yen² ~簷 *n.* eaves

~yü³ ~宇 *n.* building

WU² 無 *a.* no, none; *adv.* not; *prep.* without

~chih¹ ~知 *a.* ignorant

~ch'an³ chieh¹ chi² ~産階級 *n.* proletariat**

~ch'an³ chieh¹ chi² ko² ming⁴ ~産階級革命 *n.* proletarian revolution**

~ch'ih³ ~恥 *a.* shameless

~hsiao⁴ ~効 *a.* ineffective

~hsien⁴ chih⁴ ~限制 *n.* without limitation

~hsien⁴ kung¹ ssu¹ ~限公司 *n.* unlimited company

~hsien⁴ tien⁴ hua⁴ ~線電話 *n.* radio

~hsien⁴ tien⁴ t'ai² ~線電台 *n.* radio station

~hsin¹ ~心 *a.* unintentional

~hsing² ~形 *a.* invisible

~i⁴ ~益 *a.* disadvantageous

~ku¹ ~辜 *a.* innocent

~lai⁴ ~賴 *n.* rascal

~li³ ~理 *a.* unreasonable

~li³ ~禮 *a.* impolite

~liao² ~聊 *n.* cheerless

~lun⁴ ~論 *adv.* however

~lun⁴ ho² shih² ~論何時 *conj. & adv.* whenever

~lun⁴ shen² ma¹ ~論什麼 *pron.* whatever

210

~**shu⁴** ~數 *n.* innumerable
~**wang⁴** ~望 *a.* hopeless
~**yung⁴** ~用 *a.* useless

WU³ 五 *n. & a.* five
~**chin¹** ~金 *n.* metals
~**ch'üan² hsien⁴ fa³** ~權憲法 *n.* Five Power Constitution
~**fan³ yün⁴ tung⁴** ~反運動 *n.* five anti-movements**
~**nien² chi hua⁴** ~年計劃 *n.* five-year plan
~**yüeh⁴** ~月 *n.* May

WU³ 伍 *n.* soldier's file

WU³ 午 *n.* noon, noontime, noontide
~**ch'ien²** ~前 *n.* forenoon
~**hou⁴** ~後 *n. & a.* afternoon
~**shih²** ~時 *n.* noontime, noontide
~**ts'an¹** ~餐 *n.* lunch

WU³ 武 *a.* military, warlike
~**chuang¹** ~裝 *a.* armed
~**chuang¹ tai⁴** ~裝帶 *n.* Sam Browne belt
~**hsia²** ~俠 *n.* chivalry
~**kuan¹** ~官 *n.* military attache
~**kung¹** ~功 *n.* military merits
~**pei⁴** ~備 *n.* armament
~**shih⁴** ~士 *n.* cavalier
~**tuan⁴** ~斷 *adv.* arbitrarily
~**ch'i⁴** ~器 *n.* arms, weapon

WU³ 舞 *n. & v.* dance
~**chien⁴** ~劍 *v.* fence ; *n.* fencing
~**ch'ang³** ~場 *n.* dancing hall
~**hui⁴** ~會 *n.* ball (dance)
~**nü³** ~女 *n.* dancing girl
~**pi⁴** ~弊 *v.* cheat
~**t'ai²** ~臺 *n.* stage (theater)
~**yung³ chia¹** ~踊家 *n.* dancer

WU⁴ 誤 *n.* mistake, error
~**chieh³** ~解 *v.* misinterpret ; *n.* misinterpretation
~**hui⁴** ~會 *v.* misunderstand ; *n.* misunderstanding

WU⁴ 務 *n.* affair, business

WU⁴ 悟 *v.* apprehend, awake

WU⁴ 物 *n.* substance, thing, matter

~**chia⁴** ~價 *n.* price, value

~**chien⁴** ~件 *n.* article, thing

~**chih²** ~質 *n.* matter; *a.* material

~**chih² chien⁴ she⁴** ~質建設 *n.* material reconstruction

~**chih² wen² ming²** ~質文明 *n.* material civilization

~**ch'an³** ~産 *n.* produce, product, production

~**li³ hsüeh²** ~理學 *n.* physics

Y

YA¹ 呀 *int.* [exclamation of pain, surprise, pity, joy] ah, aha

.**YA¹** 鴨 *n.* duck

~**chiao⁴** ~叫 *v.* quack

~**jung² pei⁴** ~羢被 *n.* feather quilt

~**tan⁴** ~蛋 *n.* duck's egg

YA¹ 壓 *v.* press down, crush

~**chih⁴** ~制 *v.* suppress

~**fu²** ~服 *v.* press down

~**p'o⁴** ~迫 *v.* oppress; *n.* oppression

~**so¹** ~縮 *v.* condense

~**tao³** ~倒 *v.* overwhelm, overcome

YA² 牙 *n.* tooth

~**ch'ien¹** ~籤 *n.* toothpick

~**i¹** ~醫 *n.* dentist

~**kao¹** ~膏 *n.* toothpaste

~**k'o¹** ~科 *n.* dentistry

~**shua¹** ~刷 *n.* toothbrush

~**shui⁴** ~稅 *n.* brokerage tax

~**t'ung⁴** ~痛 *n.* toothache

YA² 芽 *n.* bud, shoot, sprout

YANG¹ 央 *n.* middle, center, half; *v.* request

~**ch'iu²** ~求 *v.* request, beg

YANG¹ 秧 *n.* rice sprout, fried fish

~**miao²** ~苗 *n.* young shoot

YANG² 洋 *n.* ocean

~**fu²** ~服 *n.* Western suit

~**hui¹** ~灰 *n.* cement

~**huo³** ~火 *n.* match

~**huo⁴** ~貨 *n.* foreign goods

~**pu⁴** ~布 *n.* calico

~**yu²** ~油 *n.* kerosene

YANG² 羊 *n.* sheep

~**chih¹** ~脂 *n.* sheep suet

~**hsien² feng¹** ~癇瘋 *n.* epilepsy

~**jou⁴** ~肉 *n.* mutton

~**mao²** ~毛 *n.* sheep's wool

~**p'i² chih³** ~皮紙 *n.* parchment

YANG² 楊 *n.* poplar

~**liu³** ~柳 *n.* willow

YANG² 陽 *a.* sunny, bright, male

~**chi²** ~極 *n.* anode (*elec.*)

~**kuang¹** ~光 *n.* sunbeam

~**li⁴** ~曆 *n.* solar calendar

~**wei¹** ~萎 *a.* sexually impotent; *adj.* impotence, impotency; *n.* impotent

YANG² 揚 *v.* raise, spread, praise

~**fan¹** ~帆 *v.* hoist a sail

~**ming²** ~名 *v.* make known

~**tzu³ chiang¹** ~子江 *n.* Yangtze River

YANG³ 養 *v.* nourish, rear, feed

~**ch'eng²** ~成 *v.* educate

~**ch'i⁴** ~氣 *n.* oxygen

~**feng¹ fang²** ~蜂房 *n.* apiary

~**hua⁴ wu⁴** ~化物 *n.* oxide

~**lao³ chin¹** ~老金 *n.* pension

~**lao³ yüan⁴** ~老院 *n.* Old People's Home

~**liao⁴** ~料 *n.* nutrition

~**nü³** ~女 *n.* adopted-daughter

~**tzu³** ~子 *n.* adopted-son

~**yü⁴** ~育 *v.* rear, bring up

YANG⁴ 樣 *n.* sample, example, model, pattern, style, kind

~**p'in³** ~品 *n.* sample, specimen

~**shih⁴** ~式 *n.* pattern, style, fashion

YAO¹ 腰 *n.* waist

~**tai⁴** ~帶 *n.* girdle

213

~**t'eng²** ~疼 *n.* lumbago

~**tzu¹** ~子 *n.* kidney

YAO² 搖 *v.* shake, move, wave

~**ch'uang²** ~床 *n.* cradle

~**i³** ~椅 *n.* rocking chair

YAO² 謠 *n.* rumor

~**yen²** ~言 n. rumor

YAO³ 咬 *v.* bite

~**chüeh²** ~嚼 *v.* chew

~**shang¹** ~傷 *v.* bite (sting)

YAO⁴ 若 *conj.* if, as if

~**shih⁴** ~是 *conj.* if

jo⁴ ho² ~何 *adv.* how

~**kan¹** ~干 *a. & pron.* some (any)

YAO⁴ 要 *v.* desire. ~¹ *v.* demand ; *a.* important

~**¹ ch'iu²** ~求 *v.* demand

~**hsia²** ~挾 *v.* coerce ; *n.* coercion

~**⁴ chin³** ~緊 *a.* important

~**jen²** ~人 *n.* VIP (very important person)

~**sai⁴** ~塞 *n.* fort, fortification

~**su⁴** ~素 *n.* element

~**t'u²** ~図 *n.* sketch

YAO⁴ 藥 *n.* medicine, drug

~**chi⁴ shih¹** ~劑師 *n.* pharmacist

~**fang¹** ~方 *n.* prescription (*med.*)

~**fang²** ~房 *n.* drugstore, pharmacy

~**fen³** ~粉 *n.* medicinal powder

~**li³ hsüeh²** ~理學 *n.* pharmacology

~**p'ien⁴** ~片 *n.* tablet (*med.*)

~**shang¹** ~商 *n.* druggist, pharmacist

~**wan²** ~丸 *n.* pill

YAO⁴ 樂 *see* **LE⁴**

YEH² 爺 *n.* grandfather

YEH³ 也 *adv.* also ; *conj.* and, also, still

~**hsü³** ~許 *adv.* perhaps, maybe, possibly

~**shih⁴** ~是 *adv.* also

YEH³ 野 *n.* desert, waste, wilderness ; *a.* wild, savage, rude

~**chan⁴ p'ao⁴** ~戰礮 *n.* field piece

~**hsin¹** ~心 *n.* ambition

~**man²** ~蠻 *a.* barbaric, brutal ; *n.* barbarian

214

~p'ao⁴ ~砲 *n.* field gun
~p'ao⁴ ping¹ ~砲兵 *n.* field artillery
~shou⁴ ~獸 *n.* beast
~wai⁴ ~外 *n.* field
~wai⁴ yen³ hsi² 外演習 *n.* field exercise
YEH⁴ 夜 *n.* night
~chien¹ hung¹ cha⁴ ~間轟炸 *n.* night bombing
~chien¹ kung¹ chi¹ ~間攻擊 *n.* night attack
~chien¹ yen³ hsi² ~間演習 *n.* night exercise
~fan⁴ ~飯 *n.* supper
~hsiao⁴ ~校 *n.* night school
~hsing² chün¹ ~行軍 *n.* night march
~li³ fu² ~禮服 *n.* evening dress
~mang² ~盲 *n.* night blindness
~pan¹ ~班 *n.* night shift
~pan⁴ ~半 *n.* midnight
~shih⁴ ~市 *n.* night market
~tsung³ hui⁴ ~總會 *n.* night club, night spot
~ying¹ ~鶯 *n.* nightingale
~ying¹ ~鷹 *n.* nighthawk
~yu² shen² ~遊神 *n.* nightwalker
YEH⁴ 業 *n.* occupation, profession, business
~shih¹ ~師 *n.* tutor
~wu⁴ ~務 *n.* task, function, job, business
YEH⁴ 葉 *n.* leaf
YEN¹ 烟 *n.* fumes, smoke, cigarette, tobacco
~hua¹ ~花 *n.* prostitute
~huo³ ~火 *n.* fireworks
~mei² ~煤 *n.* bituminous coal
~mu⁴ ~幕 *n.* smoke screen
~mu⁴ tan⁴ ~幕彈 *n.* smoke shell
~tou³ ~斗 *n.* smoking pipe
~ts'ao³ ~草 *n.* tobacco
~ts'ao³ shang¹ ~草商 *n.* tobacconist
~ts'ung¹ ~囪 *n.* chimney, stovepipe
~yeh⁴ ~葉 *n.* tobacco-leaf
YEN² 言 *v.* speak
~kuo⁴ ch'i² shih² ~過其實 *v.* exaggerate
~lun⁴ ~論 *n.* speech
~yü³ ~語 speech, language
YEN² 沿 *v.* follow. ~⁴ *prep.* along, by, through

~hai³ p'ing² yüan² ～海平原 *n.* coastal plain

YEN² 顔 *n.* color, countenance

~mien⁴ ～面 *n.* countenance

~se⁴ ～色 *n.* color

YEN² 研 *v.* grind, study

~chiu¹ ～究 *v.* study, research

~chiu¹ sheng¹ ～究生 *n.* postgraduate

YEN² 延 *v.* delay, prolong, extend, invite, spread

~ch'ang² ～長 *v.* prolong, extend; *n.* extension, prolongation

~ch'i¹ ～期 *v.* postpone

~ch'i¹ hsin⁴ kuan³ ～期信管 *n.* delay fuse

~ch'ih² ～遲 *v.* delay

~p'ing⁴ ～聘 *v.* engage (employ)

YEN² 鹽 *n.* salt

~ching³ ～井 *n.* salt well

~shui³ ～水 *n.* brine, salt water

~shui⁴ ～稅 *n.* salt revenue

YEN² 嚴 *a.* severe, stern, rigid, solemn; *adv.* very

~cheng⁴ ～正 *a.* upright (righteous)

~chung⁴ ～重 *a.* critical, serious

~han² ～寒 *n.* severe cold

~k'u⁴ ～酷 *a.* cruel, severe

~li⁴ ～厲 *a.* stern, severe

~mi⁴ ～密 *a.* close, strict

~su⁴ ～肅 *a.* austere; *n.* austerity

YEN³ 眼 *n.* eye, hole

~chao⁴ ～罩 *n.* eye-shade

~chieh⁴ ～界 *n.* field of view

~ching⁴ ～鏡 *n.* eyeglass

~k'o¹ ～科 *n.* ophthalmology

~k'o¹ i¹ sheng¹ ～科醫生 *n.* ophthalmology

~lei⁴ ～淚 *n.* tear

~lien² ～簾 *n.* eyelid

~mao² ～毛 *n.* eyelash

~mei² ～眉 *n.* eyebrow

~pei¹ ～杯 *n.* eye-cup

~t'ung² ～瞳 *n.* pupil (eye)

~yao⁴ ～藥 *n.* eye medicine

YEN³ 演 *v.* act, play, perform

~chi⁴ ～劇 *v.* act a drama

~**chiang³** ～講 v. make a speech
~**chiang³ yüan²** ～講員 n. lecturer
~**hsi²** ～習 n. exercise, rehearsal
~**pien⁴** ～變 v. develop (a situation)
~**shuo¹ chia¹** ～説家 n. orator
~**tsou⁴** ～奏 v. perform music

YEN⁴ 厭 v. dislike, hate
~**ch'i⁴** ～棄 v. reject
~**fan²** ～煩 a. troublesome
~**wu⁴** ～惡 v. dislike

YEN⁴ 驗 n. evidence, effect, proof; v. inspect, verify
~**ming²** ～明 v. verify
~**shih¹** ～屍 n. autopsy, postmortem

YIN¹ 因 conj. because
~**kuo³** ～果 n. cause and effect
~**kuo³ lü⁴** ～果率 n. causality
~**su⁴** ～素 n. factor
~**tz'u³** ～此 adv. therefore
~**wei⁴** ～爲 conj. because

YIN¹ 陰 a. shady, dark, secret
~**ching¹** ～莖 n. penis
~**kou¹** ～溝 n. sewer
~**liang²** ～涼 n. cool
~**mao²** ～毛 n. pubes
~**mou²** ～謀 n. conspiracy
~**sen¹** ～森 a. gloomy
~**tao⁴** ～道 n. vagina
~**tien⁴** ～電 n. negative (elec.)

YIN¹ 音 n. tone, voice, sound
~**hsin⁴** ～信 n. news, information
~**tiao⁴** ～調 n. tune, pitch
~**yüeh⁴** ～樂 n. music
~**yüeh⁴ chia¹** ～樂家 n. musician
~**yüeh⁴ hui⁴** ～樂會 n. concert, recital
~**yüeh⁴ tui⁴** ～樂隊 n. band music
~**yün⁴** ～韻 n. rhyme

YIN² 銀 n. silver
~**ch'i⁴** ～器 n. silverware
~**hang²** ～行 n. bank
~**hang² chia¹** ～行家 n. banker

~**hang² hu⁴ t'ou²** ~行戶頭 *n.* bank account
~**hang² yeh⁴** ~行業 *n.* banking
~**ho²** ~河 *n.* Milky Way
YIN³ 引 *n.* preface, introduction; *v.* lead, introduce
~**ch'ing²** ~擎 *n.* engine
~**hao⁴** ~號 *n.* quotation mark
~**tao⁴** ~導 *v.* conduct, guide
~**yu⁴** ~誘 *v.* entice, tempt, seduce, lure; *n.* attractiveness, temptation
~**yung⁴** ~用 *v.* quote
YIN³ 飲 *v.* drink. ~⁴ *v.* water a horse
YIN⁴ 印 *n.* stamp, seal, mark; *v.* print, stamp
~**hsiang⁴** ~象 *n.* impression
~**shua¹** ~刷 *v.* print; *n.* printing
~**shua¹ chi¹** ~刷機 *n.* printing press
YING¹ 應 *v. aux.* ought to. ~⁴ *n.* answer; *v.* reply, respond; *a.* suitable
~**¹ tang¹** ~當 *v. aux.* ought, must
~**⁴ chan⁴** ~戰 *v.* accept battle
~**ch'ou²** ~酬 *v.* entertain
~**fu⁴** ~付 *v.* deal with
~**fu⁴ ch'ing² k'uang⁴** ~付情況 *v.* meet the situation
~**sheng¹** ~聲 *n.* echo
~**ti²** ~敵 *v.* meet the enemy
~**tui⁴** ~對 *v.* answer, respond
~**yung⁴** ~用 *n.* application
~**yün³** ~允 *v.* promise
YING¹ 英 *a.* heroic, talented
~**hsiung²** ~雄 *n.* hero
~**hsiung² ch'i⁴ k'ai³** ~雄氣慨 *n.* heroism
~**li³** ~里 *n.* mile
~**ming²** ~明 *a.* clever
~**ts'un⁴** ~寸 *n.* inch
~**wei¹** ~威 *n.* English language
~**wen² fa³** ~文法 *n.* English grammar
YING² 迎 *v.* welcome, meet
~**chieh¹** ~接 *v.* meet
YING² 營 *n.* battalion, camp, business, living; *v.* manage

~chang³ ~長 *n.* battalion commander
~chang⁴ ~帳 *n.* camp tents
~chiu⁴ ~救 *v.* plan help
~fang² ~房 *n.* barracks
~li⁴ ~利 *n.* profit making
~tsao⁴ ~造 *v.* construct
~yang³ ~養 *n.* nourishment
~yang³ pu⁴ tsu² ~養不足 *n.* malnutrition
~yeh⁴ ~業 *n.* business
~yeh⁴ shih² chien¹ ~業時間 *n.* business hour
~yeh⁴ shui⁴ ~業税 *n.* business tax
YING² 蠅 *n.* fly, housefly
YING³ 影 *n.* shadow, image, vestige
~hsi⁴ ~戲 *n.* movie
~hsiang³ ~響 *n.* influence
~hsing¹ ~星 *n.* movie star
~tzu¹ ~子 *n.* shadow
YING⁴ 硬 *a.* hard, obstinate, solid
~li⁴ ~力 *n.* stress
~lü³ ~鋁 duraluminum
~mei² ~煤 *n.* anthracite
YU¹ 優 *n.* clown; *a.* excellent, abundant, excessive
~hsien¹ ch'üan² ~先權 *n.* priority
~hsiu⁴ te¹ ~秀的 *a.* excellent
~sheng⁴ ~勝 *n.* victory
~shih⁴ ~勢 *n.* superiority, supremacy
~tai⁴ ~待 *v.* treat specially
~teng³ ~等 *n.* superior class
~tien³ ~點 *n.* merit
~ya³ ~雅 *a.* gracious
~yüeh⁴ ~越 *a.* superior
YU¹ 憂 *n.* melancholy; *a.* anxious, grieved
~ch'ou² ~愁 *n.* anxiety
~lü⁴ ~慮 *n.* sorrow
YU² 游 *v.* float, ramble, swim
~hsi⁴ ~戲 *n.* game
~li⁴ ~歷 *v.* travel
~min² ~民 *n.* vagrant
~tang⁴ ~蕩 *v.* wander, ramble
~yung³ ~泳 *v.* swim; *n.* swimming
~yung³ i¹ ~泳衣 *n.* swimming suit

~**yung³ mao⁴** ～泳帽 *n.* swimming cap

~**yung³ ch'ih²** ～泳池 *n.* swimming pool

YU² 遊 *v.* ramble, travel

~**chi⁴** ～記 *n.* travels

~**hsi⁴** ～戲 *v.* play; *n.* game, play

~**hsing²** ～行 *v.* parade

~**li⁴** ～歷 *v.* travel

~**mu⁴** ～牧 *a.* nomadic

~**piao¹** ～標 *n.* sight slide

~**shui⁴** ～說 *v.* persuade

YU² 郵 *n.* post office, lodge

~**cheng⁴** ～政 *n.* post (mail)

~**cheng⁴ chü²** ～政局 *n.* post office

~**cheng⁴ ch'u² hsü⁴** ～政儲蓄 *n.* postal saving

~**cheng⁴ hsin⁴ hsiang¹** ～政信箱 *n.* post box

~**chi⁴** ～寄 *v.* mail

~**chien⁴** ～件 *n.* mail

~**ch'ai¹** ～差 *n.* postman, postboy, mailman

~**fei⁴** ～費 *n.* postage

~**hui⁴** ～匯 *n.* postal money order

~**p'iao⁴** ～票 *n.* stamp

~**tai⁴** ～袋 *n.* mail bag

~**tien⁴ pu⁴** ～電部 *n.* Ministry of Posts and Tele-
communications**

~**t'ung³** ～筒 *n.* mailbox

YU² 油 *n.* fat, oil; *a.* oily

~**chih³** ～紙 *n.* oil-paper

~**ch'i¹** ～漆 *n.* oil paint, oil color

~**hua⁴** ～畫 *n.* oil painting

~**hsiang¹** ～箱 *n.* fuel tank

~**kao¹** ～膏 *n.* ointment

~**men² t'a' pan³** ～門踏板 *n.* accelerator pedal

~**ni⁴** ～膩 *a.* greasy

~**pu⁴** ～布 *n.* oilcloth

~**ts'ai⁴** ～菜 *n.* rape (plant)

~**yin⁴** ～印 *v.* mimeograph

YU² 由 *n.* cause, reason; *prep.* from, by, through

~**shih⁴** ～是 *adv.* therefore, hence

YU³ 有 *v.* have, hold, possess, own

~**chia⁴ chih² te¹** ～價值的 *a.* valuable

~**ch'an³ chieh¹ chi²** ～產階級 *n.* bourgeoisie

~**ch'ang²** ~常 *n.* stability

~**ch'ü⁴** ~趣 *a.* interesting

~**hsi¹ wang⁴** ~希望 *a.* promising, hopeful

~**hsiao⁴** ~效 *a.* effective

~**hsien⁴ kung¹ ssu¹** ~限公司 *n.* limited company

~**hsien⁴ te¹** ~限的 *a.* limited

~**li³** ~理 *a.* reasonable

~**li³** ~禮 *a.* polite

~**li⁴** ~利 *a.* profitable, advantageous

~**ming² te¹** ~名的 *a.* famous, well-known, noted

~**neng² li⁴ te¹** ~能力的 *a.* able

~**yung⁴** ~用 *a.* useful

YU³ 友 *n.* friend

~**ai⁴** ~愛 *n.* amity

~**i²** ~誼 *n.* friendship

~**jen²** ~人 *n.* friend

YU⁴ 又 *adv.* again, also, too, moreover, further; *conj.* and

~**chi²** ~及 *n.* postscript

~**i¹ t'ien¹** ~一天 *adv.* another day

YU⁴ 右 *a. & n.* right (direction)

~**ch'ing¹** ~傾 *a.* rightist (idea)

~**p'ai⁴** ~派 *n.* rightist

~**shou³** ~手 *a.* right-hand, right-handed

YUNG¹ 擁 *v.* push, crowd. ~³ *v.* embrace

~¹ **chi³** ~擠 *v.* crowd

~**sai¹** ~塞 *v.* block up

~³ **hu⁴** ~護 *v.* support, uphold

~**pao⁴** ~抱 *v.* embrace

YUNG³ 永 *a.* perpetual, eternal, permanent

~**chiu³** ~久 *a.* permanent, perpetual; *adv.* permanently, perpetually

~**pu⁴** ~不 *adv.* never

~**sheng¹** ~生 *a.* eternal, *n.* eternity

~**yüan³** ~遠 *adv.* forever, always

YUNG³ 勇 *a.* brave, courageous, daring; *n.* valor, bravery

~**ch'i⁴** ~氣 *n.* courage

~**kan³** ~敢 *n.* valor, bravery

YUNG⁴ 用 *v.* use, spend; *n.* use, expense

~**chi⁴** ~計 *v.* use tricks

221

~chin¹ ~金 *n.* commission (money)

~chü⁴ ~具 *n.* tool, instrument, utensil

~fei⁴ ~費 *n.* expenditure, expense

~jen² ~人 *n.* servant; *v.* employ

~kung¹ ~功 *v.* study hard

~t'u² ~途 *n.* usage

YÜ² 魚 *n.* fish, letter

YÜ² 於 *prep.* at, in, on, to, by

~chin¹ ~今 *adv.* at present, now

~hsia⁴ ~下 *adv.* below

~shih⁴ ~是 *adv.* therefore, hence

~tz'u³ ~此 *adv.* hereabout

YÜ² 餘 *n.* remainder, surplus, excess

YÜ² 娛 *v.* amuse, please, enjoy; *n.* pleasure, amusement

~le⁴ ~樂 *n.* entertainment

YÜ³ 語 *v.* talk, speak; *n.* language

~yen² ~言 *n.* language, speech

~yen² hsüeh² ~言學 *n.* linguistic science

~yen² hsüeh² chia¹ ~言學家 *n.* linguist

YÜ³ 與 *v.* give. ~⁴ *v.* share; *conj.* and

YÜ³ 雨 *n.* rain

~chi⁴ ~季 *n.* rainy season

~i¹ ~衣 *n.* raincoat

~liang⁴ ~量 *n.* rainfall

~san³ ~傘 *n.* umbrella

~tien³ ~點 *n.* raindrop

YÜ⁴ 遇 *v.* meet, occur

YÜ⁴ 育 *v.* nourish, foster, rear

~ying¹ t'ang² ~嬰堂 *n.* orphanage

YÜ⁴ 玉 *n.* jade

~mi³ ~米 *n.* maize

~shu³ shu³ ~蜀黍 *n.* Indian corn, corn

YÜ⁴ 預 *v.* prepare

~chao⁴ ~兆 *n.* omen

~chih¹ ~支 *v.* advance money

~fang² ~防 *v.* prevent; *n.* prevention

~fu⁴ ~付 *v.* pay in advance

~k'o¹ ~科 *n.* preparatory class

~pei⁴ ~備 *v.* prepare; *adv.* ready; *n.* preparation

~pei⁴ tui⁴ 備隊 *n.* reserves (troops)

~suan⁴ ~算 *n.* budget

~suan⁴ chü² ~算局 *n.* Budget Bureau*

~ts'e⁴ ~測 *n.* forecast

~yen² ~言 *v.* foretell; *n.* prophecy

~yen² chia¹ ~言家 *n.* prophet

~yüeh¹ ~約 *v.* subscribe to

YÜAN¹ 寃 *v.* have a grudge, injure, oppress

~chia¹ ~家 *n.* enemy, foe

~ch'ou² ~仇 *n.* enemity

~ch'ü¹ ~屈 *n.* grievance

YÜAN² 元 *n.* beginning, dollar

~ch'i⁴ ~氣 *n.* energy, vigor

~su⁴ ~素 *n.* element

~shih³ ~始 *n.* origin, source, beginning

~shou³ ~首 *n.* head, ruler, chief executive

~shuai⁴ ~帥 *n.* Army General (*U.S.*)

~tan⁴ ~旦 *n.* New Year's Day

~tzu³ ~子 *n.* atom

~yüeh¹ ~月 *n.* January

YÜAN² 原 *n.* plain; *a.* original

~chu³ ~主 *n.* proprietor, owner

~ch'i⁴ ~氣 *n.* vitality

~kao³ ~稿 *n.* protocol

~kao⁴ ~告 *n.* plaintiff

~li³ ~理 *n.* principle

~liang⁴ ~諒 *n.* pardon

~liao⁴ ~料 *n.* raw material

~su⁴ ~素 *n.* element

~shih³ ~始 *a.* primitive

~tse² hsing⁴ ~則性 *n.* character of principle**

~tzu³ ~子 *n.* atom; *a.* atomic

~tzu³ chan⁴ cheng¹ ~子戦争 *n.* atomic warfare

~tzu³ liang⁴ ~子量 *n.* atomic weight

~tzu³ lun⁴ ~子論 *n.* atomic theory

~tzu³ neng² ~子能 *n.* atomic energy

~tzu³ shu⁴ ~子數 *n.* atomic number

~tzu³ tan⁴ ~子彈 *n.* atomic bomb

~wen² ~文 *n.* text

~yin¹ ~因 *n.* reason, cause

YÜAN² 員 *n.* member

YÜAN² 圓 *a.* round, circular; *n.* circle, dollar

~**cho¹** ~卓 *n.* round table

~**chou¹** ~周 *n.* circumference

~**chu⁴ t'i³** ~柱體 *n.* cylinder

~**chui¹ t'i³** ~錐體 *n.* cone

~**hsing²** ~形 *n.* sphere

~**kuei¹** ~規 *n.* compass

~**man³** ~滿 *a.* complete, satisfactory

YÜAN² 園 *n.* garden, orchard, park

~**i⁴** ~藝 *n.* gardening

~**ting¹** ~丁 *n.* gardener

~**yu² hui⁴** ~遊會 *n.* garden party

YÜAN² 援 *v.* rescue, quote, hold fast

~**chiu⁴** ~救 *v.* relieve (aid)

~**chu⁴** ~助 *v.* assist, help

~**ping¹** ~兵 *n.* reinforcement

~**tui⁴** ~隊 *n.* support troops

YÜAN³ 遠 *a.* distant. ~⁴ *v.* remove

~**cheng¹ chün¹** ~征軍 *n.* expeditionary force

~**chü⁴ li²** ~距離 *n.* long range

~**she⁴ p'ao⁴** ~射砲 *n.* long range gun

~**tan⁴** ~彈 *a.* over shoot

~**tung¹** ~東 *n.* Far East

~**tung¹ wen⁴ t'i²** ~東問題 *n.* problem of the Far East

~**tung¹ yün⁴ tung⁴ hui⁴** ~東運動會 *n.* Far East Olympic Games

YÜAN⁴ 院 *n.* courtyard

YÜAN⁴ 願 *n.* & *v.* wish, desire

~**i⁴** ~意 *a.* willing

~**wang⁴** ~望 *n.* wish, desire

YÜAN⁴ 怨 *v.* grumble, hate; *a.* dissatisfied

~**hen⁴** ~恨 *v.* hate

~**yen²** ~言 *a.* spiteful

YÜEH¹ 約 *v.* invite; *n.* engagement, treaty

~**hui⁴** ~會 *v.* make an appointment

~**lüeh⁴** ~略 *a.* brief, concise; *adv.* approximately

~**su⁴** ~束 *v.* restrain, control

~**shih⁴** ~誓 *v.* swear; *a.* sworn

YÜEH⁴ 月 *n.* moon, month; *adv.* monthly

~**ching¹** ~經 *n.* menses

~**fen⁴ p'ai²** ~份牌 *n.* calendar

~**kuang¹** ~光 *n.* moonlight, moonshine

~**k'an¹** ~刊 *n.* monthly magazine

~**lao³** ~老 *n.* marriage matchmaker

~**liang⁴** ~亮 *n.* moon

~**ping³** ~餅 *n.* moon cake (eaten at the Chinese Mid-Autumn Festival)

~**shih²** ~蝕 *n.* lunar eclipse

~**t'ai²** ~台 *n.* railroad station platform

~**t'ai² p'iao⁴** ~台票 *n.* platform ticket

YÜEH⁴ 越 *v.* exceed, excel, surpass

~**ch'üan²** ~權 *v.* exceed one's power

~**kuo⁴** ~過 *v.* pass over

~**yeh³** ~野 *a.* cross-country

YÜEH⁴ 閱 *v.* read, peruse, look at

~**li⁴** ~歷 *n.* experience

~**ping¹** ~兵 *v.* review troops

~**tu²** ~讀 *v.* read

YÜEH⁴ 樂 *see* **LE⁴**

YÜN² 雲 *n.* cloud; *a.* cloudy

YÜN⁴ 運 *v.* move, remove, transport; *n.* fate

~**ch'i⁴** ~氣 *n.* fortune, luck

~**ch'u¹** ~出 *v.* export

~**fei⁴** ~費 *n.* freight

~**ho²** ~河 *n.* canal, Grand Canal

~**ju⁴** ~入 *v.* import

~**shu¹** ~輸 *v.* transport; *n.* transportation

~**shu¹ chi¹** ~輸機 *n.* transport airplane

~**tung⁴** ~動 *n.* & *v.* exercise; *n.* movement

~**tung⁴ hui⁴** ~動會 *n.* athletic meeting

~**tung⁴ hsing⁴** ~動性 *n.* mobility

225

NUMBERS 數目 shu⁴ mu⁴

Cardinal Numbers 基數 chi¹ shu⁴

1	一	i¹
2	二	erh⁴
3	三	san¹
4	四	ssu⁴
5	五	wu³
6	六	liu⁴
7	七	ch'i¹
8	八	pa¹
9	九	chiu³
10	十	shih²
11	十一	shih² i¹
12	十二	shih² erh⁴
13	十三	shih² san¹
14	十四	shih² ssu⁴
15	十五	shih² wu³
16	十六	shih² liu⁴
17	十七	shih² ch'i¹
18	十八	shih² pa¹
19	十九	shih² chiu³
20	二十	erh⁴ shih²
21	二十一	erh⁴ shih² i¹
26	二十六	erh⁴ shih² liu⁴
30	三十	san¹ shih²
40	四十	ssu⁴ shih²
50	五十	wu³ shih²
60	六十	liu⁴ shih²
70	七十	ch'i¹ shih²
80	八十	pa¹ shih²
90	九十	chiu³ shih²
100	一百	i⁴ pai³
102	一百零二	i⁴ pai³ ling² erh⁴
1,000	一千	i⁴ ch'ien¹ ⌈shih²
1,030	一千零三十	i⁴ ch'ien¹ ling² san¹
1,950	一千九百五十	i⁴ ch'ien¹ chiu² pai² wu³ shih²

226

10,000	一萬	i² wan⁴
100,000	十萬	shih² wan⁴
1,000,000	一百萬	i⁴ pai³ wan⁴
10,000,000	一千萬	i⁴ ch'ien¹ wan⁴
100,000,000	一億 (一萬萬)	i² i⁴ (i² wan⁴ wan⁴)
1,000,000,000	十億 (十萬萬)	shih² i⁴ (shih² wan⁴ wan⁴)

NOTE: *The following are denominators frequently used with numbers:*

張 chang¹ *for chairs, desks, papers*
架 chia⁴ *for beds, machine guns, airplanes*
間 chien¹ *for houses, rooms*
件 chien⁴ *for things, objects*
炷 chu⁴ *for incense*
串 ch'uan⁴ *for pearls*
群 ch'ün² *for animals*
份 fen⁴ *for money, refreshments, newspapers*
副 fu⁴ *for playing cards, dominoes, mahjong*
根 ken¹ *for cigarettes, matches, sticks, grasses*
個 ko⁴ *for persons, rings, houses, schools*
口 k'ou³ *for water, rice*
管 kuan³ *for pens*
塊 k'uai⁴ *for lands, stones, cakes*
筐 k'uang¹ *for threads*
捆 k'un³ *for firewood*
輛 liang⁴ *for vehicles*
門 men² *for guns*
把 pa³ *for swords, knives, scissors, fans, locks*
盤 p'an² *for chess, food*
本 pen³ *for books*
匹 p'i¹ *for asses, donkeys, cloth, horses*
部 pu⁴ *for vehicles, books, machines*
雙 shuang¹ *for chopsticks, shoes*
扇 shan⁴ *for doors*
帖 t'ieh¹ *for medicines*
條 t'iao² *for cigarettes, handkerchiefs, streets, trousers*
挺 t'ing³ *for machine guns*
座 tso⁴ *for houses, mountains, theaters, cities*
堆 tsui¹ *for things, articles*

227

位　wei⁴　*for friends, teachers, professors, newsmen*

For Example: *If you want to say " a book "
in Chinese, you would say " i⁴ pen³ shu¹ " (一本
書); but if you want to say " a horse," you
should say " i⁴ p'i¹ ma³ " (一匹馬) instead of " i⁴
pen² ma³."* ***Care must be exercised in using the
above denominators before specific objects.***

Ordinal Numbers 序數 hsü⁴ shu⁴

1st	第一	ti⁴ i¹
2nd	第二	ti⁴ erh⁴
3rd	第三	ti⁴ san¹
4th	第四	ti⁴ ssu⁴
5th	第五	ti⁴ wu³
6th	第六	ti⁴ liu⁴
7th	第七	ti⁴ ch'i¹
8th	第八	ti⁴ pa¹
9th	第九	ti⁴ chiu³
10th	第十	ti⁴ shih²
11th	第十一	ti⁴ shih² i¹
12th	第十二	ti⁴ shih² erh⁴
13th	第十三	ti⁴ shih² san¹
14th	第十四	ti⁴ shih² ssu⁴
15th	第十五	ti⁴ shih² wu³
16th	第十六	ti⁴ shih² liu⁴
17th	第十七	ti⁴ shih² ch'i¹
18th	第十八	ti⁴ shih² pa¹
19th	第十九	ti⁴ shih² chiu³
20th	第二十	ti⁴ erh⁴ shih²
21st	第二十一	ti⁴ erh⁴ shih² i¹
22nd	第二十二	ti⁴ erh⁴ shih² erh⁴
30th	第三十	ti⁴ san¹ shih²
40th	第四十	ti⁴ ssu⁴ shih²
50th	第五十	ti⁴ wu³ shih²
60th	第六十	ti⁴ liu⁴ shih²
70th	第七十	ti⁴ ch'i¹ shih²
80th	第八十	ti⁴ pa¹ shih²
90th	第九十	ti⁴ chiu³ shih²
100th	第一百	ti⁴ i⁴ pai³
110th	第一百一十	ti⁴ i⁴ pai³ i⁴ shih²

1,000th	第一千	ti⁴ i⁴ ch'ien¹
1,110th	第一千一百一十	ti⁴ i⁴ ch'ien¹ i⁴ pai³ i⁴ shih²
The last	最後	tsui⁴ hou⁴

Decimals 小數 hsiao³ shu⁴

.3 (*point three*) *three-tenths*	十分之三	shih² fen¹ chih¹ san¹
.065 (*point zero six five*) *sixty-five thousandths*	千分之六十五	ch'ien¹fen¹chih¹ liu⁴ shih² wu³
11.25 (*eleven point two five*) *eleven and twenty-five hundredths*	十一零百分之二十五	shih² i¹ ling² pai³ fen¹ chih¹ erh⁴ shih² wu³

Fractions 分數 fen¹ shu⁴

1/2 (*one-half; a half*)	二分之一；一半	erh⁴ fen¹ chih¹ i¹; i² pan⁴
1/3 (*one-third*)	三分之一	san¹ fen¹ chih¹ i¹
2/3 (*two-thirds*)	三分之二	san¹ fen¹ chih¹ erh⁴
1/4 (*a quarter; one-fourth*)	四分之一	ssu⁴ fen¹ chih¹ i¹
3/4 (*three quarters; three-fourths*)	四分之三	ssu⁴ fen¹ chih¹ san¹
1/10 (*one-tenth*)	十分之一	shih² fen¹ chih¹ i¹
2 7/8 (*two and seven-eighths*)	二又八分之七	erh⁴ yu⁴ pa¹ fen¹ chih¹ ch'i¹

Multiple Numbers 倍數 pei⁴ shu⁴

twofold; double; twice	二倍	erh⁴ pei⁴
threefold; triple; treble	三倍	san¹ pei⁴
fourfold; quadruple	四倍	ssu⁴ pei⁴
fivefold; quintuple	五倍	wu³ pei⁴
sixfold; sextuple	六倍	liu⁴ pei⁴
tenfold	十倍	shih² pei⁴
elevenfold	十一倍	shih² i² pei⁴

229

twentyfold	二十倍	erh⁴ shih² pei⁴
fiftyfold	五十倍	wu³ shih² pei⁴
hundredfold; centuple	百倍	pai³ pei⁴

Percentage 百分率 pai³ fen¹ lü⁴

one per cent	百分之一	pai³ fen¹ chih¹ i¹
eleven per cent	百分之十一	pai³ fen¹ chih¹ shih² i¹
twenty per cent	百分之二十	pai³ fen¹ chih¹ erh⁴ shih²
fifty-one per cent	百分之五十一	pai³ fen¹ chih¹ wu³ shih² i¹
one hundred per pent	百分之百	pai³ fen¹ chih¹ pai³

The Months 月份 yüeh⁴ fen⁴

January	一月	i² yüeh⁴
February	二月	erh⁴ yüeh⁴
March	三月	san¹ yüeh⁴
April	四月	ssu⁴ yüeh⁴
May	五月	wu³ yüeh⁴
June	六月	liu⁴ yüeh⁴
July	七月	ch'i² yüeh⁴
August	八月	pa² yüeh⁴
September	九月	chiu³ yüeh⁴
October	十月	shih² yüeh⁴
November	十一月	shih² i² yüeh⁴
December	十二月	shih² erh⁴ yüeh⁴

The Four Seasons 四季 ssu⁴ chi⁴

| Spring | 春 ch'un¹ | Autumn | 秋 ch'iu¹ |
| Summer | 夏 hsia⁴ | Winter | 冬 tung¹ |

The Days of the Week 週日 chou¹ jih⁴

| Sunday | 星期日 | hsing¹ ch'i² jih⁴ |
| | 禮拜天 | li³ pai⁴ t'ien¹ |

Monday	星期一	hsing¹ ch'i² i¹
Tuesday	星期二	hsing¹ ch'i² erh⁴
Wednesday	星期三	hsing¹ ch'i² san¹
Thursday	星期四	hsing¹ ch'i² ssu⁴
Friday	星期五	hsing¹ ch'i² wu³
Saturday	星期六	hsing¹ ch'i² liu⁴

Time 時 shih²

A century	一世紀	i² shih⁴ chi⁴
A day	一 天	i⁴ t'ien¹
A fortnight	兩星期	liang³ hsing¹ ch'i²
A month	一個月	i² ko⁴ yüeh⁴
A week	一星期	i⁴ hsing¹ ch'i²
A year	一 年	i⁴ nien²
Afternoon	午 後	wu³ hou⁴
Day	日	jih⁴
Day after tomorrow	後 日	hou⁴ jih⁴
Day before yesterday	前 日	ch'ien² jih⁴
Daybreak	黎 明	li² ming²
Dusk	黃 昏	huang² hun¹
Evening	夕	hsi¹
Forenoon	午 前	wu³ ch'ien²
Last month	上 月	shang⁴ yüeh⁴
Last Year	去 年	ch'ü⁴ nien²
Morning	早 晨	tsao³ ch'en²
Next month	下 月	hsia⁴ yüeh⁴
Next week	下星期	hsia⁴ hsing¹ ch'i²
Night	夜	yeh⁴
Noon	中 午	chung¹ wu³
Today	今 日	chin¹ jih⁴
Tomorrow	明 日	ming² jih⁴
Week	星 期	hsing¹ ch'i²
Year	年	nien²
Yesterday	昨 日	tso² jih⁴

Chinese Years

Chinese years are named from the founding

of the Republic of China by Dr. Sun Yat-sen.
The chart below will indicate the names of the
years from 1912 on.

中華民國元年
  (chung¹ hua² min² kuo² yüan² nien²)
  1st year of the Republic of China   **1912**

中華民國五年
  (chung¹ hua² min² kuo² wu³ nien²)
  5th year of the Republic of China   **1916**

中華民國十年
  (chung¹ hua² min² kuo² shih² nien²)
  10th year of the Republic of China   **1921**

中華民國十五年
  (chung¹ hua² min² kuo² shih² wu³ nien²)
  15th year of the Republic of China   **1926**

中華民國二十年
  (chung¹ hua² min² kuo² erh⁴ shih² nien²)
  20th year of the Republic of China   **1931**

中華民國二十五年
  (chung¹ hua² min² kuo² erh⁴ shih² wu³ nien²)
  25th year of the Republic of China   **1936**

中華民國三十年
  (chung¹ hua² min² kuo² san¹ shih² nien²)
  30th year of the Republic of China   **1941**

中華民國三十五年
  (chung¹ hua² min² kuo² san¹ shih² wu³ nien²)
  35th year of the Republic of China   **1946**

中華民國四十年
  (chung¹ hua² min² kuo² ssu⁴ shih² nien²)
  40th year of the Republic of China   **1951**

WEIGHTS 重量 chung⁴ liang⁴

Old Standard

10 分 (fen¹)=1 錢 (ch'ien²)=*mace*
10 錢 (ch'ien²)=1 兩 (liang³)=*tael=37.8 grams*
16 兩 (liang³)=1 斤 (chin¹)=*catty=604.79 grams*

100 斤 (chin^{1})=1 擔 (tan^{4})=*picul=60.479 kilos*
=133.33 pounds

Market Standard

10 市分 (shih^{4} fen^{1}) =1 市錢 (shih^{4} ch'ien^{2})

10 市錢 (shih^{4} ch'ien^{2})=1 市兩 (shih^{4} liang^{3})
=31.25 grams

16 市兩 (shih^{4} liang^{3}) =1 市斤 (shih^{4} chin^{1})
=500 grams

100 市斤 (shih^{4} chin^{1}) =1 市擔 (shih^{4} tan^{4})
=50 kilograms
=1/2 市引 (shih^{4} yin^{3})=*110.23 pounds*

Metric System

兞=公絲 (kung^{1} ssu^{1}) =*milligram*

兣=公毫 (kung^{1} hao^{2}) =*centigram*

兝=公厘 (kung^{1} li^{2}) =*decigram*

克=公分 (kung^{1} fen^{1}) =*gram*

兙=公錢 (kung^{1} ch'ien^{2})=*decagram*

兡=公兩 (kung^{1} liang^{3}) =*hectogram*

兛=公斤 (kung^{1} chin^{1}) =*kilogram*

公噸 (kung^{1} tun^{4}) =*metric ton*

LENGTH 長度 ch'ang^{2} tu^{4}

Old Standard

10 分 (fen^{1}) =1 寸 (ts'un^{4})

10 寸 (ts'un^{4}) =1 尺 (ch'ih^{3}) =*14.1 inches*

10 尺 (ch'ih^{3}) =1 丈 (chang^{4})=*11.75 feet*

180 丈 (chang^{4})=1 里 (li^{3}) =*about 1/3 mile*

Market Standard

10 市分 (shih^{4} fen^{1}) =1 市寸 (shih^{4} ts'un^{4})

10 市寸 (shih^{4} ts'un^{4}) =1 市尺 (shih^{4} ch'ih^{3})
=0.333 meter

10 市尺 (shih⁴ ch'ih³) =1 市丈 (shih⁴ chang⁴)
150 市丈 (shih⁴ chang⁴)=1 市里 (shih⁴ li³)
　　　　　　　　　　　　　　　　=*500 meters*
　　　　　　　　　　　　　　　　=*0.31 mile*

Metric System

粍=公厘 (kung¹ li²)　　 =*millimeter*
糎=公分 (kung¹ fen¹)　 =*centimeter*
粉=公寸 (kung¹ ts'un⁴) =*decimeter*
釈=公尺 (kung¹ ch'ih³) =*meter*
粁=公丈 (kung¹ chang⁴) =*decameter*
粨=公引 (kung¹ yin³)　 =*hectometer*
粁=公里 (kung¹ li³)　　 =*kilometer*

VOLUME 體積 t'i³ chi¹

Old Standard

10 合 (ho²)　 =1 升 (sheng¹)=*1.09 liquid quarts*
　　　　　　　　　　　　　　　 =*1.035 liters*

10 升 (sheng¹)=1 斗 (tou³)
5 斗 (tou³)　 =1 斛 (hu²)
2 斛 (hu²)　　=1 石 (shih²)

Market Standard

10 市合 (shih⁴ ho²)　　 =1 市升 (shih⁴ sheng¹)
　　　　　　　　　　　　　　　　 =*1 liter*
10 市升 (shih⁴ sheng¹)=1 市斗 (shih⁴ tou³)
10 市斗 (shih⁴ tou³)　 =1 市石 (shih⁴ shih²)

Metric System

扮=公合 (kung¹ ho²)　　 =1 deciliter
竏=公升 (kung¹ sheng¹)=1 liter=*1 cubic decimeter*
籵=公斗 (kung¹ tou³)　 =1 decaliter
頔=公石 (kung¹ shih²)　 =1 hectoliter
竏=公秉 (kung¹ ping³)　 =1 kiloliter=*1 cubic meter*
　　　　　　　　　　　　　　　　　 =*1 stere*

AREA 面積 mien⁴ chi¹

Old Standard

100 方寸 (fang¹ ts'un⁴) =1 方尺 (fang¹ ch'ih³)
100 方尺 (fang¹ ch'ih³) =1 方丈 (fang¹ chang⁴)
 60 方丈 (fang¹ chang⁴)=1 畝 (mu³)=*0.1666 acre*
100 畝 (mu³)=1 頃 (ch'ing³)
540 畝 (mu³)=1 方里 (fang¹ li³)

Market Standard

10 市毫 (shih⁴ hao²) =1 市厘 (shih⁴ li²)
10 市厘 (shih⁴ li²) =1 市分 (shih⁴ fen¹)
10 市分 (shih⁴ fen¹) =1 市畝 (shih⁴ mu³)
                     =*0.1647 acre*
100 市畝 (shih⁴ mu³) =1 市頃 (chih⁴ ch'ing³)
                     =*16.47 acres*

Metric System

勎=公分 (kung¹ fen¹)   =*deciare*
安=公畝 (kung¹ mu³)   =*are=100 square meters*
頺=公頃 (kung¹ ch'ing³)=*hectare*

CURRENCIES 貨幣 hou⁴ pi⁴

The money used in Nationalist China is called New Taiwan Currency (新臺幣 hsin¹ t'ai² pi⁴) *(hereafter abbreviated NT) which consists of the Chinese dollar* (圓 yüan²) *and the dime* (角 chiao³). *The basic unit is the Chinese dollar, which equals ten dimes. They are divided into six denominations: ten Chinese dollars* (拾圓 shih³ yüan³), *five Chinese dollars* (伍圓 wu³ yüan²), *one Chinese dollar* (壹圓 i⁴ yüan²), *five dimes* (伍角 wu³ chiao³), *two dimes* (貳角 erh⁴ chiao³), *and one dime* (壹角 i²

235

chiao³). *As of the time of writing the official foreign exchange rates are as follows:**

American Foreign Exchange:

	1 US\$ =NT\$ 15.55
Pound Sterling:	1 US£ =NT\$ 43.54
Hongkong Currency:	1 HK\$ =NT\$ 2.72
Malayan Currency:	1 SS\$ =NT\$ 5.08
Burmese Currency:	1 Kyat =NT\$ 1.81
Philippines Currency:	1 Peso =NT\$ 6.64
Vietnam Currency:	1 Yüan=NT\$ 0.19
Siamese Currency:	1 Baht =NT\$ 0.74

* *Source: Central Daily News.*

FAMILY RELATIONS

grandparent
  (*parent of one's father*)   tsu³ fu⁴ mu³ 祖 父 母
  (*parent of one's mother*)
                wai⁴ tsu³ fu⁴ mu³ 外祖父母
grandfather, grandpa
  (*father of one's father*)   tsu³ fu⁴ 祖   父
  (*father of one's mother*) wai⁴ tsu³ fu⁴ 外 祖 父
grandmother, grandma
  (*mother of one's father*)   tsu² mu³ 祖   母
  (*mother of one's mother*) wai⁴ tsu² mu³ 外祖 母
granduncle, great-uncle
  (*husband of the sister of one's father's father*)
            ku¹ tsu³ 姑   祖
  (*older brother of one's father's father*)
            po² tsu³ 伯   祖
  (*younger brother of one's father's father*)
            shu² tsu³ 叔   祖
  (*husband of the sister of one's mother's mother*)
            i² kung¹ 姨   公
  (*brother of one's mother's mother*)
            chiu⁴ kung¹ 舅   公
grandaunt, great-aunt
  (*sister of one's father's father*) ku¹ p'o² 姑   婆

(wife of the older brother of one's father's father)	po² tsu² mu³	伯祖母	
(wife of the younger brother of one's father's father)	shu² tsu² mu³	叔祖母	
(sister of one's mother's mother)	i² p'o²	姨	婆
(wife of the brother of one's mother's mother)	chiu⁴ p'o²	舅	婆
father	fu⁴ ch'in¹	父	親
stepfather	chi⁴ fu⁴	繼	父
father-in-law			
(father of one's husband)	kung¹ kung¹	公	公
(father of one's wife)	yüeh⁴ fu⁴	岳	父
mother	mu³ ch'in¹	母	親
stepmother	chi⁴ mu³	繼	母
mother-in-law			
(mother of one's husband)	p'o² p'o²	婆	婆
(mother of one's wife)	yüeh⁴ mu³	岳	母
uncle			
(older brother of one's father)	po² fu⁴	伯	父
(younger brother of one's father)	shu² fu⁴	叔	父
(brother of one's mother)	chiu⁴ fu⁴	舅	父
(husband of the sister of one's father)	ku¹ fu⁴	姑	父
(husband of the sister of one's mother)	i² fu⁴	姨	父
aunt			
(wife of the older brother of one's father)	po² mu³	伯	母
(wife of the younger brother of one's father)	shu² mu³	叔	母
(wife of the brother of one's mother)	chiu⁴ mu³	舅	母
(sister of one's father)	ku¹ mu³	姑	母
(sister of one's mother)	i² mu³	姨	母
son	erh² tzu³	兒	子
daughter-in-law	hsi² fu⁴	媳	婦
daughter	nü³ erh²	女	兒
son-in-law	nü³ hsü⁴	女	婿

237

stepchild	chi⁴ erh² nü³	繼兒	女
stepson	chi⁴ tzu³	繼	子
stepdaughter	chi⁴ nü³	繼	女
brother	hsiung¹ ti⁴	兄	弟
(older brother)	hsiung¹	兄	
(younger brother)	ti⁴	弟	
stepbrother i⁴ fu⁴ (mu³) hsiung¹ ti⁴		異父(母)兄弟	
brother-in-law			

(older brother of one's husband) ta⁴ po² 大 伯

(younger brother of one's husband)

hsiao³ shu² 小　叔

(older brother of one's wife)

nei⁴ hsiung¹ 內　兄

(younger brother of one's wife) nei⁴ ti⁴ 內　弟

(husband of one's older sister)

chieh³ fu¹ 姊　夫

(husband of one's younger brother)

mei⁴ fu¹ 妹　夫

(husband of the older sister of one's wife)

chin¹ hsiung¹ 襟　兄

(husband of the younger sister of one's wife)

chin¹ ti⁴ 襟　弟

(husband of the older sister of one's husband)

chieh³ fu¹ 姊　夫

(husband of the younger sister of one's husband)

mei⁴ fu¹ 妹　夫

sister	chieh³ mei⁴	姊	妹
(older sister)	chieh³	姐	
(younger sister)	mei⁴	妹	
stepsister i⁴ fu⁴ (mu³) chieh³ mei⁴		異父(母)姊妹	
sister-in-law			

(wife of the older brother of one's husband)

sao² sao³ 嫂　嫂

(wife of the younger brother of one's husband)

ti⁴ mei⁴ 弟妹

(wife of the older brother of one's wife)

ta⁴ chiu⁴ sao³ 大 舅 嫂

(wife of the younger brother of one's wife)

hsiao³ chiu⁴ sao³ 小 舅 嫂

(wife of one's older brother) sao² sao³ 嫂　嫂

238

(*wife of one's younger brother*)	ti⁴ mei⁴	弟	妹
(*older sister of one's wife*)	ta⁴ i²	大	姨
(*younger sister of one's wife*)	hsiao³ i²	小	姨
(*older sister of one's husband*)	ta⁴ ku¹	大	姑
(*younger sister of one's husband*)			
	hsiao³ ku¹	小	姑

cousin

(*older son of one's father's brother*)			
	t'ang² hsiung¹	堂	兄
(*younger son of one's father's brother*)			
	t'ang² ti⁴	堂	弟
(*older son of one's mother's brother*)			
	chiu⁴ piao³ hsiung¹	舅 表 兄	
(*younger son of one's mother's brother*)			
	chiu⁴ piao³ ti⁴	舅 表 弟	
(*older son of one's father's sister*)			
	ku¹ piao³ hsiung¹	姑 表 兄	
(*younger son of one's father's sister*)			
	ku¹ piao³ ti⁴	姑 表 弟	
(*older son of one's mother's sister*)			
	i² piao³ hsiung¹	姨 表 兄	
(*younger son of one's mother's sister*)			
	i² piao³ ti⁴	姨 表 弟	
(*older daughter of one's father's brother*)			
	t'ang² chieh³	堂	姐
(*younger daughter of one's father's brother*)			
	t'ang² mei⁴	堂	妹
(*older daughter of one's mother's brother*)			
	chiu⁴ piao² chieh³	舅 表 姐	
(*younger daughter of one's mother's brother*)			
	chiu⁴ piao³ mei⁴	舅 表 妹	
(*older daughter of one's father's sister*)			
	ku¹ piao² chieh³	姑 表 姐	
(*younger daughter of one's father's sister*)			
	ku¹ piao³ mei⁴	姑 表 妹	
(*older daughter of one's mother's sister*)			
	i² piao² chieh³	姨 表 姐	
(*younger daughter of one's mother's sister*)			
	i² piao³ mei⁴	姨 表 妹	

nephew

(*son of one's brother*)	chih² erh²	侄	兒

Family Relations

(son of one's sister)   wai⁴ sheng¹   外   甥
(son of one's husband's brother)
                    chih² erh²   姪   兒
(son of one's wife's brother) nei⁴ chih²   內   姪
(son of one's wife's sister) wai⁴ sheng¹   外   甥
(son of one's husband's sister)
                    wai⁴ sheng¹   外   甥

niece
(daughter of one's brother) chih² nü³   姪   女
(daughter of one's sister)
                wai⁴ sheng¹ nü³   外甥女
(daughter of one's husband's brother)
                  chih² nü³   姪   女
(daughter of one's wife's brother)
                nei⁴ chih² nü³   內姪女
(daughter of one's wife's sister)
                wai⁴ sheng¹ nü³   外甥女
(daughter of one's husband's sister)
                wai⁴ sheng¹ nü³   外甥女

grandchild
(child of one's son)   sun¹ erh² nü³   孫兒女
(child of one's daughter)
              wai⁴ sun¹ erh² nü³   外孫兒女

grandson
(son of one's son)   sun¹ tzu³   孫   子
(son of one's daughter) wai⁴ sun¹   外   孫

granddaughter
(daughter of one's son) sun¹ nü³   孫   女
(daughter of one's daughter)
              wai⁴ sun¹ nü³   外孫女

grandnephew
(son of one's brother's son or daughter)
                  chih² sun¹   姪   孫
(son of one's sister's son or daughter)
                  wai⁴ sun¹   外   孫
(son of one's husband's brother's son or daughter) chih² sun¹ erh²   姪孫兒
(son of one's wife's brother's son or daughter)
                nei⁴ chih² sun¹   內姪孫
(son of one's wife's sister's son or daughter)

240

wai⁴ sun¹ 外　孫
(*son of one's husband's sister's son or daughter*)
wai⁴ sun¹ 外　孫

grandniece
(*daughter of one's brother's son or daughter*)
chih² sun¹ nü³ 侄孫女
(*daughter of one's sister's son or daughter*)
wai⁴ sun¹ nü³ 外孫女
(*daughter of one's wife's brother's son or daugh-*
ter)　　　nei⁴ chih² sun¹ nü³ 內侄孫女
(*daughter of one's husband's brother's son or*
daughter)　　wai⁴ sun¹ nü³ 外孫女
(*daughter of one's wife's sister's son or daugh-*
ter)　　　　wai⁴ sun¹ nü³ 外孫女
(*daughter of one's husband's sister's son or*
daughter)　　wai⁴ sun¹ nü⁴ 外孫女

IMPORTANT GEOGRAPHICAL NAMES OF CHINA

Anhwei 安　徽
| Anching | 安　慶 | Hofei | | 合　肥 |
| Wuhu | 蕪　湖 | | | |

Antung 安　東
| Autung | 安　東 | Hailung | | 海　龍 |
| Tunghua | 通　化 | | | |

Chahar 察哈爾
Changchiakou	張家口	Hsuanhua	宣　化
(Kalgan)		Pangchiang	滂　江
Tolun	多　倫	Yuhsien	蔚　縣

Chekiang 浙　江
Chiahsing	嘉　興	Chinhua	金　華
Hangchou	杭　州	Ningpo	寧　波
Shaohsing	紹　興	Wenchou	溫　州

Geographical Names of China

Fukien 福建

Changchou	漳州	Changting	長汀
Chinmen	金門	Chuanchou	泉州
Fuchou	福州	Hsiamen	厦門
Yungan	永安	(Amoy)	

Heilungkiang 黑龍江

Aihun	璦琿	Moho	漠河
Nencheng	嫩城	Peian	北安

Hochiang 合江

Chiamussu	佳木斯	Fuyuan	撫遠
Ilan	依蘭	Mishan	密山
Tungchiang	同江		

Honan 河南

Anyang	安陽	Chengchou	鄭州
Hsinhsiang	新鄉	Hsinyang	信陽
Hsuchang	許昌	Kaifeng	開封
Loyang	洛陽	Nanyang	南陽
Shangchiu	商邱		

Hopeh 河北

Paoting	保定	Peiping	北平
Shihchiachuang	石家莊		
Tangshan	唐山	Tientsin	天津

Hunan 湖南

Changsha	長沙	Changte	常德
Chihchiang	芷江	Hengyang	衡陽
Hsiangtan	湘潭	Shaoyang	邵陽

Hupeh 湖北

Hankow	漢口	Ichang	宜昌
Shashih	沙市	Wuchang	武昌

Hsingan 興安

Hailar	海拉爾	Lupin	臚濱
Solun	索倫	(Manchouli)	
Shihwei	室韋		

Johol 熱河

Chaoyang	朝陽	Chengte	承德
Chihfeng	赤峯	Fuhsin	阜新
Lingyuan	凌源	Pingchuan	平泉
Weichang	圍場		

Kansu 甘 肅
Chiayukuan	嘉峪關	Lanchou	蘭 州

Kiangsi 江 西
Chian	吉 安	Chingtechen	景德鎮
Chiuchang	九 江	Kanchou	贛 州
Nanchang	南 昌		

Kiangsu 江 蘇
Hsuchou	徐 州	Nanking	南 京
Nantung	南 通	Pukou	浦 口
Suchou	蘇 州	Shanghai	上 海
Wuhsi	無 錫		

Kirin 吉 林
Changchun	長 春	Fuyu	扶 餘
Kirin	吉 林	Tunhua	敦 化

Kwangsi 廣 西
Kueilin	桂 林	Liuchou	柳 州
Nanning	南 寧	Pose	百 色
Wuchou	梧 州		

Kwangtung 廣 東
Aomen	澳 門	Chanchiang	湛 江
(Macao)		Chaochou	潮 州
Hainan Is.	海 南	Hsiangkang	香 港
Kowloon	九 龍	(Hongkong)	
Shantou	汕 頭	Shaokuan	韶 關
(Swatow)		Taishan	臺 山

Kweichow 貴 州
Kueiyang	貴 陽		

Liaoning 遼 寧
Anshan	鞍 山	Chinchou	錦 州
Fushun	撫 順	Liaoyang	遼 陽
Lushun	旅 順	Penhsi	本 溪
(Port Arthur)		Mukden	瀋 陽
Dairen	大 連	Yingkou	營 口

Liaopei 遼 北
Liaoyuan	遼 源	Ssuping	四 平
Taonan	洮 南	Tungchiangkou	
Tungliao	通 遼		通江口

Nenchiang 嫩 江
Anganghsi	昂昂溪	Hulan	呼 蘭
Chichihaerh (Tsitsihar)	齊齊哈爾		

Ningsia 寧 夏
  Yinchuan   銀川

Sikang 西 康
  Yaan   雅 安

Sinkiang 新 疆
  Tihua   迪 化

Suiyuan 綏 遠
  Kueisui   歸 綏   Paotou   包 頭

Sungchiang 松 江
  Haerhpin   哈爾濱   Hunchun   琿 春
  (Harbin)   Mutanchiang 牡丹江
  Tumen   圖 們   Yenchi   延 吉

Shansi 山 西
  Taiyuan   太 源   Tatung   大 同

Shantung 山 東
  Tsinan   濟 南   Tsingtao   青 島
  Yentai   烟 臺

Shensi 陝 西
  Hsian   西 安   Hsienyang 咸 陽
  Nancheng   南 鄭

Szechwan 四 川
  Chengtu   成 都   Chungking 重 慶
  Ipin   宜 賓   Kuangyuan 廣 元
  Kuanhsien 灌 縣   Loshan   樂 山
  Tzukung   自 貢   Wanhsien   萬 縣

Taiwan 臺 灣
  Changhua   彰 化   Chiai   嘉 義
  Hualien   花 蓮   Hsinchu   新 竹
  Ilan   宜 蘭   Kaohsiung 高 雄
  Keelung   基 隆   Miaoli   苗 栗
  Penghu   澎 湖   Pingtung   屏 東
  Taichung   臺 中   Tainan   臺 南
  Taipei   臺 北   Taitung   臺 東
  Taoyuan   桃 源   Yuanlin   員 林

Tibet (Sitsang) 西 藏
  Jihkotse   日喀則   Lasa   拉 薩

Tsinghai 青 海
  Hsinling   西 寧

Yunnan 雲 南
  Kochiu   箇 舊   Kunming   昆 明

244

IMPORTANT GEOGRAPHICAL NAMES OF THE WORLD

A

Afghanistan 阿富汗
 Kabul 喀布爾
Albania 阿爾巴尼亞
 Tirana 地拉那
Argentina 阿根廷
 Buenos Aires 布宜諾斯·艾利斯
Australia 澳大利亞
 Canberra 堪培拉 Sydney 雪梨
Austria 奧地利
 Vienna 維也納

B

Belgium 比利時
 Brussels 布魯塞爾
Bolivia 玻利維亞
 La Paz 拉巴斯 Sucre 蘇克列
Brazil 巴西
 Rio de Janeiro 里約熱內盧
 Sao Paulo 聖保羅
Bulgaria 保加利亞
 Sofia 索非亞
Burma 緬甸
 Rangoon 仰光

C

Cambodia 高棉
 Pnompenh 百囊奔
Canada 加拿大
 Ottawa 渥太瓦
Ceylon 錫蘭
 Colombo 科倫波
Chile 智利
 Santiago 聖地牙哥

245

Colombia 哥倫比亞
    Bogota　波哥大
Costa Rica 哥斯達黎加
    San Jose　聖約瑟
Cuba 古巴
    Havana　哈瓦那
Czechoslovakia 捷克斯洛伐克
    Prague　布拉格

D

Denmark 丹麥
    Copenhagen　哥本哈根
Dominican Republic 多明尼加
    Santo Domingo　聖多明谷

E

Ecuador 厄瓜多爾
    Quito　基多
Egypt 埃及
    Alexandria　亞里山大港　　Cairo　開羅
El Salvador 薩爾瓦多
    San Salvador　聖薩爾瓦多
Ethiopia (Abyssinia) 愛西屋皮亞 (阿比西尼亞)
    Addis Ababa　亞的斯亞貝巴

F

Finland 芬蘭
    Helsinki　赫爾辛基
France 法國
    Lyons　里昂　　　　　　Marseilles　馬賽
    Paris　巴黎　　　　　　Riviera　里維耶拉
    Versailles　凡爾塞

G

Germany 德國
    Berlin　柏林　　　　　　Hamburg　漢堡
Greece 希臘
    Athens　雅典
Guatemala 危地馬拉
    Guatemala　危地馬拉

H

Haiti 海地
    Port-au-Prince　太子港
Honduras 洪都拉斯
    Tegucigalpa　特古西哥爾波

I

Iceland 氷島
    Reykjavik　雷克雅未克
India, Union of 印度
    Bombay　孟曼　　　　Calcutta　加爾各答
    New Delhi　新德里
Indonesia, Republic of 印度尼西亞
    Jakarta　雅加達
Iran 伊朗
    Teheran　德黑蘭
Iraq, Irak 伊拉克
    Bagdad　巴格達
Ireland, Republic of 愛爾蘭
    Dublin　都柏林
Israel 以色列
    Tel Aviv　臺拉維夫
Italy 意大利
    Florence　佛羅稜斯　　Genoa　熱那亞
    Milan　米蘭　　　　　Naples　那不勒斯
    Rome　羅馬　　　　　Venice　威尼斯

J

Japan, Nippon 日本
    Hiroshima　廣島　　　Hokkaido　北海道
    Kobe　神戸　　　　　Kyoto　京都
    Nagasaki　長崎　　　Nagoya　名古屋
    Osaka　大阪　　　　　Sasebo　佐世保
    Tokyo　東京　　　　　Yokohama　橫濱
    Yokosuka　橫須賀　　Okinawa　沖繩島

K

Korea, Chosen 韓國
    Cheju Island　濟州島　Inchon　仁川
    Kaesong　開城　　　　Koje Island　巨濟島

Munsan 汶山		Munsanni 汶山里	
Panmunjon 板門店		Pusan 釜山	
Pyongyang 平壤		Seoul 漢城	
Taegu 大邱			

L

Laos 老撾
    Luang Prabang 郎勃

Lebanon 黎巴嫩
    Beirut 貝魯特

Liberia 利比里亞
    Monrovia 蒙羅維亞

Luxemburg 盧森堡
    Luxemburg 盧森堡

M

Mexico 墨西哥
    Mexico 墨西哥

Mongolia 蒙古
    Ulan Bator 烏蘭巴托

N

Nepal 尼泊爾
    Katmandu 加德滿都

Netherlands (Holland) 荷蘭
    The Hague 海牙

Newfoundland 紐芬蘭
    Saint John's 聖約翰

New Zealand 新西蘭
    Wellington 惠靈頓

Nicaragua 尼加拉瓜
    Managua 馬那瓜

Norway 挪威
    Oslo 奧斯陸

P

Pakistan 巴基斯坦
    Karachi 喀喇蚩

Panama 巴拿馬
    Panama 巴拿馬

Paraguay 巴拉圭
    Asuncion 亞松森
Peru 秘魯
    Lima 利馬
Philippine Islands, Philippines 菲律賓
    Baguio 碧瑤   Manila 馬尼剌
Poland 波蘭
    Warsaw 華沙
Portugal 葡萄牙
    Lisbon 里斯本

R

Romania 羅馬尼亞
    Bucharest 布加勒斯特

S

San Marino 聖馬力諾
    San Marino 聖馬力諾
Saudi Arabia 沙特阿拉伯
    Mecca 麥加   Riyadh 利雅得
Spain 西班牙
    Gibraltar 直布羅陀   Madrid 馬德里
Sweden 瑞典
    Stockholm 斯德可爾摩
Switzerland 瑞士
    Bern 伯爾尼   Geneva 日內瓦
Syria 叙利亞
    Damascus 大馬士革

T

Thailand (Siam) 泰國 **(暹羅)**
    Bangkok 曼谷
Transjordan 外約但
    Amman 安曼
Turkey 土耳其
    Ankara 安哥拉

U

Ukraine 烏克蘭
    Kharkov 哈科夫

Union of South Africa 南非聯邦

  Cape Town 開普敦   Pretoria 比勒陀利亞

Union of Soviet Socialist Republics 蘇聯
(Russia, the Soviet Union)

  Moscow 莫斯科

United Kingdom 英國

  Cambridge 劍橋   London 倫敦
  Oxford 牛津

United States, United States of America 美國

  Alabama 亞拉巴媽   Alaska 阿拉斯加
                         Juneau 哲尼亞
  Arizona 亞利桑那   Arkansas 阿肯色
  California 加利福尼亞
    Hollywood 好萊塢
    Los Angeles 洛山磯
    San Francisco 舊金山
  Colorado 可羅拉多   Connecticut 康涅狄格
  Delaware 特拉華   District of Columbia
  Florida 佛羅里達   哥侖比亞特區
  Georgia 喬治亞   Guam 關島
  Hawaii 夏威夷
    Honolulu 檀香山 (火諾魯魯)
    Pearl Harbor 珍珠港
  Idaho 愛達河   Illinois 伊利諾斯
  Indiana 印第安那   Chicago 芝加哥
  Iowa 伊阿華   Kansas 堪薩斯
  Kentucky 墾塔啓   Louisiana 路易斯安那
  Maine 緬因   Maryland 馬里蘭
  Massachusetts 馬薩諸塞 Michigan 密執安
    Boston 波士頓   Detroit 低特律
                      Minnesota 明尼蘇達
  Mississippi 密士失比 Missouri 密蘇里
  Montana 蒙大拿   Nebraska 內布拉斯加
  Nevada 內華達   New Hampshire
  New Jersey 紐折爾西   紐罕什爾
  New Mexico 新墨西哥 New York 紐約
  North Carolina   North Dakota 北達科他
        北卡羅來納   Ohio 俄亥俄
  Oklahoma 俄克拉何馬 Oregon 俄勒岡

Pennsylvania　　　　Rhode Island　羅得島
　　　　賓夕法尼亞　South Carolina
South Dakota　南達科他　　　　南卡羅來納
Tennessee　田納西　Texas　塔薩斯
Utah　烏臺　　　　Vermont　洼滿的
Virginia　味吉尼亞　Washington　華盛頓
West Virginia　　　　Seattle　西雅圖
　　　　西味吉尼亞　Wisconsin　威斯康星
Wyoming　歪窩民

Uruguay　烏拉圭
　Montevideo　蒙得維的亞

V

Vatican　教庭
Venezuela　委內瑞拉
　Caracas　加拉加斯
Vietnam　越南
　Hanoi　河內

W

White Russia　白俄羅斯
　Minsk　明斯克

Y

Yemen　也門
　Sana　沙那
Yugoslavia　南斯拉夫
　Belgrade　貝爾格萊德